GOWN AND TALLITH

FIFTY YEARS OF C.U.J.S.

GOWN & TALLITH

IN COMMEMORATION OF
THE FIFTIETH ANNIVERSARY
OF THE FOUNDING OF
THE CAMBRIDGE UNIVERSITY
JEWISH SOCIETY

Edited by
William Frankel CBE
and Harvey Miller

with six original drawings
by David Weil

HARVEY MILLER PUBLISHERS
LONDON

Published by Harvey Miller Ltd
20 Marryat Road · London SW19 5BD · England

British Library Cataloguing in Publication Data

Gown and tallith: in commemoration of the fiftieth
anniversary of the founding of the Cambridge
University Jewish Society.
1. Jewish civilization
I. Frankel, William II. Miller, Harvey
909'.04924

ISBN 0–905203–81–X

Made in Great Britain
Printed and bound by
The Bath Press, Bath, Avon.

Contents

Part 4. Reports, Lists and Indexes

Foreword

AN UNDERGRADUATE AT CAMBRIDGE is surrounded by so many ancient establishments that it is not readily understood that the University is a growing body and that many institutions are of recent date. When my fellow freshman (and later my Best Man) Ansel Harris suggested that the Jubilee of CUJS be marked in some way, it was with some surprise that I realized that the Society, with its venerable and well established customs, had been formed only five years before we came up.

An informal *ad hoc* committee was formed and decided that the occasion should be marked by a dinner and the launch of a new drive to raise funds for the improvement of the facilities in Thompson's Lane. As a publisher, I undertook the production of a Commemorative Volume. The other Commemoration functions were: a Garden Party at Pembroke College, organized by the current members of the Society in June 1987; and a dinner at the Cambridge Guildhall in September 1987, under the chairmanship of Sir David Wolfson addressed by Abba Eban, the first President of the Society.

The activities of the Society have varied from year to year according to the taste of its members and the enterprise of its officers. Two constant features have been the Friday evening communal dinner and the lectures by invited guests, from the University or outside, on a wide range of subjects, principally, but not exclusively, of Jewish interest. The eve-of-Sabbath dinner, accompanied by *zemiroth* (Sabbath songs), was a joyful social occasion, and many lifelong friendships (and marriages) were initiated there.

This commemorative volume has tried to capture these two features: there are essays on the history of the Jews in Cambridge, reminiscences of the Society, talmudic, literary and political topics; the social aspect is represented by the Roll of Members, where some five hundred members have told of their postgraduate careers and their memories of CUJS.

I am extremely grateful to William Frankel CBE for his immediate acceptance of my invitation to edit the book, and to the contributors, who, although extremely busy, nevertheless found the time to add to this volume. Most of the essays appear here for the first time; some have appeared in publications that are unlikely to have come to the attention of the present readership. Dr. Raphael Loewe has made a major contribution with his history of Cambridge Jewry and list of deceased Cambridge alumni. For this essay alone this volume deserves an honoured place in every library.

David Weill, in the throes of his final year, prepared the excellent drawings which appear in this volume, and which evoke, as powerfully as many words, the memories of our student days.

The precursors to the Society are not forgotten; there are entries in the Roll of Members from graduates who were up before 1938, whose memoirs provide a fascinating glimpse into the practises before the building of the synague, and into the decision to build it. I am grateful, also, to Mrs. M. Edelman for providing the text of a previously unpublished lecture given by the late Maurice Edelman MP.

Although called *Roll of Members*, the purpose is to include anyone who attended the Services or functions at Thompson's Lane, and thereby took part in the activities of the Society. During the Second World War members of Colleges of London University were very active members.

There were no restrictions on inclusion in the Roll; anyone who came, made friends and wanted to renew contact, albeit symbolically, was welcome to be included in the Roll. At least one non-Jew replied and several people who were up before the Society was founded. The only condition was that there be no conditions; letters inviting me to participate in internal community squabbles were not answered.

At a gathering of former members one can imagine the questions: When were you up? Which College? What have you been doing since you went down? What do you remember of the Society? A questionnaire on these lines was sent out, and the replies received are presented here. As far as possible, I have left the writers' words untouched; my major editorial action has been to excise names and details of spouse and child who were not at Cambridge, except for cross-reference, restricting the entry to, for example, 'Married, two children'.

To contact former participants was no easy matter, since the records were not always meticulously kept. Every scrap of paper was examined, Minute books, supper account books etc. were scoured for names, colleges and addresses. Those contacted were asked to supply names and colleges of their contemporaries. The Colleges were most helpful in forwarding the questionnaire to former students. In this way, over 2000 letters were sent out, and some 500 replies were received.

Many former participants were not contacted because we had no correct address. I hope that the Society can in future make some provision for maintaining contact with former members. Many who were contacted did not reply because of negligence, others because they did not want to renew the connection. From the replies received, and printed in this volume, it is clear that the Society is important in life at the University. The achievements of those who did reply (about a quarter of whom live in Israel), the record of honours and prizes, of appointments to Professorial chairs and to the Bench, constitute a record of which the Society can be proud.

The Roll will bring back many memories; it renewed many contacts for me, and I am sure that it will do so for many readers. We cannot disclose addresses; if you wish to get in touch with someone, a letter sent to the Secretary of the Society (with a donation to the Building Fund) will be forwarded to the address we have; then direct contact can be established if so desired.

A debt of gratitude is owed to the College Representatives of the Society during 1987, who obtained the addresses of former members; to Katerina Harris and Hester Abrams, who extracted the preliminary lists of names; to Ann Rosen (*née* Vecht) who helped in typing the replies. Above all, thanks are due to Elliot Goodman, who as our contact with the Cambridge students, responded promptly and effectively to every request that I made. Inevitably, much of the work fell onto my two-fingered typing, and

I would like to acknowledge the forbearance of my wife, who, although from the other place, accepted uncomplainingly my spending night after night in the service of CUJS.

I have taken the opportunity to give permanent home, in this volume, to the Preface to the Book of Memorial, which was prepared, in proof form only, for the occupation of the new Synagogue. The names listed in the Book of Memorial are included in Dr. Loewe's list. The Preface sets out very clearly the underlying concepts guiding the Society, and it is to be hoped that each succeeding generation of students leading the Society will use it, and help to reduce the *Sin'at Chinam* which, the Talmud tells us, was the cause of the destruction of the Second Temple.

Harvey Miller

Part One

Historical

Raphael Loewe

Cambridge Jewry:
The First Hundred Years

Early Origins

IN MEDIEVAL ENGLAND the navigable rivers constituted major arteries of communication, whence the importance of Oxford and Cambridge; the former as an administrative as well as a commercial centre. Cambridge — on the edge of the fens, but linked by the Cam and Ouse with the Wash at King's Lynn — was important for local trade, but for the King's business it was overshadowed by Northampton, Colchester and Norwich. It was the need for credit generated by business, and the availability of a royal castle on the spot in case of trouble, that attracted Jews to Oxford* and Cambridge** early in the twelfth century.

Around the same time there began — first in Paris — a movement in which the cathedral schools emancipated themselves into embryonic universities, and Jews were involved in financial transactions regarding the foundation of the two earliest colleges — Merton, at Oxford, in 1267 and Peterhouse, at Cambridge, in 1265. Jewish scholars were living in both Oxford and Cambridge up to the expulsion in 1290 and it is inherently likely that some clerks intent on biblical studies or the background to the New Testament will have engaged them in discussion***, but no written evidence of such scholarly interchange is known.

*See C. Roth. *The Jews of Medieval Oxford*, Oxford Historical Soc., New Series. 9. 1951; EJ 12. 1534f.

** See H.P. Stokes. *Studies in Anglo-Jewish History*, Edinburgh, 1913, pp. 103f; EJ 5. 69 (C. Roth).

***See C. Roth. *op cit.*, pp. 149f.

Although in the early sixteenth century there was no Jewish community in England, the reformation was pregnant with significance for the Jewish future there, and not least for a shoulder-rubbing association with the (by now) much enlarged universities. One object of Henry VIII was to use Oxford and Cambridge, instead of the Church, as the training-ground for future servants of the crown; another was to provide a scholarly underpinning for the evolving theology of anglicanism. The first object meant the up-grading of the arts degree, no longer thought of as but the preparation for the study of divinity. Although the new learning inserted Greek, and at least in theory Hebrew, into the curriculum, the essential component for the B.A. degree at Cambridge was (and long remained) mathematics — in studying which students, seated on three-legged stools, would wrangle: whence the term 'tripos' to indicate the final examination (now in any subject) and the designation of all mathematicians placed in the first class as 'wranglers'. As regards the second, Henry founded professorships of Hebrew at Oxford and Cambridge, and by the time King James' Bible was published (1611) the scholars in Oxford, Cambridge and Westminster who produced it had been able to acquire a Hebrew expertise reflected in their debt to the standard Jewish commentators*. Their competence was mainly due to the availability by then of Hebrew grammars in print, dictionaries and Latin translations of a few important rabbinic texts. But it was in part assisted by a few ex-Jewish converts (e.g. Emmanuel Tremellius**) from overseas who were occasionally available as tutors. After Jewish resettlement under Cromwell faithful Jewish scholars sometimes visited Cambridge regularly to teach Hebrew, as did Isaac Abendana (brother of the Sephardi *Haham* in London) already in the seventeenth century, or resided there permanently, as did Israel Lyons in the eighteenth.

It was not until the nineteenth century that Jews began to aspire to a university education in England. The exclusion of all

---

*See R. Loewe. 'Jewish Scholarship in England'. *Three Centuries of Anglo-Jewish History*. ed. V.D. Lipman. London. 1961. pp. 125f.. EJ 8. 9f; G. Lloyd Jones. *The discovery of Hebrew in Tudor England; A third language*. Manchester. 1983.

**For those mentioned by name see the alphabetical list of deceased Cambridge Jewish Graduates. etc. in the Appendix, page 167.

non-anglicans from Oxford and Cambridge led to the foundation (in 1826) of what is now styled University College London. It is true that there had been a few late 18th-century Jewish trail-blazers at Cambridge, emanating (if we ignore converts to Christianity, or the near descendants of such) from largely assimilated families at home or slightly less assimilated ones in the West Indies. Jewish participation in university life was feasible (if one disregards the absence of a substantial Jewish community and consequent problems of dietary observance) provided that one did not seek to take a degree, which involved acquiescence in a trinitarian formula.

An option open to young men with the necessary social standing was to join a college as a 'fellow commoner', sharing the fellows' table and being exempt from academic requirements. Arthur Cohen, who entered Magdalene as a fellow commoner in 1849 on the Prince Consort's introduction (instigated by Moses Montefiore) did in fact read the mathematical tripos and took his B.A. — the first Jew to do so — as a 'non-declarant' in 1858; he took his M.A. in 1879, by which time Jews could have the words *in nomine Dei* substituted for reference to the trinity. Cohen represents the emergent Jewish professional class of Victorian England. James Sylvester, the future Savilian Professor at Oxford who had already taken a first in mathematics in 1831 but who likewise deferred taking his degree, is the harbinger of a different stratum — those who would, in their careers, swell the ranks of the professionals but who started with no advantages of wealth or even middle-class social establishment, but who ascended the ladder through sheer intellectual ability. Nathaniel Mayer Rothschild (later the first Lord), the first of his family to go up to Trinity, matriculated in 1859 but did not take an examination or graduate, although after the Act of Parliament of 1856* he could have done so. However, with a view to breaching such entrenched anglican defences as remained, the Rothschilds afforded finan-

---

*The Act of 1856 opened BA degrees at Cambridge to Jews, Muslims etc. without violence to their conscience; the 1871 Tests Act similarly opened higher degrees, fellowships and university appointments. At Oxford, the matriculation formalities at the commencement of university residence had likewise involved Christian formulae; this barrier had been removed earlier, by an Act of 1854. I am grateful to Judge Finestein for confirming these details.

cial sponsorship to Numa Hartog, who emerged from the mathematical tripos in 1859 as Senior Wrangler; all such restrictions were removed by the Religious Tests Act of 1871. In 1866 Solomon Schiller-Szinessy was appointed teacher (subsequently reader) of Talmudic and Rabbinical Literature, thereby becoming the first Jew to hold a formal university post as distinct from being privately or informally engaged to provide instruction in Hebrew. Alongside the later stages of the struggle of Jews (and other non-anglicans) for admission to the universities on equal terms there marched the endeavours of women to achieve the same. Of the women's colleges, Newnham was founded in 1871 and Girton, two years its senior, moved to Cambridge in 1873, although neither was formally incorporated into the University until after the Second World War. Both colleges attracted Jewish entry early on; Hertha Ayrton (*née* Marks) who became a distinguished scientist went up to Girton in 1876.

Jews in the Town

OUTSIDE THE UNIVERSITY there was a small Jewish presence in Cambridge to sustain these early students. Since the eighteenth century there had been a few Jewish residents who were, it seems, maintaining a synagogue (perhaps for occasional rather than regular assemblage) before 1778.* There was certainly a tiny congregation worshipping in a rented room on the site of the Union Society's premises from 1847, and after 1873 in Regent St. About 1888 it moved briefly to Petty Cury and around the turn of the century — by which date students constituted a significant factor in mustering a weekly quorum for worship — to a room over a china shop (Messrs. Barrett) on the south-west corner of the Market Place. Thence they migrated to a studio in a garden at Camden Terrace (Park Terrace), to move again shortly before 1913 into premises behind a cycle-shop opposite the en-

* See H.P. Stokes. *Studies in Anglo-Jewish History*, Edinburgh, 1913, pp. 233f; C. Roth. *The Rise of Provincial Jewry*. London. 1950. pp. 42f.

trance to Sidney Sussex College. That remained their home until the opening of purpose-built premises in Ellis Court (a name now lost) in Thompson's Lane in 1937. Numbers were always exiguous, and in view of rival attractions undergraduate attendance at synagogue was variable. It was not until early in the twentieth century, when Israel Hersch opened a boarding-house that attracted Jewish boys from London and elsewhere to the Perse School, that a regular sabbath *minyan* during term-time could be more or less relied upon by those concerned to find one. In 1899 C. Fox and H.M. Adler had led a *putsch* against the permanent Jewish residents, the undergraduates thereafter taking over the running of the synagogue.*

The Student Body

THE JEWISH STUDENTS came from a cross-section of the community and from homes differing widely both in synagogal allegiance and in the degree of Jewish observance. For all except those most staunchly committed, the availability in Cambridge of a conventicle lacking all aesthetic attraction — in contrast to the environment — will scarcely have provided a sheet-anchor for their Jewish identity. For many of them — perhaps most — the link will have been the interest (and domestic hospitality) afforded by the successive readers in rabbinics — S. Schiller-Szinessy, S. Schechter and above all by Israel Abrahams — as well as by Redcliffe and Nina Salaman in their home at Barley, some twelve miles out of Cambridge.

At the beginning of the century, church-going on Sundays was still a significant feature in the Cambridge social rhythm. The successive readers in rabbinics constituted a nucleus for the synagogal activities of the exiguous Cambridge Hebrew Congregation, and also, through the hospitality of their homes, a mute prompting to the less committed of their responsibility towards the Jewish counterpart of their college chapel. Few of that gener-

* See H. Loewe. *Israel Abrahams*, Cambridge. 1944. p. 77.

17

ation are now left: but many will have learned from them of the powerful and lasting influence of this unobtrusive chaplaincy service.

Once religious tests and compulsory chapel had been abolished two major challenges to the Jewish conscience (if we leave aside until later increased long-term risks of inter-marriage) were occasioned by the Cambridge system and its traditions. To one of these, the dietary aspect, we shall return; the other concerns the possible clash of examination time-tabling with the sabbath or festivals. A significant proportion of the early Jewish students — at a guess, perhaps more than half of the 20-30 in residence at any time up to 1914 — came from homes that took sabbath-observance seriously: not a few had been educated in London at St. Paul's School, attractive to Jewish parents since it held no classes on Saturdays. An arrangement was at some time nego-tiated with the university administration (I would suppose at the initiative or sponsorship of Schechter, and perhaps Israel Gollancz) under which for examination papers scheduled for a Saturday or Jewish festival (in effect *Shabu'oth*) Jewish students might employ an amanuensis and dictate their scripts, thereby remaining within the letter of the law. Abrahams — perhaps more sensitive than his predecessors to the impression that such legal subterfuge might leave on Christian colleagues whose own spiri-tuality he appreciated and respected — introduced the private invigilation system, still current, by which students would write their scripts before or after the day concerned, remaining incom-municado in his home or that of one of the few other Jewish dons. The moral afforded by this facility (and by the tolerance of the University in sanctioning it, despite substantial inconvenience) will have spread beyond those who were its direct beneficiaries, some of whom down the years have taken it all too readily for granted.

It was thanks to the encouragement of Abrahams and his predecessors that Jewish student life evolved three university societies which, in complementing the Cambridge Hebrew Con-gregation that was responsible for maintaining the synagogue, could provide a focus for the Jewish identity of those for whom worship in synagogue was either unattractive or unmeaningful. These were the university branch of the Anglo-Jewish Association, the Zionist Society, and a forum for the discussion of religious, literary, and other Jewish topics which, after Schechter's departure for New York in 1902, formally constituted itself as the 'Schechter Society'. It is symptomatic of the pre-1914 atmosphere that Abrahams and others (who entertained reservations about Herzlean Zionism) felt it right to support the Zionist Society no less than the others. Activities would revolve round week-end invitations — generally jointly by one or more of the societies together with the congregation — to a visiting speaker, mostly clerical but sometimes a lay communal leader. The visitor might address more than one of the society meetings and also give a sermon either on Friday evening or Saturday morning. Costs were still relatively slight, apart from the rent for synagogue premises, for which the dons and non-university residents had often to chip in to balance the budget. Otherwise, the society concerned had to find the cost of a hotel room for Friday night, the return fare (if necessary) from London, and the service of tea or coffee from the college kitchens for a meeting in an undergraduate's rooms or e.g. in the Old Combination Room of Trinity College. The printing of a programme-card each term cost little, and sabbath lunch hospitality would be provided either by one of the few Jewish families or by students in one of their own rooms. Before 1914 the subscription for the Cambridge Hebrew Congregation was ten shillings a term and in the thirties that for the combined society was about the same. Some students, coming from immigrant families in the East End of London, or from Manchester, might find difficulty in affording even this, but since the majority then came from (financially speaking) middle-class homes, solvency was usually contrived.

With the building of the present synagogue in the mid-thirties the situation changed. There were by then probably 50+ students (out of a larger, indefinable Jewish *quantum*) concerned to identify with Jewish life in the University, and the three societies and the Hebrew Congregation found it appropriate to amalgamate as the Cambridge University Jewish Society, pooling their income and making it less easy for the loosely committed to make the existence of four organizations the excuse for joining none. Those responsible, under the leadership of Robert Waley Cohen, for providing a purpose-built synagogue for which rent would not be payable, did not think through the financing of the maintenance of the fabric etc on an undergraduate subscription. Nor could the much more intense use of the building, with consequent heavy wear and tear, occasioned by the influx of a refugee and evacuated community during the Second World War have been foreseen. The availability of a synagogue with an attached hall and catering facilities meant that all previous activities continued at an increased momentum. Some time after Israel's emergence into statehood in 1948 a need was felt for an Israel Society, which came into existence as an independent entity on entirely secular premisses, and (as far as I am aware) admitting non-Jews so desiring to membership. The only formal link of the present Jewish Society with its four progenitors is its constitutional obligation to stage a 'Schechter Lecture' every year.

Kashruth

THE PROVISION, ATTACHED to the synagogue, of a kitchen and a hall suitable for dining likewise transformed, in due course, the extent to which the degree of resoluteness necessary for the observance of the dietary laws at Cambridge, as an aspect of Jewish identity, might unduly tax a student's loyalty. However, for decades before the thirties many students brought up to a substantial strictness in *kashruth*-observance had managed to make adequate arrangements for their feeding.* Before outlining these, we must note certain aspects of both the Jewish and the general situation that have changed since 1945, and which will place earlier arrangements for *kashruth*-observance in perspective. On the Jewish side, of those in Anglo-Jewry who respected

* See R. Loewe. 'The Evolution of Jewish Student Feeding Arrangements in Oxford and Cambridge'. *Studies in the Cultural Life of the Jews of England.* ed. D. Noy and I. Ben-Ami. Folklore Research Center Studies. v, Jerusalem. 1975. pp. 165f.

the dietary laws both in the home and outside it, there were few (even amongst the Anglo-Jewish ministry) who concerned themselves, outside their own home, regarding the utensils in which food was prepared or served: the great majority would not hesitate to consume fish, or an egg, in an ordinary restaurant. The prevalence of a significantly greater sensitivity in this respect is due to demographic changes in Anglo-Jewry consequent upon the upheavals caused by Hitler and the Second World War: and it ought to be evaluated alongside the numerically far larger abandonment, or near-abandonment, within Anglo-Jewry of dietary observance altogether.

As regards non-Jewish Cambridge, the dining together of fellows of the college and the student body was regarded as part of the educational process (similarly to the obligatory dining of law-students at the inns of court). The regulation that students must take their evening meal 'in hall' on at least a minimum (usually five) nights each week not only promoted mutual education in social *mores*, but also ensured that the impecunious student would be in effect prevented from risking his health by going short on food. By the time that Jewish undergraduates were becoming a feature of the Cambridge scene (*Cohen of Trinity*, by Amy Levy*, appeared in 1889) a few Muslims and Brahmins had also been going up to the University, and these had their respective dietary laws. College kitchens found it no great trouble to accommodate such requirements and tutors were sympathetic to matters of conscience. With such arrangements all but a handful of Jewish students up to 1939 were satisfied. Rationing problems during the Second World War, combined with the insistence by some Jewish students that the standard of *kashruth* thereby attainable was inadequate, induced some tutors to exempt them from the requirement to dine in hall altogether. The aftermath of the war, increased student numbers, and the frequency since then of students being already married, eventually consigned to near-

*The Gentleman's Magazine. 266. no. 1901. May, 1889. pp. 417-24; reprinted in
J. Leftwich. Yisröel, The First Jewish Omnibus. 1933. pp. 50-58. The author had herself
been at Newnham. Although the piece is valuable evidence regarding Jewish
integration in university life, it does not reflect the existence of any sense of local
communal identity amongst Jewish students.

oblivion regularity of communal dining with some degree of formality as an instrument of social education.

Communal dining, at least in the atmosphere of the sabbath, with opportunity for more leisured recitation of the post-prandial grace accompanied by *zemiroth*, is likewise an instrument of Jewish social education: and the early trail-blazers at Cambridge, some of them familiar with it from their home background, were loth to forgo so powerful a factor in fostering the spirit of *Shabbat*. They would consequently foregather in each other's rooms for their sabbath meals. My father (H. Loewe), who was at Queens' at the beginning of this century, told me that one arrangement, perhaps typical, was for a group of four students to have a fixed arrangement, according to which during the eight weeks of term each would be host to the others for two sabbaths, getting fried fish etc sent up from home (the railway parcel service was then cheap and efficient). At some date — my guess would be in the early 1920s — these groups coalesced, making arrangements with one of the local cafés to serve a fish meal each Friday during term. After the communal supper, on perhaps three or four occasions during each term a visitor would speak and discussion would follow. When the synagogue in Thompson's Lane was being planned, the culinary arrangements were designed to meet not much heavier use than for the weekly suppers, or for full catering on the rare occasions that Passover fell during term. Almost from the outset, however, they were required to bear an increased load. The extent to which, in recent decades, the synagogue has become the centre where a minority of Jewish students take a daily main meal has meant that, for them, the erstwhile centrality of the college has been largely eroded. It has also meant that because catering has come to dominate the use to which the building is put, the synagogue now looks more like one of Pharaoh's store-cities than the Alexandrian synagogue that was one of the wonders of Jewish antiquity: and arguably more Jewish students are kept away by its *ethos* than are attracted by it. Student diehards rarely envisage the long-term consequences of their enthusiasm.

Periods and Moods

T H E T W O W O R L D wars each constituted a watershed in the make-up and *ethos* of Cambridge Jewry. No doubt the surviving minute-books would help to recreate the atmosphere of the three periods — pre-1914, 1919-39 and post-1945 — if the evidence in them were properly used, e.g. by correlation of attitudes recorded from discussions in committee with what is retrievable of their proponents' other activities in Cambridge and in their subsequent careers. That task I must leave to others. A flavour of the pre-1914 period may be caught in the pamphlet recording the celebration in 1909 of the twentieth year of the Cambridge Hebrew Congregation;* it prints Israel Abrahams' commemoration sermon in the Cambridge synagogue, and also (in loving prolixity) the proceedings over which Israel Gollancz (then an English don at Christ's) presided, and the guests at which included Hermann Adler (Chief Rabbi), Moses Gaster (*Haham*), and Morris Joseph (of the Reform Synagogue), their speeches being reproduced verbatim. The students' drinking-song in Latin, *Gaudeamus igitur juvenes dum sumus*, was sung, with the addition of topical allusions by L[eonard] S[tern] — to be killed in the war — to those who maintained the *minyan* ('*floreant decemviri*') and to those more conspicuous by their absence from synagogue ('*qui negligunt...discent congregare*'). Before the first war, a capacity to savour such witticisms could be presupposed in a Cambridge audience. After 1918 there was still a significant, albeit attenuated number of Jewish students who were either reading classics or had done so in the sixth form at school; after 1945, Jews virtually gave up the subject. A much greater gulf was caused by the terrible casualty-rate amongst young officers, which substantially eroded the *continuum* of experience of integration in Cambridge university life. Whereas Albert Polack, who had matriculated at St John's in 1911, returned to complete his degree in 1920, his brothers Benjamin (King's, 1909-13) and Ernest (St John's, matriculated

---

Celebration of the Twentieth Anniversary of the Foundation of the Cambridge Hebrew Congregation. Cambridge Jewish Publications. 2. 1909.

1912) were both killed. The death of Israel Abrahams in 1925 meant that Jewish students lost a focal point of religious leadership; his readership was not filled — for lack of funds — until the appointment of Herbert Loewe in 1931.

But despite the feelings of the older generation that in 1914 an era had come to an end, there was in the general atmosphere of Cambridge in the twenties a much greater continuity than survived the upheaval of the Second World War. It ought not be supposed, from the general tenor of what has been written here, that no vestige of anti-semitism was to be detected in the University. Some residual, social anti-semitism did occasionally manifest itself, but it is significant that H.M. Abrahams' biographer considers that he would have found this motif overplayed in the film (*Chariots of Fire*) that portrays the beginnings of his athletic career.* Two major features characterized post-war opinion amongst the Jewish student body, the increasing size of which included a growing component of children of refugees from Russia who had arrived around the turn of the century. One feature (already operative in embryo before 1914) was an awareness of the rapidly developing importance for the future of Judaism of Palestine under the British Mandate. The Inter-University Jewish Federation of local Jewish societies, founded in 1919, had Zionism at the forefront of its objects from the outset. Left-wing sympathies were still liberal in complexion rather than labour, and evinced themselves (at least in the later twenties) in an unease, widely felt in student circles, at the alleged harshness towards Germany of the terms of the Versailles Treaty. There was little involvement in communism or radical socialism, even though it is possible that contemporary committee lists of the Socialist Society etc may include a number of Jewish names (e.g. that of M.L. Perlzweig); and, despite the 'working-class' (in an idiosyncratically Jewish sense) background by now of quite a lot of Jewish students, it is to be surmised that during the General Strike of 1926 some of them will have been volunteering, alongside

---

* Abrahams did not live to see the film. Norris McWhirter (*DNB, 1970-80*. Oxford. 1987. p. 2) writes that 'Abrahams, on his own testimony, would have regarded such a [n antisemitic] portrayal as over-fanciful'.

their gentile compeers, to help maintain transport and other public services.

The significant move of Jewish student opinion to the left began after 1933, and was largely fuelled by the lethargy of the conservative-dominated national governments in the face of Hitler's internal anti-semitism and his territorial aggression abroad. To the extent that such lethargy, or inaction, was substantially inspired by fear of Soviet Russia, whilst the Labour Party was itself flirting with pacifism, the Communist Party in Cambridge — as elsewhere — appeared to offer the young the only rallying-point that viewed nazism realistically. The increasing trickle to Cambridge of German-Jewish research students (some of them, like E.B. Chain, or D. Daube, destined for future fame), of established scholars and scientists and, after 1937, of teenagers sent for safety out of Germany; and alongside it, the British Government's hypersensitivity towards Arab opinion and increasingly restrictive policy on Jewish immigration to Palestine, culminating in the White Paper of 1939 — all this meant that by then, the political sympathies of Jewish students were almost solidly with the Labour Party. At the outbreak of war, Cambridge and its environs became an evacuation area. The synagogue's catering and other resources had immediately — with the onset of the high holidays — to bear a burden for which they had not been designed, and students (reinforced by the evacuation to Cambridge of the London School of Economics and some other London colleges), together with the local Jewish residents, had hastily to contrive such educational arrangements for schoolchildren in the countryside as petrol-rationing etc made feasible. Herbert Loewe, who had exhausted his strength in working for refugee relief and whose leadership had set the wheels of this improvization in motion, became terminally ill, and died at the onset of the Battle of Britain.

The evacuated community included a number of business people from London. Since under war-time conditions the student body had a very rapid turnover, the non-academic section of the Cambridge Jewish community, which provided continuity, came effectively to dominate the synagogue. The fact that the student body retained some sense of a corporate entity was largely due to the leadership of William Frankel, a future editor of the *Jewish Chronicle*, then a law student at the London School of Economics. Another London student (of University College) likewise evacuated to Cambridge was Hayim Herzog, whose later service to Israel was to culminate in its presidency.

The result of this *bouleversement* has been that, since the war, Cambridge Jewry — including its student component — has come to think of itself rather a satellite, or miniature version, of a conventional suburban community instead of (as it had hitherto self-consciously been) *sui generis*. Before 1914, and to a lesser extent up to 1939, Jewish students had felt that their Cambridge experience contributed not only to their individual Jewish self-awareness, but also to their collective Jewish self-expression — an attitude epitomized in the wearing to synagogue of the academic cap and gown conventional not only in college chapels, but on all public or semi-formal occasions. The breach in continuity meant that that sort of consciousness was largely lost. The virulence of German anti-semitism, especially after the exposure at the end of the war of the gas-chambers, imbued many Jewish students with an emotional alienation from that very European culture the history and literature of which some of them were themselves making the object of their own academic studies. This feeling was intensified by their solidarity with, and increasing involvement in Israel, the mood of which, despite a top-dressing of western technology and Sephardi Hebrew pronunciation, was still of a predominantly east-european complexion. Fascination with things Israeli, especially if folk-generated and resistant to conventional western categories of thinking and aesthetic canons, came to usurp the gravitational pull of the European classics, both ancient and modern, and the formalism that is part of their idiom. The experience which the European tradition enshrines came to be felt to be not (or not primarily) relevant. Application to learning modern Hebrew provided the obvious channel for this emotional re-orientation and self-distancing from Europe — not least because, paradoxically, it had ingested precisely that European cast of mind reflected in syntax from which young Jews had often convinced themselves that they were emancipated. With the natural categories of traditional Hebrew they, like most of their contemporaries, had become impatient. They were thus, on the whole, dismissive of the traditional Cambridge approach to Hebrew as being, effectively, a classical language alongside of Greek and Latin, with a rabbinic and medieval extension worthy of academic interest in the same way that Byzantine Greek might be. Cambridge still then conferred no more academic attention on modern Hebrew than it did on modern Greek; and to many young Jews this disregard seemed eloquent of what they thought of as an essential divergence, or even incompatability, of Jewish and western values, priorities, and categories of self-expression.

It is of course true that this attitude is not so very different from that which has characterized much of English youth in the last quarter of the twentieth century. The Suez War, Vietnam, and the impotence of the religious establishment, Christian and Jewish alike, in the face of such moral challenges as genocide and mass-starvation, are no doubt contributory causes. The point that is here being made is that the factors mentioned above stimulated an iconoclasm amongst Jewish students rather earlier than occurred amongst their gentile compeers; and the circumstance that — unlike the latter — they had available an alternative, Hebrew cultural tradition which, in an over-simplified form for the most part, was being brought to their attention with all the educational and other promotional techniques that Israel's publicity machinery had available, meant that Jewish student rejectionism tended to be earlier and more self-assertive (albeit no less self-deceiving) than the environmental variety. It is of the nature of iconoclasm to dissemble its tacit retention of much of the accumulated intellectual and cultural store, for the articulation of which traditional forms provide convenient categories.

Jewish Identification

IN THE FOREGOING we have been mainly concerned with the institutional organization of Jewish student life at Cambridge and its varying complexion. But it is pertinent to note that at the very least since 1945 it has been a minority only of those students who must be reckoned to possess Jewish status that has seen fit to identify itself with the Cambridge University Jewish Society or its predecessors. Moreover, although membership of the Society may be taken as a significant pointer, case-histories will show that it is certainly not an invariable prognostication of life-long Jewish commitment. Nor should the responsible historian ignore the Jewish significance within the University of those, whether students or professors and college dons, who remained aloof from organized Jewish activities, since nearly all of these (not least the few that have endeavoured to dissemble their Jewish origins altogether) will have been a significant opinion-forming factor amongst educated circles in regard to Judaism, refugee problems, Zionism and British policy towards Palestine/Israel. In view of the substantial Oxbridge element in the British establishment, the significance of this interaction needs no underscoring.

It follows that before we address ourselves to the effect of Cambridge experience on students' Jewish consciousness in terms of a life-time's commitment, it is appropriate to survey — briefly, and of necessity impressionistically — Jewish participation in the wider university scene. We may start with strictly academic matters. The intellectual ability of a high proportion of Jewish students is reflected in election, by open examination, to entrance scholarships to colleges, in the class attained in tripos examinations, the winning of university prizes and scholarships and, after 1920, proceeding to work for a Ph. D. degree. Evidence insofar as concerns those by now dead is assembled in the appendix to this article. Their choice of subject would probably repay further study if their results were correlated with the statistical patterns of annual tripos records. Thus, noteworthy among the earliest Jewish women to go up to Newnham and Girton seems to be an interest in natural science. Amongst the men, before 1914 classics (sometimes followed by law) was regarded as a useful basis for a professional career, analogously to the generally prevailing view, as was also mathematics — historically, the pre-eminent arts subject at Cambridge. Apart from future ministers and a handful of future professional academics, very few Jews read for the Oriental Languages Tripos in which Hebrew could be offered alongside another language. Lionel Barnett, destined to become one of the leading British indologists, read classics. The early interest of Jews in newly introduced academic disciplines may be noted. Thus, the Economics Tripos was first examined in 1905; in 1907, the six Part 1 candidates included two Jews — G. Levinstein and Eva Spielmann.

Colleges, apart from Trinity and St John's, were quite small in numbers — until 1914, a single sitting at dinner was the norm — so that fellow-students were all at least acquaintances. Of the four focal college activities (to leave aside tutorial teaching) the chapel may be here ignored, and communal dining in hall has already been considered. There remain the multifarious college societies and sport, and the extension of these activities in university societies and teams. Jewish participation in college debating and other societies may be presupposed, but would require research into minute-books and college magazines to document. The same applies to sport at the college level; the Jewish performers who, like H.M. Abrahams and his brothers, made the university teams and even national headlines, are noticeable by their rarity: this perhaps reflecting Jewish tardiness (until their schooling was in this respect reinforced by Jewish youth clubs, or Maccabi) in maturing a capacity for team-effort. The same no doubt applies to dramatics. One recalls the occasional Jewish actor in the triennial Greek play (initiated by Walston, an archaeologist of Jewish origins), or in the more frequent productions of the Footlights — Jonathan Miller's launching-pad.

If one looks at the other cross-university association, as has been noted above, the Socialist Society was attracting significant Jewish recruitment from around 1930. The Conservative counterpart, the Pitt Club with its own premises, operated on the lines of a London club and, being more exclusive, attracted few Jewish students; whatever their politics, these found their natural milieu in the Union Society. Its weekly debates, which attracted as visiting speakers political figures and others of the first rank, gave opportunity both to practice the art of public speaking and also, if one had an eye on a political career, of catching the eye of some front-bench parliamentarian. Indeed, up to about 1939 the Unions at Oxford and Cambridge were regarded by the national parties as a place for talent-spotting. Arthur Cohen, in 1853, was the first Jew to attain its presidency; amongst his Jewish successors are numbered Edwin Montagu (1902), A. Kean (1935), and Greville Janner (1952)*. A number of others — in particular A.S. Eban — prepared themselves in the Union for public office in the national life of Great Britain or Israel, as well as for leadership in Jewish and other communal spheres.

More important, however, although less tangible than the foregoing in regard to Anglo-Jewish history, has been the educative potential of the plethora of informal social activities, through which many a young Jew or Jewess who had gone up to Cambridge from an almost exclusively Jewish environment has learned to feel at ease in a pluralistic society. The implications of this as pertinent to the inter-marriage rate will be considered below.

Commitment

W H A T, T H E N, O F the impact of three or more years' university experience at Cambridge on Jewish consciousness and commitment? Clearly, we are confronting here questions that cannot be properly addressed otherwise than by taking into account the whole of the subsequent career of those concerned; and to that extent, the list of deceased Jewish graduates etc. assembled in the appendix to this article may provide the Anglo-Jewish historian with some useful source–material. Proper evaluation of it would demand far more space than is here available, but the following avowedly impressionistic reading of the evidence may be put on record.

I have no doubt that Cambridge has enabled some to discover for themselves a Jewish awareness, or to deepen what had been a conventional or even but a nominal Jewish awareness; and that

Recollections of the Cambridge Union 1815-1939. ed. P. Cradock, Cambridge. 1953

in some cases such enrichment has steered those concerned into maintaining an intensified Jewish identity through synagogue attendance, communal service, emigration to Israel, work for Soviet Jewry, interest in Jewish history, etc. But I should be much surprised if this plus is not outweighed by those, coming either from lukewarm backgrounds or from homes of intense Jewish commitment and observance, who, after Cambridge, have in effect opted out of the Jewish community. However, crude statistics are not of much help here. More significantly, I am not disposed to think that membership of the Jewish Society, or of any of its forerunners, will have greatly affected the individual outcome. An important (but by no means an absolute) indicator is afforded by choice of a marriage-partner; and for this, part of the evidence lies to hand, since the two older colleges for women, Newnham and Girton, have published registers in which maiden and married surnames are cross-indexed. Of the women listed below, something over 50% married out and, had the living been included in the survey, the figure would have been much higher still. Information regarding the men is more haphazard, depending upon their meriting listing in *Who's Who*, etc. (although again, college magazines could yield information). My impression from such information as has come my way is that the inter-marriage rate of Cambridge Jewish men has been higher than that for women; and as regards more recent graduates, whose own halakhic status as Jews could not be challenged, my guess is that it will have been a minority that have married Jewish spouses. No doubt the same picture holds good for the entire Anglo-Jewish community to-day, but it has to be recognized that the tendency began earlier among those scions of the Jewish middle classes, and the upwardly mobile children of immigrant parents who, by dint of sheer intellectual ability, won scholarships to Cambridge in the face of keen competition.

Jewish students, or at any rate those who have organized themselves into university Jewish societies, tend to take themselves much more seriously as future leaders of the community than, *mutatis mutandis*, their gentile compeers have done; and they have constantly protested at the lack, or inadequacy, of subvention with which the Jewish community has been prepared to provide them for self-training in their future role. To what extent have those at Cambridge made good the claim? In the strict sense of leadership, it seems exaggerated. True, the current President of the Board of Deputies, Dr Lionel Kopelowitz, began his apprenticeship in communal service as synagogue secretary (*shamash*) of the Cambridge Jewish Society, and his immediate predecessor is also a Cambridge man. But of Cambridge Jewish graduates who have achieved positions of eminence in British life, it is a minority, albeit a respectable one, that has accepted positions of responsibility either at the top, e.g. Robert Waley-Cohen, or in what might be called the 'middle management' levels of voluntary communal service (synagogue wardenship, office in the Welfare Board, etc.). But to put matters in this way gives an unfair picture, inasmuch as the Anglo-Jewish community's unique situation means that it owes at least as much to the inconspicuous leadership of the family man (and his wife) who sustain the loyalty to Judaism, world Jewry and Israel of their own children and circle of friends. Many such persons, even though not in the public eye, generally secure the posthumous accolade of a brief obituary note in the *Jewish Chronicle*; and the number of names listed below followed by reference to such notices speaks for itself.*

Some other significant indicators are more difficult to assess. If one thinks of Israel, one is immediately reminded of some of the early settlers who managed without the supportive apparatus of modern immigrant absorption, such as Michael Lange and his wife, Nita Bentwich; or of H.M. Wiener, L. Billig, and A. Yellin (the last of whom came up to Cambridge from the old *Yishuv*, and rowed in the Christ's boat), all three of whom were killed by Arabs for their zionist and ecumenical ideals (Wiener left legacies to Moslem institutions in Palestine). But it is probable — at the least — that these, like many more recent graduates who have gone on *Aliyah* or who have spent a period of voluntary service in Israel, did not owe their zionist vocation to Cambridge; rather, they

---

*It is of course the case that the *Jewish Chronicle* notices the deaths of eminent Jews whose connection with Judaism and community was non-existent. There are a few such cases (e.g. Leonard Woolf) amongst those listed in the appendix to this article, but statistically they are insignificant.

contributed the skills and intellectual training that they had gained there (Billig, for example, was a most gifted Arabic scholar at the Hebrew University). Nonetheless, students intending *Aliyah* will whilst at Cambridge have been mutually supportive; and for others, a collective Jewish student identity has contributed to their noteworthy response at times when Israel has needed volunteers or defence against calumny.

And so we come back to the ultimate — but imponderable — question; how far has experience at Cambridge contributed to the maintenance, intensification, evaporation or the deliberate jettisoning of Jewish commitment? As suggested above, each must answer for himself in retrospect across the lengthening years. The historian will best confine himself to assessing those whose lives can be surveyed *in toto*. But anyone who attempts an assessment, whether of the dead or of the living collectively, ought not be mesmerized by institutional membership. Unwillingness to attend the university synagogue need not imply lack of religious response, since attendance itself may sometimes mean no more than herd-instinct. Before 1939 — and indeed after the war — traditionalist and reform Jews managed to worship together, on orthodox lines, in the Cambridge synagogue. The emergence in recent years of two parallel congregations, traditionalist and reform, probably tells the observer more about collective intransigence, or about the aesthetics of congregational worship, than about serious theological thinking. A university education ought to afford the Jewish student the opportunity, and the challenge, to attempt some serious thinking in regard to the inter-relationship of Judaism, with its universalistic and domestic ethical ideals, membership of the House of Israel, and the necessity or propriety of Jewish independent statehood. But students who rally to combat campus anti-semitism posturing as anti-racialism depend less on their own reflection on such matters than on slogans and hand-out material; and are inclined to treat the availability of the latter as discharging them from the moral obligation to engage in fundamental thinking for themselves.

If I may hazard a personal impression, it is that in all but a very few cases decisions regarding commitment to a Jewish identity or a preparedness to let it atrophy will have been reached by young men and women before going up to the University. Experience there may change the complexion of the expression of such identity or solidarity but will not affect it fundamentally. Tensions regarding choice of a marriage-partner will certainly be heightened, but they are essentially not different from the tensions inherent in a pluralistic society (including those, like Israel, where pluralism is concealed by a label); although it is probable that young women at the university encounter greater pressures of this nature than men. Participation in, or aloofness from, a Jewish Society will, in the long run, not affect issues that concern faith, rhythm and *regimen* of life and Jewish solidarity.

From this point of view, it should be instructive to compare the Jewish involvement of those now dead, listed in the appendix, with the response (and particularly any failure to respond, should the Editor see fit to reveal it) of those living who were circularized with a view to securing data for the preparation of this volume. Some of the dead would no doubt have been surprised — and a few of them indignant — to find themselves included in my list; similarly, failure to respond to the questionnaire could be inspired by a conviction that the angelic clerk charged with keeping up to date the Book of Life can manage well enough without having to refer to a kind of Cambridge Jewish *Who's Who*.

The cosmopolitan provenance of Cambridge Jewry is hardly surprising, although the appearance — albeit briefly — of a Sassoon from Baghdad as early as 1864 is worth observing. The contribution of Jews educated at Cambridge to the Anglo-Jewish community, to world Jewry, to Israel, and, in the case of a very few, to Jewish thought and scholarship, has been a worthy one. It might therefore be thought a pointless exercise, and perhaps invidious, to try to explore in what way, and to what extent, one can isolate what Cambridge Jews have contributed that Cambridge itself made it possible for them to give, or to give more effectively. Any such enquiry regarding a given individual demands a sensitivity on the part of the historian or biographer that can transcend measurement by card-membership. It is a reasonable question to ask in the case of those who have risen to prominence; for example, how much could S. Brodetsky have given to Zionism, A.S. Eban to Israel, Abraham Cohen to Anglo-Jewry, A.S. Diamond to English reform Judaism or M.L. Perlzweig to international Jewry had they not taken their first steps towards their chosen professions at Cambridge, or been subtly moulded or polished by its atmosphere? In the case of such as these, the evidence is there — not only in their writings and public actions, but equally in the method and mood of their respective responses to criticism. But the question here posed is no less real in regard to the contribution — arguably a far more important one — of those who have not become household names or scholars of international reputation. One of the most poignant entries in the list appended to this article concerns Martha Pereles (*née* Ullmann), who spent 1909-10 at Newnham. She was a teacher in Jewish schools in Czechoslovakia who died in a concentration camp. One would like to think that memories of pre–1914 Cambridge, blending with other sources of spiritual strength, may have helped her find a serenity at the end, to take a vicarious pride in which is the privilege, as well as the challenge, of those of us who have survived.

The fact that such questions as these rarely yield answers hardly matters. The very fact of formulating them may be but a way of asking just what we ourselves have received from Cambridge, and to what extent we are duly grateful for it. And by way of illustrating the suggestiveness of raising the question, I conclude by citing two examples; the first because its very inconclusiveness must warn us against any temptation to romanticize, and the second because it can illustrate the intricacy of Jewish involvements in what Cambridge is and does, as well as the combination of subtlety and disciplined research that is needful in order to substantiate its presence.

Chaim Weizmann's son Michael was at King's from 1934-1937. I do not recollect ever having seen him in the synagogue or at any Jewish function, although I believe that he was president of the university Zionist Society for one term. When the war came, he joined the Royal Air Force, and unfortunately he was killed in 1942. It is idle to speculate to what extent, had he lived, his Jewish awareness might have matured and his Cambridge experiences might have informed it.

Several members of the Mond family went to Cambridge (see appendix). Their Jewishness was not disavowed, but their Jewish consciousness had in effect evaporated until, after the Balfour Declaration, Alfred Mond (later Lord Melchett) became fired by Zionism. After the rise of Hitler his two children by a non-Jewish wife formally adopted Judaism. It may therefore be supposed that Francis Mond (son of Emile, not a Cambridge man), who went up to King's in 1912 but transferred to Peterhouse, will hardly have felt sufficient Jewish identity to seek out Jewish activity with a view to sustaining it. He, too, was killed, in the Royal Flying Corps, in 1918. In the following year his father established in his memory the Francis Mond professorship of Aeronautical Engineering at Cambridge — only the second such chair (by a matter of months) to be founded in this country. Its first occupant was Bennett Melville Jones,* a scientific article by whom introduced the concept of an ideally streamlined aircraft with minimum drag: and this led to the evolution of the monoplane with retractable undercarriage. Other work by Jones concerned aircraft stability and the avoidance of stalling. When, in 1935, some in Cambridge tried to get the University to decline a benefaction to extend the work, partly on pacifist grounds and partly out of concern lest it make Cambridge a target in time of war, Jones stated publicly that 'at present it is neither our intention nor our desire ... for research specifically devoted to [a military] end'. Nevertheless, by 1937 he was concentrating on the military aspect, and during the war he was an important member of a team that evolved an improved gyroscopic sight for air-gunnery which, when put into operation on D-Day 1944, doubled the success-rate.

How this work would have progressed had there not been funds to found the Cambridge chair, and the extent to which the Nazis were able to avail themselves of Jones' research in building up the efficiency of the *Luftwaffe*, are questions that it is beyond my own competence to address; but it seems clear that, in any event, the

---

*See *DNB. 1971-80*. pp. 453f; *Biographical Memoirs of the Fellows of the Royal Society*. 23. 1977. pp. 253f.

greater accuracy in air-gunnery was in itself one of the material factors in deciding the last major set-piece battle of the war. In the present context it is also relevant to note that in Cambridge Jones gave lectures for the faculty of mathematics, and may well have been heard by Sydney Goldstein of St John's, an applied mathematician and keen zionist who graduated in 1925. Goldstein, who himself taught at Cambridge from 1931, worked during the war on aerodynamics, subsequently becoming professor of mathematics at Manchester until, in 1951, he joined the technology institute of the Haifa Technion, where it seems reasonable to suppose that his aerodynamical expertise will have contributed to Israel's survival. Francis Mond's blood was surely not shed in vain; and, problematic though it be, the historian and philosopher of Judaism cannot evade the challenge of finding room within his scheme for such paradoxes as this.

C. M. Rose & P. L. Jackson

A Glance over the Records
C.H.C. 1888 – 1937
C.U.J.S. 1937 – 1987

T HE VOLUMINOUS RECORDS of the Cambridge Hebrew Congregation and the Cambridge University Jewish Society are now held in the University Library as Add. Mss. 8394 – 5. The Archive consists principally of C.U.J.S. General Meeting and Committee Meeting books since 1937, and in addition, the records of the Society's four predecessor organizations, the earliest dating from 1888. The material in the C.U.J.S. records alone is substantial! The first three volumes of General Meeting minutes from 1937 – 67 each contain around five hundred pages, and there are many hundreds of loose leaves and sheets. This account therefore provides no more than a brief and highly personal sketch of the history of the C.U.J.S. and its principal predecessor, C.H.C. The more detailed account that the subject deserves awaits a future historian.

In 1847, the Jewish Chronicle announced the formation of a congregation worshipping at Mr. Lazarus Cohen's house, in Hobson Street. After a series of moves summarized in Professor Loewe's article, the Congregation moved to 3 Thompson's Lane, its present home in 1937.

From the end of the nineteenth century, the times of the Services were fixed termly. This flexible approach led to the *Shabbat* morning Service sometimes being set to commence at midday. As will be outlined below, there was also considerable flexibility in the form of the Service itself. From about the same time, termly preachers were invited. The Chief Rabbi was a frequent visitor, although the Synagogue was not under his jurisdiction. Many notable visitors were invited, perhaps the most outstanding being Professor Albert Einstein, although there is no record of him actually speaking. Finance was a recurring problem for the Congregation — it is described in 1912 as 'bankrupt' — so that in 1936 it was suggested that only bachelors be invited to address the Society so as to cut down on the expenses for visitors. This was rejected on the grounds that the Congregation did not run a marriage agency.

An annual dinner in commemoration of Solomon Schechter, renowned for bringing the Cairo Genizah to Cambridge in 1897, was first mooted as early as 1925. Three of these dinners actually took place in 1927 – 9, but the practice thereafter lapsed, to be revived twenty years later. Other projects were equally short-lived, or have been forgotten: in 1930, it was decided that a *shabbos goy* be procured to open and close the Synagogue; elsewhere, it seems that a porter at Sidney Sussex College was paid for such a service. In 1932, the formation of a small choir was proposed, but no more is heard of it in the Congregation's records. An earlier project which bore fruit was a club for Jewish boys in Bethnal Green, first planned in 1920. In that year also, the Congregation adopted an Austrian child, while for the benefit of its own number, a Jewish Exhibition had been established in 1897. This had an annual value of £70, the exhibitioner having to have the ability to read the Service and the *Torah*. The exhibition is now funded through the Jewish Memorial Council.

It is hardly necessary to record that many elements of Jewish life in Cambridge have not significantly changed. For example, complaints about talking during the Service were lodged in 1912, while the question of the segregation of the Ladies' section was first raised in 1921. Four years later, a perennial problem was left, as ever, unsolved: a proposal that *Shabbat* morning Services begin more promptly was rejected as being impracticable. This was at least an improvement on the suggestion in 1912 that early morning Services be discontinued 'on the grounds that no real necessity for them existed', which was 'gently but firmly opposed'.

Elsewhere in this volume are related the events that led to the formation of C.U.J.S. The early years of the Society were overshadowed by the grim events in Europe: in March 1938, a joint meeting was held with the other University religious and political Societies to discuss 'The position of Jews in Central and Eastern Europe'— an event which attracted four hundred people, and was well reported in the Press. Later in the same year, an appeal was made on behalf of German refugees and it was decided that every member should pay 2/6d per term to enable refugees to attend communal suppers.

The outbreak of War in September 1939 immediately plunged C.U.J.S. into crisis. In October, the Senior Treasurer painted a very gloomy picture of the Society under wartime condition and said that 'he did not think it beyond the bounds of possibility that the Society would have to forego its functions and just keep the Synagogue open, and perhaps the reverse'. Although this view proved to be unjustifiably pessimistic, the task of obtaining speakers had its problems. The imposition of rationing, made the provision of food for the Friday night meal an 'acute difficulty'. The rise in the Jewish population was not totally without its benefits. Among the evacuees were the Jewish members of the London University colleges, who, in October 1939, were given full membership of C.U.J.S. They appear to have been a particularly vibrant group, and by the Michaelmas term 1942, formed a majority of the members and Committee of the Society, although the Cambridge members blocked the appointment of a London president. Amongst this influx was a certain Vivian (*Chaim*) Hertzog, then a law student at University College London.

The war years, however, had their lighter moments. During *Succoth* in 1940, it was proposed that 'the roof should be opened'. This was carried with acclamation and two members were despatched to execute this mission. The first result of this was a shower of water in the centre of the room, which caused the occupants of this portion to evacuate hurriedly. This was followed by a shower of apples, which fell further afield. Throughout this, the Secretary had been persevering heroically to say a few words, but alas, through the open patches of the covering a member could be seen, apparently eating and what spectacle could the Secretary provide to compare with this?

Much of the Society's history has been shaped by its ownership of the Synagogue. Independent of all external Jewish authorities, the C.U.J.S. thus has a unique responsibility. The maintenance of the Synagogue building and the organizing of Services has, therefore, not surprisingly, always loomed large in the Society's affairs, and has sometimes led to problems.

Disputes between Orthodox and Progressive elements of the Cambridge Jewish community have a long history. Apparently, the Services followed the Spanish and Portuguese ritual from 1888 for about two years. Thenceforth, a flexible form of the *Ashkenazi* ritual was adopted, based on the Singer's Prayer Book, with various portions of the Service being omitted or read in English. Frequently, the *Haphtarah* was read in the vernacular, while sometimes only the first part of the *Sidra* was read, albeit in Hebrew. For a few years during the 1920s, indeed, the triennial scheme of reading the Torah was adopted, certain parts of Leviticus and Deuteronomy being omitted. More serious problems arose in 1949-52: despite the fact that the Progressive members of the Society were permitted to hold services on *Shabbat* afternoons, a proposed joint service with the local Unitarians aroused fierce opposition, and was prevented only by the intervention of the Chief Rabbi. In 1952, the Society agreed to hold Reform Services on alternate Friday nights, but general dissatisfaction led to the creation of a compromise Service: basically Orthodox, but with some of the prayers recited in English. Some Orthodox members felt so strongly about this innovation that they conspicuously walked out, but by 1958 C.U.J.S. had returned to a fully Orthodox Service, and has remained Orthodox to this day. Relations between Orthodox and Progressive members of the Society have, nevertheless, remained excellent.

Relations with the Residents have also been a delicate question, with C.U.J.S. sometimes feeling its control of the Synagogue to be under threat. This issue first raised its head during the War, with the increased number of Residents. By October 1941, following obstruction by some Residents during the High Holydays' Services, relations became so strained that the outgoing committee informed its successor that 'strong-arm methods were advisable in dealing with these elements'. In 1956, following the refusal of the Residents to accept an increase in their subscriptions to the Synagogue, a cautious response was urged on the Society since 'if we tried to get a guaranteed permanent increase from the Residents, this could give a certain faction of them, at present quiescent, a handle to gain control of the Synagogue, which was undesirable'.

The Seventies brought new problems. The Society's growing financial difficulties, together with the first moves to build a new Synagogue, stimulated plans for the Residents to become full members of the C.H.C. (C.U.J.S. in its capacity as the Synagogue), with a committee divided equally between residents and students. In November 1977, a proposed new Constitution to this effect was placed before the Termly General Meeting, but was rejected, the majority feeling that it would reduce the students to the rank of 'second-class citizens'. At present the cost of maintenance is divided between the Cambridge Jewish Residents' Association (35%), the Cambridge Traditional Jewish Congregation (40%) and the C.U.J.S. (25%).

For many members, the most important feature of C.U.J.S. is the daily Kosher lunches it provides by means of the Cambridge Jewish Restaurant. The daily canteen was quite unforeseen when the Society was founded, the Synagogue's kitchen facilities being merely intended to enable the Society to hold communal Friday night meals. These had been held since 1924, mainly in Thurston's Cafe, opposite Emmanuel College, at a cost of 2/6d for a fish meal. Other venues were the Waffle Cafe in Petty Cury, and Mindel's Continental Cafe, a short-lived kosher restaurant in Green Street. In 1943, however, the increase in the number of students and residents and in the general level of religious observance, together with the inability of colleges to provide good vegetarian meals during the War, led to the demand for a daily canteen during term-time. Despite some objections that this was akin to 'turning the Synagogue Hall into a restaurant', the canteen was opened in the Michaelmas term 1943 and was soon declared 'an unqualified success'. Indeed, by 1948, it was reported that, 'from being primarily a means of providing kosher food to Orthodox members of the Society, it had become a social institution, holding the Society together.'

The Society has always seen the promotion of education as one of its foremost concerns. Over the years, C.U.J.S. has operated many educational schemes, from the Jewish Study Group of the 1950s to the current Jewish Learning Exchange. Mention should also be made of the C.U.J.S. Library, founded in 1956, in memory of Herbert Loewe (1882 – 1940), Reader in Rabbinics in the University, which continued to flourish thanks to its many generous benefactors.

In fifty years, there have been many memorable meetings and distinguished speakers. The Chief Rabbi, Lord Jakobovitz, has spoken to the Society on several occasions, continuing a tradition, dating from the beginning of the century. Among other notable speakers were Martin Buber and David Ben Gurion; in November 1986, a hundred and fifty people crowded into the Synagogue to hear a speech delivered by the Society's first president, Mr. Abba Eban. In addition, since 1945, C.U.J.S. has organized an annual lecture in memory of Dr. Solomon Schechter.

At times, the behaviour of the members has not been all that could be desired. In 1948, for example, the President complained 'that the conduct of the Society during the term and at the meeting was deplorable. Behaviour at suppers and meetings was so bad as to be ascribed only to ignorance of civilized manners'. However, the committee itself has not always been free from dispute and criticism. In June 1949, the Society was informed that 'Louis Bourbon ruled without the States-General — he was foully murdered. Nicholas Romanov ruled without the Duma — he was foully murdered'. The president was 'ruling without the committee, *nu?*'. In 1963, another hapless president was accused of intimidating the tellers at an election, it being alleged that he had 'deliberately obliterated identified marks on a ballot paper, argued, threatened and otherwise interfered with the right of the tellers to run the election'. Individual committee officers have also sometimes been less than punctilious in performing their duties.

Thus, to mention but one instance, the Synagogue Secretary of the Lent term 1963 offered the following explanation for his lack of activity: 'I have been lazy, but then I said so at the start, and no one believed me!'

A Society, of course, is the composite of its members, and inevitably, it is never possible to please all of the people all of the time. Certainly, it is difficult not to feel no sympathy for the exasperation of the Secretary who penned the following report on a debate at a General Meeting in December 1948: 'Various members felt that the Society was too academic, too sordid, too historical, too undistinguished, too formal, too informal, too religious, too political, too cliquish, and too Jewish. The writer feels that there is a fable of Aesop which has some relevance but cannot remember what it is'.

Yet, for all this, the final word should be left with the Secretary who chronicled the Society's first meeting on 9th June 1937: 'The meeting concluded with expressions of pleasure, delight and amusement'. So have many more since.

Robert Waley Cohen

Selig Brodetsky

Israel Finestein

Cambridge Contrasts:
Waley Cohen and Brodetsky in Snapshot

RARELY CAN TWO people, holding high office at the same time, have so graphically illustrated the diversity of their community.

Sir Robert Waley Cohen (1877-1952) of Emmanuel College, was a prominent member of the Victorian Anglo-Jewish pluto-aristocracy. He was a descendant of Levi Barent Cohen, the Dutch Jewish merchant who settled in London in the 1760s, two of whose daughters married Sir Moses Montefiore and Nathan Meyer Rothschild. Waley Cohen's maternal grandfather was Professor Jacob Waley, Professor of Political Economy at University College, London, the chairman of whose crucial Finance Committee Waley Cohen was with pride to become.

Professor Selig Brodetsky (1888-1954) of Trinity, was born in the Ukraine, arrived in England in 1893, and in his early years looked upon the straitened circumstances and lowly social rank of his parents as part of the natural order of things. At Cambridge he became all too keenly conscious of the disparities. He ceased to regard them as fetters to personal or professional advancement, but retained a marked, though usually concealed, sensitivity on this score. Brodetsky loved England, and had a high estimate of the value to the world of British social democracy and parliamentary government.

Waley Cohen was managing director of Shell, and for a generation until his death dominated the United Synagogue, which his uncle, Lionel Cohen, had founded in 1870. He gave the impression

of being ready to devote limitless time to the affairs of the synagogal body. One never knew which of the two organizations he
took the more seriously.

He believed in communal forward-planning and rationaliza-
tion, and consciously followed his uncle's celebrated example of
both retaining the vision and mastering the detail. As Vice-President and President of the United Synagogue, he supervised its
huge expansion numerically and geographically. He was well
aware that the fate of this strikingly Victorian body, deeply English in character and style, was ultimately bound up with the new
children and grandchildren of the ghetto.

It was a matter of policy on his part to establish friendly
working relations with the rabbis and spokesmen of the Eastern
European newcomers. He did not publicly deride Yiddish, as some
of his notable predecessors had done. He did not frown on talmudic
learning, as some of them had been wont to do. He sought to
anglicize by trying to meet their requirements and by encouraging
their access into, and communal training within the union.

Waley Cohen was a communal autocrat who preferred to use
democratic forms. He expected to get his own way. His flair for
chairmanship was frequently demonstrated at unruly Council
meetings of the United Synagogues. To see his massive frame
confronting his critics while with bland skill he quieted them with
authority and condescension, was an education in finesse. He
allowed his natural irascibility to be called into play when necessary. His hidden impatience with argument would then emerge.
Few were prepared to withstand his ire or ignore the immensity
of his experience and devotion. He made no pretence to be an
orthodox Jew. Yet he seems to have regarded the survival capacity
of Anglo-Jewry as linked with the maintenance and sound management of the established institutions of orthodoxy. These senti-
ments were reinforced by family pride and traditions. His religion
was deeply personal.

Where Waley Cohen had gone to school at Clifton and enjoyed
his membership of its Jewish House (founded by the Cohens),
Brodetsky attended the Jews' Free School and the Brick Lane
Talmud Torah. Where Waley Cohen had a natural *hauteur*,

Brodetsky had an instinctive ebullience. The latter was a Zionist by birth and rearing, and a devotee of Weizmann. Waley Cohen had considerable respect for Weizmann's pragmatism and talent for public relations, but he remained a firm opponent of political Zionism. He was commercially involved in the strengthening of the industrial and technical infrastructure of Mandatory Palestine. He joined in practical schemes for the improvement of the life of the Yishuv. But he deemed the idea of Jewish statehood to be an imprudent departure from the spirit and objectives of the emancipation.

His public disputes on this issue in the 1940s with the then Chief Rabbi, Dr. Hertz, were painful to both parties, unsparing to either, and wasteful of public energy. Waley Cohen did not support the Government's restrictions upon Jewish immigration into Palestine, but at no time prior to 1948 did he abandon the anti-Zionist position widely shared within the old governing families and those who took their fashion from them. He felt the pain of the Jewish people. In desperate times he searched for practical remedies within the framework of his citizenship and ideology.

Just as Waley Cohen went out of his way to establish bonds with the new immigrant community, so Brodetsky never lost his genuine respect for the *noblesse oblige* of the old leadership. When he was President of the Board of Deputies, he was not deterred by his Zionism from resisting what he regarded as efforts by the Zionist bureaucracy to subvert the independence of the Board. He was highly self-conscious as a successor to Montefiore in that office, and was zealous to sustain the visible independence and public standing of the Board.

Brodetsky combined with the Presidency of the Board the post of political head of the Jewish Agency in London. Waley Cohen and others considered that this was a self-defeating combination from the Board's point of view, and unhelpful to the Jewish community. Brodetsky, who had been a member of the Executive of the World Zionist Organization since 1928, saw no conflict between the two posts. He inevitably faced serious disaffection and criticism from a variety of directions. When, in 1949 after ten years as President he settled in Israel, it was with a sense of relief, only to find that his notion of his new role as President of the Hebrew University proved most controversial in Jerusalem, and peace of mind eluded him.

When Brodetsky headed the Mathematics Tripos List in 1908, he became an instant celebrity. He retained his air of precocity all his life. It sharpened his sensitivity to public criticism. His election as the first academic to the Presidency of the Board — he was Professor of Applied Mathematics at Leeds University from 1924 to 1949 — enhanced his sense of celebrity. This was reinforced by his acute awareness that he was also the first of the new immigration to achieve that office. He was without arrogance, but the contrast between his sense of achievement and his subjection to the sharp darts of dissension, grieved him.

He was the most popular public speaker in the Jewish community. Banter, Yiddish quippery, and an unaffected approachability, helped him to prick pompous balloons and strike chords of mutual recognition of ideas among what used to be called the masses. He was a master of the common touch and a born teacher.

By example and personal influence, Brodetsky's role in encouraging the self-identification of Jews at the Universities was considerable. He welcomed the movement, in which Waley Cohen was a leading figure, to erect adequate and independent premises for the Cambridge University Jewish Society and the Synagogue. The provision in the scheme that the students should manage the Synagogue appealed to him. He shared Waley Cohen's view that the congregation should be comprehensive and not sectarian, while retaining its recognizably traditional character.

Both men ran exceedingly busy public lives. Brodetsky's was probably the more strenuous, if only because of his substantial Zionist political work and his heavy travel between London and Leeds. It was an impressive sight to see him, with his improbable broad-rimmed trilby and laden briefcase, rotund of figure and rubicund of countenance, striding along from Great Russell Street to Tavistock Square from Jewish Agency to Board of Deputies with a distinctively jaunty air. It was not unknown for him to continue, in a taxi to King's Cross, a discussion begun at Woburn House, to be cut short only on the platform as the Leeds train drew out. Was Leeds an interval to Bloomsbury, or was Bloomsbury the interval? One never quite knew.

In 1908, in honour of his academic distinction, the Maccabeans arranged a public dinner for Brodetsky in the West End. The chairman on that occasion was the Right Honourable Arthur Cohen, KC, an aged kinsman of Waley Cohen, the favourite nephew of Montefiore and a former President of the Board of Deputies. Arthur Cohen had studied mathematics at Cambridge more than fifty years earlier. Because of his religion Arthur Cohen was barred from graduation until the passage of the Cambridge University Reform Act of 1856. The impact of this association with the old man remained with the young mathematician far into later years.

Brodetsky's career is bridge-like in many respects. On one side of the bridge is the striking presence of Waley Cohen. The bridge itself is colourful, sometimes resplendent, and always repays study.

Part Two

Reminiscences

8th November 1925. Gonville and Caius College, Cambridge
Chaim Weizmann and the Committee of the C.U. Zionist Society

Chaim Herzog

A Link with Israel

I WAS AN ACTIVE member of the congregation and the Synagogue in the early years of the World War. I was again connected with the Synagogue when stationed on a course during my army service in St. John's College. The period early in the War was a flourishing one for the Synagogue, since two Jewish student bodies, those of Cambridge and those of London University, merged in the Cambridge University Jewish Society and also in the Thompson's Lane Synagogue.

I recall with nostalgia our Friday night dinners and Shabbat Services. We had many cultural activities as part of the active life of our community. I can recall in particular one of our meetings which was addressed by David Ben-Gurion, later Israel's first Prime Minister.

Many of my former contemporaries are here in Israel, such as Professor Domb, Professor of Physics at Bar-Ilan University, and Professor Marco Cain, Professor of Urology at the Hebrew University Hadassah Medical School. Both Judge Helmut Lowenberg, Late President of the District Court of Tel-Aviv, and Professor Yaacov Talmon (formerly Fleischer when at Cambridge) the world renowned historian, passed away, unfortunately, some years ago.

One of the highlights of our social life was, undoubtedly, the Purim Spiel, which was so successfully staged and which in fact has remained a vivid memory in the minds of all who were present. It was originally done some years earlier by Mr. Gershon Ellenbogen. However, a group of us — William Frankel, later Editor of the Jewish Chronicle, Helmut Lowenberg and myself — adapted the scenario, text and lyrics to the times through which we were living and to the developments in Anglo Jewry, which were reflected in the show. If I am not mistaken, I acted as *Shadchan* in the play.

We were at the University at the beginning of the War. While we were aware of the suffering of European Jewry from the ravages of the War, we were not yet aware of the horrors of the Holocaust. Many of us were busy on international student forums in the task of representing the Jewish community in Palestine and the Jewish State on the way. Many of us were to experience the War in its full ferocity. Little did we dream at that time that we were contemporaries of a Holocaust which would destroy a third of our people, and that we would be privileged to live to see the rise of an independent sovereign Jewish State from the ashes of War. Many of us were to be part of the struggle for the realization of this dream.

What we experienced in our student lifetime must surely be a challenge and an inspiration to the student of today. We need you in Israel. Your contribution can be immensely important. You are not being asked to come to help drain swamps. You are being asked to come to a free democracy which has achieved a marked degree of sophistication in the fields of technology, electronics, agriculture, nuclear medical equipment, solar energy etc.

The infra-structure which has grown up in Israel provides more than ever a basis for *aliya* on the part of the English Jewish student. Here we as Jews achieve a fulfilment that cannot be achieved by Jews elsewhere.

Thompson's Lane represents for us all our commitment to our traditions and our awareness of being one people. I trust those instincts which motivated our link with Thompson's Lane will motivate you to join us in Israel.

Aryeh Newman

The CUJS 1941-44[*]

A Jewish Microcosm
(A personal view by a past president)

THIS IS A PERSONAL recollection of the CUJS during the Second World War in the tranquil perspective of some forty years distance. It cannot but be a personal rather than bird's eye view, since by accident of birth and academic ambition I became one of the participants in that scenario. While I shall endeavour to focus on the general characteristics of the CUJS landscape, even a landscape must etch in the individual objects that give it body. The names of some individuals will be writ large in the scenario I am about to describe, the names of others of possibly equal distinction or distinctiveness will not qualify for even a mention. But that is an unavoidable consequence of the selectivity of the human observational apparatus.

Perhaps the most general observation of significance regarding the role of the CUJS during those crucial war years is that it came to represent, as in no other preceding period, a microcosm of Jewish life in the world at large and Anglo-Jewry in particular. My starting point will, therefore, consist of a brief review of the Jewish ideological and historical environment.

Emancipation and equal rights in an open society, continued and increasing antisemitism against a backcloth of conflicting nationalisms on the one hand, and universal brotherhood and internationalism on the other, presented the Jewish student with

[*] This article includes excerpts from my article: *Jewish Identity: Cambridge 1941-44* that appeared in The Cambridge Review vol 10, no. 2276 Oct. 1983, by kind permission of the publishers Taylor and Francis Ltd., the copyright holders.

options and dilemmas that still continue to exercise his mind. In 1941-44 these were overshadowed by the hideous climax of anti-semitic agitation: the Holocaust, and by the not entirely uncon-nected struggle for Jewish sovereignty in the Palestinian Homeland.

The Jewish student population of the War years reflected, too, the ideological currents at work in the Anglo-Jewish community as well as the successive waves of immigration into the country and their progressive but different forms of acculturation. For the prepogrom Anglicized section of the community who had come to Britain mainly from Germany in the early and middle nineteenth century, the English public school system and Oxbridge con-stituted, for those able and inclined to take advantage of them, the principal formative elements in their education. Intermar-riage was rife, and indeed regarded by many as a natural consum-mation of a conscious process of assimilation, the 'extinguishing of the tribe painlessly by intermarriage.'* Here and there, sur-vived the relics of an attempt to forge and retain a faintly Hebraic, ethical, possibly monotheistic culture which substituted occa-sional worship in or at least formal membership of a synagogue for the respectable churchgoing of their Christian counterparts. The products of this wave of immigration had all but opted out of the Jewish community in which, oddly enough they still held the leading positions. The *noblesse oblige* public activities of these Anglo-Jewish notables on behalf of their co-religionists was their substitute for Jewish practice and knowledge.

Their contribution to laying the institutional foundations for a corporate Jewish student life at Cambridge however should not be underestimated. It was the institutional commitment of such figures as Sir Robert Waley Cohen, a former Emmanuel man, which brought into being the Cambridge University Synagogue and its amenities long before Hillel foundations were even dreamt of. But without the influx of the products of the mass immigration from East Europe at the turn of the century bringing with them a vibrant Jewishness these amenities would have become a monu-

*From a short story by Gilbert Frankau entitled 'An Outlier from his Tribe' in *Yisroel. The First Jewish Omnibus*, edited by J. Leftwich (London: John Heritage 1934) p. 134

ment of wood and brick, under-exploited and reserved for special occasions. As it was, the communal-minded efforts of this disappearing aristocracy came at a strategic turning-point in the history of Anglo Jewry, when the descendants of the East European wave of immigration were beginning to take over the community leadership.

Unlike their Anglicized predecessors they came from homes where observance of the Sabbath and festivals and the dietary laws in varying degrees, the speaking of *Yiddish*, some religious schooling on Sundays and weekday evenings after school till barmitzvah, were the norm. A few like myself had private teachers and later attended Eastern European-style Talmudic colleges. The religious observance and Jewish knowledge wore thin for lack of practice as these first generation Britons went into the wider world, particularly when they literally stormed the citadels of academe to satisfy a thirst for scholarly distinction and professional qualification engendered as much by a religious respect for learning as by years of deprivation and persecution. An intense Jewish feeling often remained, transmuted into a passion for social reform, a communist utopia or Zionism. Parents who delighted in their sons' distinction deplored their alienation from Jewish traditional *mores* and were haunted by the spectre of intermarriage, which spelt for them the annihilation of all that was near and dear to them. For this reason the corporate life of the Cambridge college system did not appeal to many parents, and they preferred universities nearer home which kept their children within the family orbit, within sight of the familiar landmarks. The number of observant Jews going up to Cambridge was for this reason always very small.

The war years, however, brought a more intensely Jewish element into the student body as a result of the larger residential Jewish community which was swelled by evacuees from the Blitz and by students of the London University colleges transferred to Cambridge for the duration, particularly from the London School of Economics. This element was reinforced by the influx of refugees from Nazi persecution. For the first time there appeared among the undergraduate and graduate body products of the synthesis of German culture and Jewish orthodoxy, a synthesis fostered in their country of origin in a Jewish school system which combined a systematic training in both Jewish and secular subjects. A paler reflection of this day school began to strike roots in Britain just before the war and qualified for state aid in the postwar period. The graduates of these schools have indeed changed the Jewish face of the university campus today.

The focal point of Jewish identity at Cambridge was the University Jewish Society which at the time was a roof organization for all activities Jewish, including many of those sponsored by the local Jewish residents. The committee included a Zionist Convener, a Supper Secretary to whose time-honoured Friday night Sabbath dinner chore was added a daily kosher 'British Restaurant', then subsidized by the Ministry of Food, which is still in existence and Synagogue and Meetings Secretaries, all on the synagogue premises at Thompson's Lane. With the change in character and composition of the student body and residential community, the University synagogue became pronouncedly orthodox, that is less English and decorous and more foreign and fervent in the eyes of the Anglicized establishment of an earlier age, represented by the seemingly permanent Senior Treasurer, the famous educational psychologist Charles Fox (1876 – 1964). As an M.A. of the University he would also invigilate members of the Jewish student body who did not wish to sit for examinations on the Sabbaths and holidays. Perhaps his first encounter with the changed and, for him, disconcerting new elements in Jewish life was when I presented myself at his home on the Sabbath-eve complete with a prepacked kosher cuisine for the day prepared by the wife of an interned orthodox German refugee rabbi who earned her living by running a modest home-from-home restaurant for the growing number of students wishing to keep the dietary laws or simply enjoy Jewish food and company. The other two students who turned up complemented the new archetypal pattern of the Jewish student body. One was the son of the Russian-born Zionist leader Professor Selig Brodetzky, the other the son of the head of Clifton college public school's Jewish house, the Jewish educational response of a previous age.

It was not long before 'Charlie' Fox was replaced as Senior Treasurer by a German refugee, an orthodox Jew, David Daube then already a distinguished member of the Law and Divinity faculties who, whenever necessary, intoned the lengthy Biblical lesson prescribed by Orthodox rite straight from the unpointed Scroll, a performance not regarded as coming within the duties or competence of previous incumbents. The active members of the Society included a goodly number of 'Palestinians', usually Jewish students from the continent who had come to study at London or Cambridge from or on their way to Palestine. Many of them later became prominent in Israel in the political, judicial, military and academic fields. Among them was Chaim Herzog, the Israeli President.

Debate at Society meetings was fast, furious and entertaining, attended by scores of students. Battle was mainly joined between the left, right, centre and religious supporters of Zionism who were in the majority and their opponents. The latter came mainly from the Liberal Jewish elements and the utopian left-wingers and universalists, both of whom regarded any form of Jewish nationalism as a fascist heresy. Since their Jewish commitment and background was, in the first instance, of an attentuated and sporadic nature, these elements remained on the fringes of the Jewish Society. The ultra-orthodox, who regarded Zionism as a pseudo-messianic blasphemy, were unrepresented at the university for the simple reason that no one from such circles would have risked his hereafter by entering its precincts.

Nevertheless in accordance with the pluralist spirit of the CUJS their fringe views were represented amongst the variety of speakers invited by the Society. No ideological trend was ignored, no personality too controversial. On the contrary, the preference was quite naturally in an effervescent student body for the controversial, for the *enfant terrible*, providing that the individuals concerned were willing to address a specifically Jewish student body. And there were such refusals, on principle. One example comes to mind, Professor Harold Laski whose Saturday morning lecture at LSE proved a formidable counter-attraction to the synagogue service. Indeed one particular Sabbath morning epitomized the split in Jewish life within one Anglo-Jewish family. Neville Laski a former President of the Jewish Board of Deputies on his way to the synagogue in Thompson's Lane to say *Kaddish* for his father bumped into his brother Harold on his way to give his Saturday morning lecture. No importunings could prevail on the universalist-socialist Harold Laski to address a specifically Jewish Society. But that did not prevent the Society from enjoying and baiting a number of varied and colourful figures all united by their consistent and sometimes venomous anti-zionism. They included left wing Victor Gollancz, the devout monotheists of the Liberal Jewish establishment, Lily Montagu and Basil Henriques and Agudist representative Harry Goodman. Then there were the Zionist speakers and above all the harbingers of the Holocaust like Dr. Schwartzhart the Jewish representative of the Polish government in exile who was among the first to bring to the students direct documentary evidence of the mass extermination. Its impact was indelible and undoubtedly influenced the lives of students who later took part in the rehabilitation of camp survivors and the rebuilding of Jewish life in Eretz Israel.

Characterization of people in terms of their background and origins provides a neat labelling device but can never give a true or complete picture, since so many overlapping influences are at work. There was, too, the call of military duty which drastically curtailed the amount of time most students could remain at the University or had at their disposal during the period they were up. For some this meant total concentration on essential studies to the detriment of outside interests, to others, an eagerness to take advantage of whatever expressions of Jewish camaraderie and culture were available before the inevitable break with civilian life and venture into the unknown.

Among the first and second generation Jewish students of Russian origin at Cambridge one could see their efforts to come to terms with conflicting loyalties. There were those whose parents, not unlike their nineteenth century predecessors from Germany, had given them the minimum of Jewish education, packing them off to a public school and thence to Cambridge. Some impelled by ethnic or religious considerations compromised by sending them to the Jewish house at Clifton or Perse. Once at university most strove to integrate themselves into college life, kept clear of the Jewish Society but occasionally dropped in for a Friday night meal, perhaps out of genuine nostalgia for Jewish company, or to quote Gilbert Frankau again, 'to exchange clan courtesies'* or even out of more utilitarian motives. These included tentative approaches to see how easy or difficult it might be to become elected president of the Society before going down, in this way boosting parental pride without prejudicing their own efforts to shine socially outside the Jewish domain. Some succeeded as a result of their oratorical and intellectual gifts in making a distinguished political and public career for themselves usually at the expense of their Jewish commitment. Others, less gifted, retained the Jewish option for the advantages it might still bring them. Both suffered from the love-hate relationship which characterizes the alienated of all minority groups.

During those early forties, however, the keynote of Cambridge Jewish life was not alienation but a return to the sources. An emergency committee for Jewish education centred in London catered for the religious needs of Jewish children evacuated from the Blitz to the Cambridge area. A rabbi from a London synagogue, a Cambridge man, returned to the University Town to supervise the programme. Students helped in teaching chores and the running of youth groups. Both the students and members of the allied forces benefited from the activities of the Jewish chaplains seconded to the Cambridge area, nearly all of whom turned out to be Cambridge graduates. They were intensely Zionist, first generation in Britain and products of a combined rabbinic and university education. One of them, Bernard Casper (now Chief Rabbi of Johannesberg) was appointed senior chaplain to the Jewish Brigade, the Palestinian Jewish units that saw service in the Mediterranean and European campaigns.

The Society and community as a whole was fortunate in the personality of the head of Hillel house, the Jewish house at the Cambridge school of Perse. Harry Dagut, himself the product of Oxbridge and an East European rabbinic and intensely zionist

*Op. Cit. p. 129

home. He regularly brought his 'boys' to the synagogue and contributed his own unique blend of Jewish dignity, good humour and tradition.

No description of CUJS life would be complete without a reference to the role of the 'refugee' rabbis and scholars from the continent. The most distinguished among them were Professor Samuel Kraus and the venerable chief Rabbi of Vienna, Rabbi Taglicht. There were others too, less renowned, who played an important part in hosting Jewish students, lecturing to them and teaching the many Jewish boys and girls scattered in and around Cambridge, evacuated from the blitz or refugees themselves from the Nazi scourge. This atmosphere of intensified Jewishness was epitomized in the activities of an unusual figure in Cambridge Jewish life—Rabbi K. Kahana Kagan of Fitzwilliam, a refugee rabbi from Lithuania whose wife and children perished in the Holocaust. He was a kind of Talmudic virtuoso who in his late forties had come up to Cambridge with the avowed aim of perfecting his almost nonexistent English and acquiring that minimum of academic status within the Jewish community to enable him to spread his message of Talmudic learning amongst its academic élite. His weekly lecture at the University Synagogue was a pedagogic *tour de force*. Enthusiasm and complete mastery of the subject more than compensated for the curious pidgin of Yiddish syntax, phonology and newly-acquired English vocabulary interlaced with Talmudic and Roman legal terms which served as Kahana's medium of communication. During the three years he was up until he obtained his long-coveted academic qualification of M. Litt on the subject of usufruct in the Talmud, his lectures on Sabbath afternoons attracted a small but select audience of graduates and undergraduates, some encountering the subject for the first time.

He himself rarely attended the synagogue service. But one such visit is worthy of note, when he transformed the traditionally solemn and decorous Simhat Torah service into an ecstatic Yeshiva style dancing in honour of the Torah learning he so single-mindedly and enthusiastically promoted. His presence at the University gave me the opportunity to continue my rabbinic studies under his guidance. When I had to make up a term of residence after finishing my final English tripos examinations, my study of the Talmud and religious codes for rabbinic ordination under his aegis was accepted as a recognized course of study by Emmanuel, something I think quite unique in the history of that Protestant establishment. Rabbi Kahana's status was indeed enhanced by his Cambridge immersion and he was duly appointed Professor of Talmud and Codes at Jews' College London, conducting its first course for full rabbinic ordination. During his sojourn at the University, Kahana's Talmudically-stocked brain soaked up a knowledge of Roman and British jurisprudence which enabled him to produce a seminal comparative study of Roman, British and Jewish law entitled *Three Great Systems of Jurisprudence* (London; Stevens, 1955)

To sum up, the CUJS with its varied cultural activities, its canteen and multi-purpose hall, all managed by the students themselves, provided an invaluable training for many in conducting religious services, in experience of communal administration and leadership. But first and foremost, the CUJS during those war-torn years constituted a successful experiment in pluralist Jewish living (worthy of emulating in our more polarized times) where all who regarded themselves as belonging to the community of whatever shade of observance or ideology could find their niche and fruitfully interact with each other.

*As a past president of the CUJS, at the time, the Anglo-Jewish historian and Judge, Israel Finestein QC later wrote: 'It was at that time a remarkable and self-conscious example of *broadchurchmanship*' (personal communication 8.1.84).

D. Weil

Julia Neuberger

Being Hooked

C AMBRIDGE IN THE late 1960s. It was then much more politically active than now. There were the odd sit-ins, and there was even the Garden House Riot. It all seems a bit misty now, but the issues were quite clear at the time.

It was a strange place to go as a doubting Jewess at that date. I was not at all comfortable. I came from a religious Reform background. I had had a bar–mitzvah and a confirmation. I had, as I saw it, humoured my father whilst still at home, and gone to services with him. I had even, though unwillingly, been Senior Jewish Prefect at my school, and had to run Jewish prayers.

What freedom then to go to Newnham, a college so opposed to religious organizations that it boasted no chapel but merely a quiet room (where I later conducted services for the Cambridge Reform community). What joy to have it all open to one — the Union, the Labour Club, the Cambridge Poverty Action Group, Shelter. There were college activities and university ones, with new friends everywhere. I was constantly in a whirl of activity. There were always more parties, more meetings, more events, than I could possibly manage in a term. By the end of term I would go home and sleep exhaustedly for a week.

Nothing Jewish so far, you may have noticed. It is true I was not very interested, despite valiant attempts by select members of the Jewish society to make me so. Instead, I was learning Biblical Hebrew academically for the first time. It was a soft option in comparison with Arabic, which I couldn't read, or Aramaic, which I could not understand. At least I had done 'O' level Classical Hebrew not too many years before. And my main subject, Assyriology, the study of ancient Babylon and Assyria, could not be studied alone. So there I was, professing total disinterest in things Jewish, studying Hebrew for large parts of the day!

The trouble was that I became interested again. Of course I kidded myself it was academic, and that it was nothing to do with me being Jewish. I went to a service or two at the synagogue, and that put me off again — as any service has done where women are separated and considered of no consequence as far as a *minyan* is concerned.

But even then my interest grew. Assyriology was looking less and less of a serious option, as Iraq became impossible for Jews to go to (there were public hangings of Jews in Baghdad and Basra), and Turkey became closed to British archaeologists temporarily, in the wake of what was called the Mellaart affair. (James Mellaart, a British archaeologist, was thought by the Turks to have stolen finds from a site.)

Hebrew was the obvious choice as my main subject for Part II. And yet there I was, an uncomfortable, uncommitted Jewess, not at all sure I could read Hebrew without some religious involvement.

Then Nicholas de Lange came to teach. He was thinking of finishing his rabbinic studies through Leo Baeck College himself at the time. He transformed Jewish studies for me. The history came alive. I became fascinated by medieval French Jewish-Christian relationships. I learned about RaDaK, and about Yedaiah Rederei. Medieval Jewish Provence became a living world. David Kimeli was a friend and even Judah ibn Tibbon a close acquaintance. I wanted to trace the links between the Cathar heretics in Christianity and the Jews of that liberal golden age in Provence. I wanted to follow the course of translation of Greek medical and philosophical writing into Arabic, then Hebrew and then Latin or old French. For a brief period — a few months at most — Jewish life in medieval southern France became more important to me than real life. I read voraciously. I knew all the street names mentioning Jews in most of the region. I had discovered mentions of Jews in letters by archbishops dating back to Agobard of Lyons. I was hooked.

Not, of course, that I would have admitted being hooked. That would have been far too embarrassing. I was, after all, still claiming that my interest was purely academic. Yet at this time I began, furtively at first, to get back into organized Jewish life. I went to the Progressive Jewish Students group, with friends who were thrilled I had joined them but all too keen to say: 'I told you so'. We went to the Jewish Society on alternate weeks after our service, and the other weeks we would eat informally with Nicholas de Lange, bringing our own dishes, sharing, eating vegetarian, singing and *benching* in a *chavurah*–like atmosphere before I knew what a *chavurah* was.

We had marvellous *Shabbatot*. Gradually, I was able to admit I was enjoying them. A couple of months later I told Nicholas over dinner that I was finding religious meaning in them. My life was becoming enriched. I could once again admit to being a practising Jewess. I hurried to telephone my father, whose reaction was predictable: 'So what? I knew that was what would happen....'

Through all this I jogged along at Cambridge, happy, and much involved in all the university had to offer. I was Chairman of Cambridge Shelter. I had just served on a committee of inquiry into corruption in the Cambridge University Labour Club. Yet Judaism, and Jewish friends, were playing an increasing part in my life, and the enthusiasm, the thirst for more, was there.

The Jewish studies element of my Hebrew course began to take precedence over the rest. I became engrossed in medieval Judaism and Jewish history. I began to read widely in the works of Rambam and Ibn Ezra, Rashi and Radak, and draw comparisons with contemporary non–Jewish literature.

My friends became fascinated too. We read medieval texts late into the night on *Shabbat*. We celebrated festivals together, with services and food. The *chavurah* atmosphere grew. We became closer.

None of this had prepared me for the rabbinate, however. It was Nicholas de Lange's idea. (He has been remarkably influential in my life, introducing me to my husband as well!) He thought it would be a good thing, in terms of 1066 and all that, if I were to study for the rabbinate. My protests were considerable. I did not think women were rabbis; I, who had campaigned with other Labour Club members against sex discrimination and for equal pay legislation, knew only too well that religious bodies were not to be included. Those two parts of my life — the political, anti-discrimination side, and the religious, albeit progressive, side — had always seemed destined to stay apart. Women rabbis? I was not even sure that I liked the idea myself.

Nicholas persisted. I agreed to try, by travelling to London one day a week for courses at the Leo Baeck College, notably Rabbi Dr Louis Jacob's Talmud class. What overwhelmed me completely was the support I received from all sides, even the most unlikely quarters. Orthodox friends from the Jewish Society, with whom I had kept in touch though I saw them relatively rarely, wished me well and promised help with Aramaic texts (I had not studied Aramaic at this stage) if I needed it. Christian Hebrew lecturers changed the timetable to allow me to have a clear day in the week. My old friend Dr Sebastian Brock, who had by then moved to Oxford, but had spent much of the first year trying to make me understand the *Kamatz Katan*, taught me some basic Palestinian Jewish Aramaic. Professor Emerton, Anglican divine and Regius Professor of Hebrew, provided me with some American Jewish bible commentaries. My cousin, Dr Erwin Rosenthal, gave me working texts of *Mishnah* and *Midrash Rabbah* and *Tanchuma*. The list went on and on.

What was amazing about it is that even those who could at the very least have been expected to be negative about women rabbis, and who were, on the whole, fairly dismissive of non–orthodox Judaism, gave wholehearted support. I do not know why. But I can hazard a few guesses. Firstly, I think that the whole small Jewish student community (there were many Jewish students, but only a few played a part in the community) was thrilled in the early 1970s that any of their number wanted to continue further with Jewish studies. Secondly, although there was a clear divide between orthodox and progressive students, there were close friendships across the divide, and we did eat together and celebrate together a few times a term. Thirdly, there were those amongst the orthodox who felt that Jewish women had not been given sufficient opportunities to study, and that they could see no objection to the type of studying I was to do — as opposed to the role-model I was to take on — at the Leo Baeck College.

Whatever the reasons, and I shall probably never know them in full, the students who played any part in the life of the Jewish Society were immensely supportive. I look back on that, after ten years of a career where the community appears to be polarizing to a remarkable degree, with enormous pleasure and affection. I do not believe it could happen now. The lines are far more sharply drawn, and the Cambridge adult community would be less receptive to such thinking than they were then.

But in those glorious, heady days of the late 1960s and early 1970s, things were different. There was a tolerance and a friendship. We did not need to agree, but agreeing to disagree was perfectly acceptable. Cambridge then was an exciting place in which to rediscover Judaism. I have no regrets that it was there and then that I was fully awakened to the excitement of the world of medieval Jewry. I only regret that those who come after me will not be able to experience that tolerance, learn about orthodoxy or progressive Judaism by being part of both, receive help from both sides, and support in what they choose to do.

Thompson's Lane, in my time, did not look or sound like a bastion of 1960s liberalism. There were no sit–ins, and there was no active student union (Cambridge Students' Union as opposed to the Union Society) involvement. The hippy culture appeared not to have impinged at all. And yet the good things of that time had coloured the atmosphere of the synagogue enormously. It was tolerant, warm, supportive and witty. It was liberal (note the small l) in its attitudes and encouraged debate.

The 1980s have been different in kind. We live in a much less liberal age. We are all less tolerant. I just hope that Thompson's Lane can retain its old cool academic objectivity and liberalism, and give support and friendship to others who are finding their way back into Judaism.

Cyril Domb

Jewish Life at Cambridge in the 1930s and 1940s

I CAME UP AS an undergraduate in 1938, a year after the formation of the Cambridge University Jewish Society and the opening of the new Synagogue in Thompson's Lane.

When I arrived to take up residence at Pembroke in 1938 there was already a well established tradition of committed observant Jews in the 1930's. A story was told of Maurice Plotnick who on arrival at Trinity explained to his bedmaker that he was an eccentric, he lit candles in his rooms Friday evenings, and kept separate dishes for meat and dairy foods. 'It's all right, Sir' came the reply, 'I've had Jewish gentlemen before'. Maurice Pryce was one of the most brilliant young mathematical physicists at Cambridge in the early '30s (he went on to become an FRS at a very young age and Wykeham Professor of Physics at Oxford). Pryce was my first mentor during the war years, and told me quite proudly that he had acted as a *Shabbat Goy* for Joe Gillis during his years at Trinity, switching off the light in Joe's room before retiring on Friday night. But perhaps the most sophisticated *halachic* story of this period related to two undergraduates, one of St. John's the other of Trinity, who are reputed to have approached one of the porters with a small token payment to buy rights in the College, so that they could arrange an Eruv for the two colleges, and carry between each other's rooms on *Shabbat*.

The organization of Jewish life at Cambridge was unique. There was virtually no permanent community and no Rabbi, and all Jewish activities were in the hands of the students. The introduction to the *Book of Memorial* mentions a series of incidents which led to a vote of censure on Senior members of the University and townsmen who were holding office in the Cambridge Hebrew Congregation. This led to the resolution passed by the Congregation in 1899 that in future no graduates or townsfolk were eligible for office, for voting, or for attendances at meetings unless specially invited to be present for some definite purpose. This resolution was zealously observed, and during my time as an undergraduate the students were proud of their independence and lack of affiliation with any other synagogue body. Despite the influx of large numbers of wartime evacuees from London, the direction of the Synagogue remained in their hands. Services were run by a small group of fully observant students, but many of their less–observant or non–observant colleagues would attend regularly. Out of consideration for the latter the *Shabbat* morning services started at 10:30 am with *Keriat HaTorah* and finished by noon to enable those who wished to attend a 12 to 1 lecture. Members of the University were expected to wear academic dress for Synagogue services. The *Keriat Ha Torah* was shared amongst those who were capable of reading, and for example I can well remember Aubrey Eban, who was a senior graduate student when I first came up, taking his share regularly, even though he was far from being observant.

Cambridge always attracted young people of ability, and my own contemporaries included (besides Aubrey Eban) David Tabor, a leading young Zionist thinker who later became Professor at Cambridge and the world's leading authority on friction, Bernard Casper, who later became Chief Rabbi of S. Africa, Anthony Epstein, who is currently Foreign Secretary of the Royal Society, Chaim Herzog, now President of Israel (who was evacuated to Cambridge with University College, London) and William Frankel, later editor of the *Jewish Chronicle* (who studied at the London School of Economics, also evacuated to Cambridge). CUJS attracted most of the leading personalities and speakers of Anglo-Jewry; but they were often a little taken aback by the eloquence and sophistication of the votes of thanks proposed perhaps by Eban and seconded by Tabor.

Eban's brilliance as a thinker and speaker was already well developed, and few of us doubted that he was destined for an outstanding career. During my first year he conducted a study circle on the Middle East, in which the participants were clearly overawed by his detailed intimate knowledge of the subject. Since the audience participation was minimal he described the study circle as a division of labour in which he performed the study and the others made the circle. On many occasions he demonstrated his remarkable facility for an appropriate turn of phase. At a CUJS meeting several speakers had expressed disappointment with the level of reporting in the columns of the *Jewish Chronicle*. 'It describes itself as the Organ of Anglo-Jewry' quipped Eban. 'This is not quite accurate—it is in fact the Mouth–Organ of Anglo–Jewry!'

A few Jewish dons attended Synagogue services regularly. Notable among them were Herbert Loewe, Reader in Rabbinics, David Daube, a young Fellow of Caius who afterwards became Regius Professor of Roman Law at Oxford, and Charles Fox, a well known educational psychologist. And of course all CUJS Shabbat morning services were attended by Harry Dagut and the boys of Hillel House at Perse School.

Several eminent senior members of the University were crypto–Jews whose identity became apparent when their full names appeared in official documents. The distinguished Trinity mathematician Abraham Samuelovitch Besicovitch was a Karaite Jew who had swum across the Volga to escape from Russia. Despite his reputed pride in his non–conformist ancestry, he never made contact with CUJS. There was an argument among the students as to whether Prof. Postan, Professor of economic history, married to the well known non-Jewish historian Eileen Power, was himself Jewish or not. The issue was resolved when his first names appeared in print—Michael Moishe!

During the vacation when the students were absent there was little Jewish activity. In fact *Rosh Hashanah* and *Yom Kippur* nearly always fell at the end of the long vacation and it was not always easy to put together a *Minyan*. David Daube told me of one occasion on a *Yom Kippur* when it was felt inadvisable to allow for any break in the service since the *Minyan* might not re-convene! He faced the challenge of a four hour gap between *Musaf* and *Neilah* in which to conduct the *Minchah* service; but, he added, he came from Freiburg, a community whose special pride was *Piyutim* and deliberate prayer; he was delighted to demonstrate publicly that a Freiburger could rise to the occasion. This must surely be a world record for the length of a *Yom Kippur Minchah*.

The character of the community changed dramatically in 1939 with the outbreak of war when a large number of London Jewish evacuees descended on Cambridge. It was of great importance to CUJS that the control of Jewish activities associated with the Synagogue should remain in the hands of the students. Among the most eminent of those who settled in Cambridge was the Chief Rabbi, Dr. J.H. Hertz who took up lodgings at the Bull Hotel. The officers of the Society informed him politely but firmly, that whilst they had the greatest respect for his person and his Office, the Cambridge Synagogue was independent and unaffiliated. Dr. Hertz took this in good part, and did not interfere with the student organization of the services. However he had no inhibitions about expressing his views on various aspects of the services forthrightly and vigorously. He was particularly peeved with the custom which Herbert Loewe maintained of reading out during *Yizkor* the complete list of names of deceased members of Cambridge Jewry from the Unnamed Martyr of 1144 up to contemporary times. Hertz expressed his conviction that some of those on the list belonging to the medieval period were not Jews at all, and he persuaded Cecil Roth at Oxford to investigate the matter. He was delighted when the latter produced some positive evidence to support his claim.

An unusual personality who appeared on the Cambridge scene during the war years was Rabbi Kopul Kahana. He was an outstanding Lithuanian talmudist with a photographic memory who knew the whole of the *Babylonian Talmud* by heart. In fact he gave a public demonstration of his remarkable ability to some of the students, asking them to pick any volume of the *Talmud*, and fix a pin at some point of the page; he would then recite the text at the same point any desired number of pages later.

He had come to Cambridge with no previous formal training to study Roman Law. By good fortune he made contact with Mr. Turner of the Cambridge Law School who very soon appreciated that Kahana could not fit into the conventional pattern of studies, and persuaded the University authorities to waive the first degree and allow him to proceed to a thesis. It says much for the elasticity of the University administration at Cambridge that such a procedure was permitted.

Rabbi Kahana proceeded to commit the whole of the Roman Legal Codex to memory, and made very rapid progress with his studies, and Turner was delighted to find his faith justified. But after a little while Kahana began to disparage Buckland, the major Cambridge authority on Roman Law, at first by occasional remarks, then with more vehement criticisms. Turner suggested to Kahana that he was only a beginner in the field, and that he needed to devote much more careful attention to Buckland's writings before offering any criticism. But Kahana could not be suppressed, and a story was current among the students that during one of the interchanges Kahana challenged Turner to open Buckland's classic treatise at any page, and he was sure that he would find an error. Turner chose a particular page, and Kahana (who was very short sighted) pushed the text to his eyes, moved it rapidly to and fro, and stopped in triumph — he had found a mistaken reference!

Kahana was awarded the degree of M. Litt at Cambridge and continued for many years to interest himself in Roman Law. He was appointed to head the Rabbinical department of Jews' College, where he taught *Halachah* to several generations of Anglo-Jewish ministers, and trained them for their Rabbinical diploma. When asked why he had come to Cambridge in the first place he replied 'I knew that the Jews in England would respect me only if I had first obtained the respect of the *Goyim*'.

It is appropriate, finally, to draw attention to the close relationship which has existed for many decades between Cambridge and the Land of Israel. The *Book of Memorial* already contains the names of three former Cambridge students who were killed in Arab riots — Harold Marcus Wiener, Levi Billig and Avinoam Yellin. Of my own Cambridge contemporaries at least ten are now living in Israel, a proportion which is well above that of normal *aliyah* in Anglo-Jewry.

CUJS group 1941 (? Cricket team in a match with Perse)
Left to right:
Top row: William Margulies, Lionel Wolman, Marco Caine, Gerald Sklan, Cyril Domb, Albert Cherns, Basil Sklan, Monty Richardson, Solly Cohen
Bottom row: Asher Weingarten, ? Crystal, Harry Dagut, Leon Galkoff, ? Levine.
(Six of them became Professors)

Part Three

General

Abba Eban

The Central Question*

ISRAEL HAS NEVER been more secure against external menace and never more vulnerable to domestic folly. There is no existential danger from hostile Arab armies. Egypt has removed itself in its own interest from the cycle of recurrent wars. Jordan does not seek military involvement in the anarchy of Lebanese politics, and the Syrian threat can be contained by deterrent power and vigilance. Terrorists are a threat to individual Israeli lives, but not the life of the Israeli state. The American-Soviet balance creates an international environment favourable to Israel's stability. The global relationship, moving toward a possible era of détente, does not imply a Soviet threat to Israel's existence. In these conditions, the darkest shadow hanging over Israel comes from within itself.

Most tragedies in history are self-inflicted. Israel's peril would arise from the stupendous folly of accepting a structural defect through the permanent incorporation of the West Bank and Gaza into the Israeli state. There does not exist on the face of the inhabited globe a single country that resembles what Israel would look like if it were to exercise a permanent jurisdiction over 1,300,000 members of a foreign nation owing no devotion to our flag, our tongue, our name or our national vision, and recognized by all the governments of the world, including that of Israel, as a separate nation endowed with a specific particularity within an Arab context. If we were to hear that Holland had decided to incorporate four million unwilling Germans into its society, or that the United States wished to have a permanent jurisdiction over

*This article first appeared in TIKKUN, Vol 1, No. 2, San Francisco, Nov. 1986

90 million rebellious Russians, we would assume that those countries had decided to resign from world history. Yet there are still some Israelis and friends of Israel who speak as if the annexation of the West Bank and Gaza were a serious option.

To Israel's great fortune the national consciousness is awakening to this danger. The most significant development in Israeli politics during the premiership of Shimon Peres has been the irreversible decline of the annexationist idea. The experience of 19 years has proved two things beyond a reasonable doubt: there is not, and, in all probability, there will never be, a Knesset majority for the application of Israeli sovereignty to all the territories of the West Bank and Gaza; and there is no prospect that Israelis will ever form more than four or five percent of the total population of those areas. Annexation has failed both the juridical and the demographic test.

The evidence for these conclusions is cumulative. In September 1984 all previous commitments to the ultimate application of Israeli sovereignty to Judea, Samaria and Gaza were expunged from the coalition agreement on which the Peres-Shamir government of national unity bases its mandate. Permanent Israeli rule in the West Bank and Gaza is no longer official Israeli doctrine and no accredited spokesman of our country has a right to propound it as a national consensus. (Not all the Israeli envoys in the western hemisphere show awareness of this change.) In June of 1984 the Labour party conference had unanimously adopted resolutions declaring that the incorporation of the administered territories into Israel and the refusal to entertain any territorial concessions 'would violate the nation's Zionist principles, undermine its moral foundations, contradict its democratic character and thwart any possibility of peace in the future'. The text went on to say that 'the settlements located in the heart of the Arab populated areas not only fail to serve Israel's security needs, but constitute a security problem and a heavy economic and political burden' and that, accordingly, a government headed by Labour will not establish settlements in densely populated Arab areas in the heart of Judea, Samaria and Gaza that are not expected to remain under Israeli sovereignty...'

Over 1,030,000 Israelis voted for this and even more vigorous anti-annexationist platforms in the 1984 elections which enabled Shimon Peres to head the incoming government. Two years later, as prime minister, he successfully sought a unanimous Labour party conference resolution (April 10, 1986) defining 'the termination of Israeli rule over the 1,300,000 Palestinian Arabs in the West Bank and Gaza' as the aim of any peace negotiation. The resolution went on to propose the establishment of a Jordanian-Palestinian state 'which would also include the populated Arab areas of Judea, Samaria and Gaza that would not be included in the State of Israel under a peace agreement.' It was at this meeting that Peres turned to the Palestinians and exclaimed: 'We recognize you as a people!'

Disenchantment with annexation in the labour movement has been paralleled by the action of some prominent Likud politicians, including the mayors of Tel Aviv, Rehovot, Dimona and the chairman of the World Zionist Organization who formed a new 'liberal' party with a platform advocating the principle of 'territory for peace.' The party has a doubtful prospect of independent existence, but its very formation recalls the fact that not everyone in Likud supports political or territorial radicalism. There is a great deal of compromise potential in the liberal wing of Likud. Israeli sovereignty in an undivided Eretz Israel still survives in Likud's official platform and rhetoric, but there is encouraging evidence that it is a slogan rather than a serious program of action. The Likud parliamentary party has always avoided the kind of legislation that would translate the annexation rhetoric into reality. On March 7, 1986 the Knesset rejected a formal motion to apply Israeli sovereignty to Judea, Samaria and Gaza. Only eight of the one hundred and twenty Knesset members supported this proposal, five of them being members of Techiya and one being Kahane! The massive opposing majority was composed of Labour members who believe that annexation is undesirable in principle and Likud members who believe it to be impossible in practice. Likud members were also unwilling to absorb the juridical and electoral consequences of enfranchising a vast Arab population which would take virtual command of the parliamentary balance of power and would, incidentally, generate a great leftward swing in the Knesset's centre of gravity. Both on national and on party grounds the Likud party is totally inhibited from actually voting annexation into law.

Another circumstance that exposes the fragility of the annexationist rhetoric is that the Likud party is formally committed to support the Camp David accords concluded in 1978 between Menachem Begin and Anwar Sadat. This is the most renunciatory text ever signed by a Zionist or Israeli leader in relation to the Land of Israel. It totally excludes any idea of incorporating the West Bank and Gaza into the State of Israel, decides that the permanent status of those territories shall be determined by agreement between Egypt, Israel, Jordan and the elected representatives of the Palestine people, insists that any agreement must satisfy 'the legitimate rights and just requirements of the Palestine people', insists further that any agreement on the future status of the West Bank and Gaza be subject to Palestinian ratification and requires the 'withdrawal of the Israeli civil and military administration' during an interim period in which the Palestinians shall exercise 'full autonomy' in the West Bank and Gaza.

It is beyond any resource of the English language to express a greater incompatibility than that which separates the Camp David text from any idea of permanent Israeli rule over the entire territory of the West Bank and Gaza. Whatever the inter-party rhetoric may be, it is a fact that the avoidance of annexation is the dominant theme of Israel's official jurisprudence.

The international news media and, especially, Diaspora Jews tend to exaggerate the strength of annexationist opinion and to underestimate the range and depth of public support for a peace settlement based on territorial compromise. The lack of progress in this direction is not the result of inherent Israeli obduracy, it is the consequence of the Arab refusal to enter a substantive negotiation. Israelis react in one way to theoretical fantasies and in another way to concrete diplomatic prospects. The dramatic change that ensued when Anwar Sadat made his voyage to Jerusalem illustrates the speed with which ultimative platforms and conditions melt away under the influence of operative encounter.

To understand why other Arab states have not put this Israeli syndrome to the test we must evoke the sharp contrast between the Zionist and the Palestinian diplomatic traditions. Chaim Weizmann's advice to his associates used to be: 'If a document or proposal is thirty percent in our favour, put the thirty percent in your pocket and argue about the rest.' The Palestinian national movement has invariably taken the contrary attitude. If a proposal was 80 percent in its favour it could be trusted to reject it with total vehemence. Professor Yehoshafat Harkaby, who first analyzed the Palestine Covenant with ruthless realism has now reached the conclusion that this attitude no longer prevails. In his masterly work Fateful Decisions (Hebrew, Am Oved, Tel Aviv 1986) he diagnoses an elusive pluralism in which the old fundamentalism might cease to be decisive in the policies of the Palestinian national movement. This is the implicit assumption behind the urgent effort of Shimon Peres to bring the possibility of a converging interest to the test of a negotiation process. If Israel were able safely to disengage from the tasks of ruling the densely populated Arab areas of the West Bank and Gaza, it would not only be making a concession to Palestinian rights; it would also be serving Israel's values and interests. We may even be approaching a point at which the burden of this coercive rule would weigh more painfully on Israel than on any part of the Arab world. Asked by an interviewer in an Israeli newspaper (Ma'ariv, October 3, 1986) whether, in the absence of a peace agreement in the next decade or two, an Israeli leader might have to give up territories unilaterally in order to disengage from the disenfranchised Arab population, Peres replied: 'Whoever says that would be telling the truth...'

Clearly, this is no zero sum game in which a gain for one side would automatically mean a sacrifice for the other. The movement of opinion in Israel away from annexation has come not in response to Arab pressure, which is surmountable, or to international influence which is negligible, but rather as a result of deep Israeli reflection on the structural fallacy inherent in the present condition. The security of a nation-state depends not exclusively on its territorial configuration, but also and mainly, upon its inner cohesion, the rhythm of solidarity between its citizens, the capacity to share common memories and devotions. In the historic 1947 U.N. debate, when an Arab delegate urged that 'Arabs and Zionists should be **forced** to accept the *axiom* of a single state,' the Canadian delegate quietly remarked; 'Mutual consent is necessary for living together. Without consent there must be separation.' Ironically, it was the Zionist camp which then applauded that remark.

Those among Israel's friends and supporters who are advocating political passivity, in which the present Israeli structure continues to congeal, do not seem to understand the consequences of their complacency. There is no political structure in the world marked by such discontinuity as that which describes the relations between the area of Israeli law and the areas and populations under military administration. They live in different worlds of experience and aspiration. Their allegiances flow in opposite directions. The kind of Israeli government which would envisage permanent rule over the 1,300,000 Palestinians is not the kind of government that would offer them the right to vote and to exercise their real numerical weight in our political system. History has created such a duality of national identities between the river and the sea that any unitary framework is bound to be coercive and morally fragile. While Zionist radicals profess to believe that the bigger Israel becomes, the more Zionist and Jewish will it be, the truth is that we have reached a point whence the bigger that we become, the less Jewish and Zionist will Israel be.

It is astonishing to find so many Diaspora Jews indifferent to the question of whether or not Israel is to be a land of double jurisdictions, as it inevitably is under the present condition, or whether there is a Jewish duty to require the affirmation of the principle of consent. In the areas of Judea, Samaria and Gaza today there are 1,300,000 Arabs and less than 50,000 Israeli settlers. The Arabs cannot vote or be elected at any level, have no degree of juridical control over the government that determines the conditions of their existence, have no right of appeal against the judgments of military courts, are not free to leave their land with assurance of a right to return, are not immune from judgments of expulsion from their birthplace and homeland, have no flag to revere, do not possess the same economic and social conditions as their Jewish neighbours, nor the same status for their newspapers and universities. The 50,000 Jews and those who might come in their wake have a totally different set of rights and immunities. Instead of the basic Jewish social injunction *Hoq echad yihyeh lachem*, there is a society in the West Bank and Gaza in which a man's rights are defined not by his conduct or by any egalitarian principle, but by his ethnic identity. This is precisely the condition from which the French and American revolutions saved or protected the Jews during their century of emancipation, enabling them to emerge from the ghetto and to join in the wonder and innovation — and also the challenge — of the outside world. This may be inevitable in the absence of a peace settlement, but it is not a long-term Zionist vision.

Despite all its importance, the issue of individual rights is not decisive. For the Palestinians today as for the Jews in 1948 the issue is one of national self–expression. It is anachronistic as well as wildly unrealistic for Meron Benvenisti to urge an Algerian solution, such as that which inspired the French colonialists to believe that to make the Algerian nationalists citizens of metropolitan France would win respite from the painful necessity of territorial separation.

Israel can only affirm its membership in the democratic family of nations today by asserting the provisionality of the present dual jurisdiction. This ceased to be a fully convincing argument after 1977 when the idea of permanent rule entered the Israeli political lexicon from which Shimon Peres is now attempting to exclude it.

I do not deal here with various diplomatic expressions that could be given to the doctrines of disengagement or 'territory for peace'. The Camp David autonomy, the Palestinian-Jordanian state advocated in the Labour platform, the unilateral autonomy proposal bequeathed by Moshe Dayan, proposals in the same sense made recently by Israeli ministers such as Yaacov Tsur and Gad Yaacobi and, above all, Shimon Peres' conscious revolt against quiescence and inertia all show that thoughtful minds are moving away from immobilism. The immediate task is ideological: to combat and defeat the vogue of status-quoism. What is at stake is not 'the Palestinian problem,' but the Israeli problem. What is Israel, what is its nature, what is its vision, what are its dimensions, where are its boundaries, what is its human composition, what is the degree of its commitment to its Jewish character and its democratic vocation? No other state in the world community has so many existential marks of interrogation hanging over its life and obscuring its forward march.

The issue cannot be determined by marginal interests or *avant-garde* pressures. There are now less than 50,000 Jews in the West Bank and Gaza. This means that they have multiplied at a rate of about 400 families a year over the past two decades during a period in which the Arab population has grown by 200,000! The spectacular marginality of this phenomenon in Israel's social and cultural enterprise refutes the preposterous idea that the 50,000 may dictate the destiny and policy of the four million who reside in the area under Israeli law. I have read ridiculous magazine articles announcing that 'armed revolt' by this group would inhibit an Israeli government from adopting a 'peace territory' approach even if such an approach became operational. Those who write and speak in this way are not always conscious of the insult that they inflict on Israel's statehood by ascribing impotence and frivolity to its institutions. Today — when the myth of Kahana has subsided into derision, with serious doubt that he can even ensure his own individual re-election — is no time to be intimidated by a demonology that would make puny illicit squatters the determinant factor in deciding Israel's political and moral future. A movement whose members have been caught attacking mosques four decades after the Nazi assault on Jewish synagogues does not merit any degree of deference. It is part of the problem and the malady; it is not part of any solution.

What must be resisted is the corrupting effect of a spurious Zionist deviationism on the nation's spiritual condition. The idea of exercizing permanent rule over a foreign nation can only be defended by an ideology and rhetoric of self-worship and exclusiveness that are incompatible with the ethical legacy of prophetic

Judaism and classical Zionism. The spiritual father of that movement described the 1,300,000 Arabs in Judea, Samaria and Gaza as illicit squatters who infiltrated in the seventh century into what they should have known to be a totally Jewish country, so that they are merely squatters who took possession when the owner happened to be abroad. Accordingly 'they have no rights or lands or homes and are entirely at our disposal to deal with as we see best.' Therefore, 'any decision by an Israeli government or parliament to concede any part of the territory of Eretz Israel is to be regarded as null and void by any citizen or soldier...'

This seditious nonsense deserves therapeutic treatment, with all possible patience and concern. But no other nation in the world is being asked to put its decision-making process under the influence of ideas which can only add to the sombre lineage of Jewish self-destruction. We must be inspired and guided by our history, but inspiration and guidance are vain if they lead to suicidal zealotry. What we must not do with our history is to try to repeat it. The great Ben Gurion refused to name military units after Masada, Betar and Bar Kochba since he considered it bizarre to name regiments after failures. Nobody would name a French regiment after Waterloo.

Our road points to crucial survival, not to another heroic martyrdom. We cannot dictate the conduct of our foes or even of our friends, but we can at least keep the sanctuaries of reason intact and arm ourselves with a rationality the lack of which is written in the death of past kingdoms.

Benjamin Disraeli. Portrait by Count D'Orsay, 1834

Maurice Edelman

The Hebraic Spirit in Literature: Disraeli*

TO TALK OF THE Hebraic spirit is in itself to beg for a definition. Is it the whole body of thought expressed in the Bible and the interpretative writings of Talmudists? Or is it something much more elemental, a simple summary of the lofty theology and ethics for which Jews in their history have been prepared to go to the stake? Is it something highly complex which only scholars can unravel, or is it a basic intuition which enables a pallid Jew from the sophisticated North to share his prayers with a darker Jew from the Yemen, and recognize a common heritage? As I hope to illustrate, Disraeli, attached as he was by an unbreakable cord to his ancestry, had a lifelong preoccupation with achieving a synthesis between Judaism and its derivative cultures. At its worst, his aim was to rationalize the contradictions in his situation — the exoticism of the Jew who wanted to identify himself with everything English, the outsider who wanted to be an insider, the challenging aspirant who still saw himself like his own Alroy as a Prince of the Captivity.

But at his best, Disraeli was concerned with the basic and universal expressions of the Hebraic spirit — law and justice, compassion and the practice of charity, and an unquenchable faith in Divine inspiration.

*Edited version of a previously unpublished lecture delivered at the Weizmann Institute at Rehovot in June 1965.

Isaac Disraeli, the father of Benjamin Disraeli, was born in 1804 to Miriam Basevi. Isaac's father, Benjamin D'Israeli, had come to England in 1748 from the Italian Jewish colony of Canto in Ferrara. His second wife was Sarah Siprut de Gabay Villareal, descended on one side from the Spanish Jewish house of Ibn Kaprut and on the other from the Portuguese Jewish family, the Villareal. Isaac D'Israeli was a member of the Bevis Marks synagogue in London until 1813, when he quarrelled with the synagogue elders, and thereafter allowed his three sons and daughter to be baptised. Benjamin Disraeli was himself baptised at the age of *Barmitzvah* at St. Andrews, thus formally completing his divorce from Judaism and, as events proved, permitting himself the political career which British laws at the time would otherwise have denied him.

Yet, Isaac's resignation from Bevis Marks wasn't wholly a resignation from his interest in Judaism. As late as 1833 he published *The Genius of Judaism*, a study of Jewish history, with special reference to the growth of the Talmud. That Disraeli himself (as I shall now refer to Benjamin) preserved, and indeed strengthened throughout his life, his attachment to his Jewish heritage derives in no small part from his father's example.

It was Goethe who described his work as 'fragments of a great confession.' This is, I think, true of all artists, but of no one more than Disraeli who, seeing his own life as a romance chose the romantic form in which to describe it. So it is that when Disraeli spoke or wrote about Jews his imagery and his ideas were a mixture of ancestral memories, exotic fantasy and Byronic posture, all related to the situation in which he found himself as an English gentleman of Spanish and Portuguese Jewish origin professing the Christian faith. Disraeli was, of course, a great myth-maker and like most romantic myth-makers he invented for himself an elaborate ancestry. One of his favourite fantasies was to see himself as a descendant of the Venetian doges. In his early political life he often chose the Venetian oligarchy as an example of an autocratic system which English gentlemen should shun.

But even if his Venetian genealogy was suspect, no one could doubt, nor did he seek to blur the fact, that he was a Jew. In his early life he consciously heightened the distinctiveness of his Jewish features by his exotic dress. He made a parade of his apartness. But later in his political career, his purpose was to integrate rather than to separate himself. Disraeli's aim in his writing about Jews was to relate the Jewish past to his Christian present. If it led him sometimes into absurdity, it also enabled him to enunciate some sublime and prophetic truths about the Jewish people, as relevant today as when he said them. For example, in *Tancred* he says of the Jews in exile, celebrating the Feast of Tabernacles, 'A race that persists in celebrating the vintage, although they have no fruits to gather, will regain their vineyards. What sublime inexorability in the law! But what indomitable spirit in the people!'

What breathes most clearly through Disraeli's work is a Messianic faith, a belief in the destiny of the Jewish people related to his reverence for their past. In his political life, for all his courage, there were moments when the jeers of his opponents, especially of those who wanted to perpetuate the civil disabilities of the Jews, wounded him. O'Connell called him a descendant of one of the thieves on the Cross. At first he was disposed to take on the protective colouration of his Christian background. 'In the debate on the Jew question,' he wrote in a letter to his sister, 'nobody looked at me and I wasn't at all uncomfortable, but voted in the majority with the utmost sangfroid.' But he was to be ashamed of that passage in his life. And his choice of heroic Jewish figures, expressed in *Coningsby* by Sidonia, in *Alroy* by the hero himself, and in *Tancred* by Tancred's own identification of his nobility with semitism, was an act of defiance. Disraeli, 'the Ibis that wandered into the woods of Buckinghamshire', could never be an Englishman of Anglo-Saxon stock. He was an onlooker even when he was a participant. He could admire Eton, the medieval tradition of almsgiving and the English aristocracy. But his own roots were elsewhere. That is why he projected himself through literature into a rich and glorious Jewish past, where his heroes were extrapolations of himself, and from which he could claim that the principles and traditions of Christianity derived. In Germany, romantic medievalism and Fichte's antisemitism went together.

In England Disraeli turned his medievalism towards the Holy Land.

In 1830, at the age of twenty-seven, Disraeli began a voyage to the East in search of his spiritual patrimony. This is how he describes Tancred, the Christian son of Lord Montacute, in search of his Semitic heritage in Palestine.

'Why was he here? Why was he, the child of northern isle, in the heart of the stoney Arabia, far from the scene of his birth and of his duties?... Was it a morbid curiosity or the proverb restlessness of a sated aristocrat that had drawn him to these wilds? Had he no connection with them? Had he not from his infancy repeated, in the congregation of his people, the laws which from the awful summit of these surrounding mountains, the Father of all had himself delivered for the government of mankind? These Arabian laws regulated his life. And the wanderings of an Arabian tribe in this 'great and terrible wilderness' under the immediate direction of the Creator, sanctified by his miracles governed by his counsels, illumined by his presence, had been the first and guiding history that had been entrusted to his young intelligence, from which it had drawn its first pregnant examples of human conduct and divine interposition, and formed its first dim conceptions of the relations between man and God.'

Tancred, for all his Christian-British ancestry, is essential the Jewish Disraeli in search of faith and eternal principles. Before leaving for Jerusalem, he has an affectionate discussion with his father, Lord Montacute — a projection of Disraeli's own rationalist father — who wants him to go into Parliament. Tancred is reluctant: he wants faith. His father complains, 'You are going into first principles.'

Disraeli-Tancred replies in a flash, 'Give me then second principles: give me any!'

Action, with Disraeli, had to be related to ideas. Eventually with a sigh his indulgent father — so we might imagine Isaac Disraeli — embraces him, thinking — and I quote from *Tancred* 'The House of Commons would have been just the thing for him. He would have worked on Committees and grown practical!'

But no, he had to go to Jerusalem.

Well, Tancred does set off for Jerusalem, but before going he has a chat with the all-wise Jew Sidonia, who is to provide him with introductions and a letter of credit. He asks Sidonia how to get there.

'It is no longer difficult to reach Jerusalem,' Sidonia replies. 'The real difficulty is the one experienced by the crusaders — to know what to do when you have arrived there!'

I have the feeling that it is a problem which has presented itself to many another tourist ever since.

Disraeli, absorbed in the clamour and colour, the exotic sounds and scenes of the East, wanted to equate Arab and Jew, and having done so to describe them as the authors of what he called 'the Semitic principle' from which the West derives its laws. He was drawn to the Arabs with an enthusiasm which has persisted among certain Englishmen to this day. He saw them as 'Jews on horseback', and valued their austere and virile lives. Significantly, the heroines of his Oriental romances tend to be Jewesses rather than Arabian maidens, perhaps because he saw them in the image of his own sister and had no opportunity of meeting their Arab counterparts. Disraeli was one of the first English writers and travellers — Lady Hester Stanhope was another — to give glamour to the desert, to discover its beauty, to esteem its wanderers and to engage in a love-affair with an imagined Arabia. Splendid in literature, it has, I think, been sometimes responsible for what I might call the Byronic fallacy in its application to Middle East politics.

Disraeli affirmed the sympathies between the north, as he called the British Isles, and Palestine. He also regarded Christianity as the fulfillment of Judaism, but he seemed to have little trust in the speed of Jewish conversion. Thus, he says of the English Bishop in Jerusalem when Tancred arrives there

'He was delighted to have an addition to his congregation which is not too much, consisting of his own family, the English and Prussian Consuls, and five Jews whom they have converted at twenty piastres a week. But I know that they're about to go on strike for higher wages!'

Disraeli was a realist as well as a romantic, a politician as well as a novelist, a moralist as well as an aesthete. There is scarcely a single passage of poetic ecstasy about the desert or Arabia that doesn't end in reference to the conditions of his contemporary Jews with some implicit or subjective relevance to himself.

'Never complain, never complain!' was one of Disraeli's political dicta. But in literature it was otherwise. If his complaint was dignified and his explanations arguable, he still found it necessary in at least four of his books, *Coningsby, Alroy, Tancred* and *Lord George Bentinck*, to return to his two-fold vindication of his people and of himself. The civil disabilities of the Jews in England were the source in him of an obsessive indignation which he felt all the more strongly since he saw the British way as life as a Semitic derivative. 'The life and property of England,' he wrote in *Tancred*, 'are protected by the laws of Sinai. The hardworking people of England are secured in every seven days a day of rest by the law of Sinai. And yet they persecute the Jews, and hold up to odium the race to whom they are indebted for the sublime legislation which alleviates the inevitable lot of the labouring multitude!' Then Disraeli, in the person of Tancred, continues: 'Vast as the obligations of the whole human family are to the Hebrew race, there is no portion of the modern populations so much indebted to them as the British people. It was 'the sword of the Lord and of Gideon' that won the boasted liberties of England; chanting the same canticles that cheered the heart of Judah amid their glens, the Scotch upon their hillsides, achieved their religious freedom.'

They were thoughts which General Orde Wingate was to recall at a later date.

You will remember that in Disraeli's Parliamentary opposition to the civil disabilities of the Jews, Lord George Bentinck — another Judaeophile who was to anger his colleagues — was his remarkable friend and ally to the point where defying on this issue the Party he had hitherto led, Bentinck finally resigned his leadership. His late translation from being an otiose country gentleman to being a vigorous political leader is one of the curiosities of Parliamentary history. But his espousal of the cause of religious and civil liberty, especially that of the Jews, might belong to the history of miraculous conversion, were it not for his intimacy with Disraeli. He is immortalized in Disraeli's political biography, *Lord George Bentinck* where Disraeli sets out the arguments against Jewish civil disabilities which he used in enlisting Bentinck's sympathy. Disraeli begins by repeating the theme which recurs in many paraphrases throughout his literary work. The civilized world, he says in effect, owes its civilisation to the Jews. Why then are the Jews persecuted? Is it because of the Crucifixion? As if anticipating the Ecumenical Council, Disraeli replies that the charge of deicide is neither historically true nor dogmatically sound.

Then he turns to the effect of persecution on the Jews. 'Persecution,' he says, 'though unjust, may have reduced modern Jews to a state almost justifying malignant vengeance.'

Among the infamous classes, Disraeli goes on, there will always be found Jews. 'In this they obey the law which regulates the destiny of all persecuted races; the infamous is the business of the dishonoured.'

Disraeli never sought to separate himself from his less fortunate fellow Jews. Yet he wanted to affirm the origin of their shortcomings. But, Disraeli continues, the Hebrew has survived all his trials.

'Though a material organization of the highest class may account for so strange a consequence, the persecuted Hebrew is supported by other means. He is sustained by a sublime religion, Obdurate, malignant, odious and revolting as the lowest Jew appears to us, [note the *us*] he is rarely demoralized. Beneath his own roof his heart opens to the influence of his beautiful Arabian traditions. All his ceremonies, his customs and his festivals are still to celebrate the bounty of nature and the favour of Jehovah. The patriarchal feeling lingers about his hearth. A man, however fallen, who loves his home, is not wholly lost. The trumpet of Sinai still sounds in the Hebrew ear, and a Jew is never seen upon the scaffold, unless it be an *auto da fé*'.

Note, too, Disraeli's recurrent use of the word 'sublime'. It is the essential religious word of his vocabulary, a word with a mystical connotation of that which transcends man's experience and reaches to the *SHECHINA*, the Divine Presence.

Indeed, if the Hebraic spirit in Disraeli's writing were to be defined rather than illustrated, I would say that it lies in the application of the attributes of God to the world of man. Loving-kindness, charity, grace and holiness — those are the qualities which Disraeli the novelist sought to interpret, and Disraeli the politician to express through institutions and laws. Yet Disraeli, so moving when he deals with human rights, was capable of enunciating some curious social doctrines.

'The native tendency of the Jewish race,' he says, 'who are justly proud of their blood, is against the doctrine of the equality of man.... Their bias is to religion, property and natural aristocracy and it should be the interest of statesman that this bias of a great race should be encouraged and their energies and creative powers enlisted in the cause of existing society.' He was writing, of course, in an age of revolution when even in the secure society of England there were fears of violent social change.

Disraeli was much occupied with the idea of aristocracy — an idea which at its worst was concerned with the social snobbery of an outsider but at its best with the search for noble sources of authority. He loved great houses, terraces with peacocks, splendid vistas and ancient elms. He loved the aristocratic bearing of Young England, a movement which he could lead but to which he could never belong. Though he wasn't born to it, he still liked to think that the English aristocracy had derived from the Semitic aristocracy which was his own heritage, and he preached the connection with the enthusiasm which others in the 19th century gave to proving that the British were the Lost Tribes of Israel.

There was a gap between the influences of his Jewish ancestry and the British stock of his colleagues and followers. He was English in every respect of his external life. He rode in steeple-chases as a young man; his English prose was admired and imitated; he had a house and an estate at Hughenden with his own church; the country gentlemen followed him; he aggrandized the nation whose Prime Minister he became; he earned a Queen's affection. But the gap remained. He tried to close it by claiming that Jews were natural conservatives, that Christianity was the completion of Judaism, and that, as he put it in Lord George Bentinck's biography, 'The Jews represent the Semitic principle;

all that is spiritual in our nature.' Still the gap would not close. Disraeli, though honoured and lauded as no other statesman except Wellington whose prime distinction was as a soldier — Disraeli to his end remained a man apart, alien in his literary idealism though naturalized because of his pragmatic politics. At first an eccentric he was accepted because the British love eccentrics in moderation. At last, he was accepted because his eccentricity had become a dominant fashion.

The contribution of Disraeli to 19th century politics was what he alternatively called faith or fidelity acting as a reinforcement to action. What he saw in the English — and he was chiefly concerned with the English — was courage and pragmatism. Perhaps it would now be called realism. But as Tancred points out to his father, realism alone leads to incoherence in a nation's life. Disraeli's eccentricity drew attention to himself. Once it was drawn, he was in a position to argue in favour of ideas and policies as a framework for action. It was an alien mode of thought — the logos preceding the act of creation — a semitic mode as Disraeli might have said. But a nation reared on the Bible couldn't fail to like it. The Queen liked it. Her Empire grew from an idea. And Disraeli's idealism became the framework of much that was greatest in Britain's 19th century achievements.

Disraeli believed in the aristocratic principle. Prevented by his birth from a physical identification with the aristocracy of England, he sought to express it in his daring identification with the aristocracy of the Jewish people.

Was his preoccupation with the aristocracy of the Jewish people merely a subjective justification for the status he claimed in English society? In part I think it was. Disraeli was one of the first to state the terrible principle, 'Race is everything.' In the biography of Lord George Bentinck, he has a passage which includes some of the most disastrous fallacies of the 19th century racial theorists — those which led in turn to the evils of the 20th century racialists. 'The influence of a great race will be felt,' he writes. 'Its greatness does not depend upon its numbers, otherwise the English would not have vanquished the Chinese, nor would the Aztecs have been overthrown by Cortez and a handful of Goths. That greatness results from the physical organization, the consequences of which are shown in its energy and enterprise, in the strength of its will and the fertility of its brain. Let us observe what should be the influence of the Jews, and then ascertain how it is exercised.

The Jewish race connects the modern populations with the early ages of the world, when the relations of the Creator with the created were more intimate than in those days, when angels visited the earth and God himself spoke with man. The Jews are the trustees of tradition and the conservators of the religious element. They are a living and the most striking evidence of the falsity of that pernicious doctrine of modern times — the natural equality of man.' Observe how he recurs to the theme. 'The political equality of a particular race is a matter of municipal arrangement, and depends entirely on political considerations and circumstances; but the natural equality of man now in vogue, and taking the form of cosmopolitan fraternity, is a principle which were it possible to act on it, would deteriorate the great races and destroy all the genius of the world.' Then he deals with an issue of modern concern. 'What would be the consequence,' he says, 'on the great Anglo-Saxon republic, for example, were its citizens to secede from their sound principle of reserve and mingle with their negro and coloured populations? In the course of time they would become so deteriorated that their states would probably be reconquered and regained by the aborigines whom they have expelled, and would then be their superiors!' The original anti-Communist Disraeli might also be thought a proto-racialist.

The principle of 'apartness' is, of course, one which Jews may approve as an act of religious preservation; racially, as history has proved, it has led to evil conclusions. It is the ultimate decadence of the doctrine of a Chosen People. Yet it is also in flat contradiction of the spirit of the Prophets which is the essence of the Hebraic spirit. And so I must emphasize the strange dichotomy in Disraeli's thinking. On the one hand, he was a spokesman of aristocracy: on the other, he made Tory democracy articulate. Conservative in all his principles and an enemy of revolution, he was nevertheless a reformer, an advocate of progress. In a Biblical phrase, he drew the attention of the affluent 19th century to the Two Nations, the England of the rich and the England of the poor. The Jewish ethic worked powerfully in the British statesman, if not in the literary theorist. But the vision that haunted him was that of the Messianic figure, the redeemer of the oppressed and rejected, transcending in his personality all the petty affects of ordinary men, the descendant and equal of the heroes and judges and kings of Israel.

In his novel *Coningsby*, two figures side by side represent two halves of Disraeli's nature, though Coningsby himself is commonly supposed to represent Lord Littleton, and Sidonia Baron Alfred be Rothschild. There were things that Disraeli valued more than money. Intellect and authority were two of them. In his youth, Disraeli had shown some disrespect for money, and till his mature age was careless in his treatment of it. But at close quarters and personified in a Rothschild, he could esteem it more. Sidonia, the mysterious, remote, all-seeing, all-knowing figure who first appears in *Coningsby* is what Philip Guedalla has called 'Disrothschild.' He is power made flesh. But it is a benevolent power. It is the power of man which in its perfection is God-like. When Coningsby, the tyro-Disraeli, talks to Sidonia, the master-Disraeli, about greatness, Sidonia says:

'The age doesn't believe in great men because it doesn't possess any. The spirit of the age is the very thing that a great man changes.' Coningsby is doubtful. 'What,' he asks, 'is an individual against a vast public influence?' And Sidonia replies with a single word, 'Divine.'

Whatever the faith he professed, Disraeli believed in the divine nature of man which permitted an infinite development and fulfillment. Not for him the sad doctrine of predestination and original sin. Not for him the doctrine of men beyond the limit of God's grace. He believed in the perfectibility of man, and in the possibility of a dialogue between God and man because of the divinity they share.

Nothing moved Disraeli so much as the fervour of faith: and in that fervour nothing so much as the dedication of the Jew to his past, the quality which, despite all persecution and vilification, made the humblest Jew a prince on his religious occasions. Thus in *Tancred* he says:

'Conceive a being born and bred in the Judenstrasse of Hamburg or Frankfurt, or rather in the purlieus of our Houndsditch or Minories, born to hereditary insult, without any education, apparently without a circumstance that can develop the slightest taste, or cherish the least sentiment for the beautiful; living amid fogs and filth, never treated with kindness, seldom with justice, occupied with the meanest, if not the vilest toil, bargaining for frippery, speculating in usury, existing for ever under the concurrent influence of degrading causes which would have worn out, long ago, any race that was not of the unmixed blood of Caucasus, and did not adhere to the Laws of Moses; conceive such a being, an object to you of prejudice, dislike, disgust, perhaps hatred. The season arrives, and the mind and heart of that being are filled with images and passions that have been ranked in all ages among the most beautiful and the most genial of human experience; filled with a subject the most vivid, the most graceful, the most joyous, and the most exuberant; a subject which has inspired poets, and which has made gods; the harvest of the grape in the native regions of the Vine.

He rises in the morning, goes early to some Whitechapel market, purchases some willow boughs for which he has previously given a commission, and which are brought, probably, from one of the neighbouring rivers of Essex, hastens home, cleans out the yard of his miserable tenement, builds his bower, decks it even profusely, with the finest flowers and fruits that he can procure, the myrtle and the citron never forgotten, and hangs its roof with variegated lamps. After the service of his synagogue, he sups late with his wife and his children in the open air, as if he were in the pleasant villages of Galilee, beneath its sweet and starry sky.'

The sweet and starry sky of Galilee was an element that Disraeli had seen and remembered from his 1830 voyage. It was the inspiration of his epic novel *Alroy*, written shortly after his journey to the East — certainly not the best of this novels, certainly not the most mature, but certainly expressing in the most ardent form the Hebraic nostalgia that was to last through

Disraeli's life. Alroy, the Jew of Baghdad, the reputed descendant of David, the Prince of the Captivity, raised a banner of revolt among the Jews in the 12th century. In incantatory prose, Disraeli describes the heroic march of Alroy at the head of a Hebrew army with his sister Miriam at his side, his discovery of the sceptre of Solomon, and his eventual capture and execution. The story is full of purple patches, but what is striking is Disraeli's sensitivity — perhaps an atavistic sensitivity — to the inwardness of the Jewish religion, as for example, in this description of the advent of the Sabbath after the Jews had fought a great battle.

'When the sun set, the Sabbath was to commence. The undulating horizon rendered it difficult to ascertain the precise moment of its fall. The crimson orb sunk behind the purple mountains, the sky was flushed with a rich and rosy glow. Then might be perceived the zealots, proud in their Talmudical lore, holding a skein of white silk in their hands, and announcing the approach of the Sabbath by their observation of its shifting tints. While the skein was yet golden, the forge of the armourer still sounded, the fire of the cook still blazed, still the cavalry led their steeds to the river, and still the busy footmen braced up their tents, and hammered at their palisades. The skein of silk became rosy, the armourer worked with renewed energy, the cook puffed with increased zeal, the horsemen scampered from the river, the footmen cast an anxious glance at the fading twilight.

The skein of silk became blue; a dim, dull sepulchral, leaden tinge fell over its purity. The hum of gnats arose, the bat flew in circling whirls over the tents, horns sounded from all quarters. The sun had set; the Sabbath had commenced. The forge was mute, the fire extinguished, the prance of horses and the bustle of men in a moment ceased. A deep, a sudden, an all-pervading stillness dropped over that mighty host. It was night; the sacred lamp of the Sabbath sparkled in every tent of the camp, which vied in silence and in brilliancy with the mute and glowing heavens.'

The novel is also notable for a large number of Talmudic references and notes, some of which Disraeli certainly derived from his father. One of his Talmudic footnotes which I like very much concerns the eleven Jewish doctors invited to a splendid supper by King Pirgandicus. Then, on pain of death, they were given the choice of eating pork, of taking a pagan mistress or of drinking wine consecrated to idols. After some discussion, the doctors decided that the first two choices were forbidden by the Law of Moses, the third only by the Rabbis. So they drank the un-kosher wine — and finding it very good, drank too much. When they woke up the next day, they found themselves in the arms of their pagan mistresses, with the remnants of a pork feast in front of them. Their sudden death in the course of the year proved, Disraeli underlines from the Talmud, that the Word of God and of the Rabbis have something in common.

Disraeli himself, was, I suspect, intrigued by Talmudism — but sceptical. Yet he could not feel a benevolent interest in it as a basic element in his Jewish heritage.

From time to time in the West, the question is posed of writers who are Jews — 'Are you a Jewish writer?' For my own part, I believe that a Jew is one who recognizes his community of historic experience with those others who in their past have identified themselves, or been identified, as Jews. By that definition, who can doubt that Disraeli was a Jewish writer? His was the passion of an aristocratic nature which saw his ancestors as a nation of kings and judges, who saw the inwardness of his contemporary Jews, condemned for the most part to degradation who still contained in themselves the divinity of a people chosen to transmit a divine message.

If Coningsby ends his message to Young England with the words, 'Dare to be great!' it is because Disraeli conceived greatness in the trumpeting tones of a man who had looked on his native land from a mount in Zion.

David Daube

A Jewish Prayer*

To Käthe Zhao

I N 1 9 4 2 O R 1 9 4 3 , when I was doing humanitarian war work in England, I met a protestant chaplain — I am not sure what his name was, Watson, I think — who felt the need for a more seriously engaged Christianity. Two of his hopes were that the Church would help in improving the social order and in replacing enmity by understanding in relations with Jews. Remember that the welfare state was still in the future and that antisemitic doctrines which dominated the continent had some impact even in Britain. Today he would find many flourishing bodies with whom he could link up — especially in the U.S.A. At that time, it was uphill labour. He founded a group 'The Nails', so called because the members were always to carry four nails in a pocket, so as not for one moment to forget about Jesus's sacrifice and the demands flowing from it. He planned a publication where their goals were to be set out in detail; and he asked me, then leading a strictly traditional Jewish life, to contribute an article on how far co-operation between us was possible. Before this volume was ready, the group evaporated. He moved away and we lost touch.

* This is part of an article first published in Rechtshistorisches Journal, ed. Dieter Simon, Frankfurt am Main, vol 6, 1987, pp. 194 ff.

But I found a carbon of my typescript and shall here reproduce it without the slightest revision. After that, some reflections.

'The Nails' and the Jews
by David Daube
(Fellow of Gonville and Caius College, Cambridge)

I. The object of the movement called 'The Nails', to judge by a perusal of its Code, is a closer association of the Christian religion with the common life in our industrialized society. The sponsors of the movement realize that even those who are true Christians at heart are more and more apt to regard religion as something to be practised only on certain definite occasions. The notion of religion as the great principle by which all actions, private or public, must be governed is rapidly disappearing. To revive it, and thereby to make Christianity a living factor in the modern world, is the purpose of the new movement.

II. For that section of Judaism which is strictly observant, and which for the sake of brevity will be termed orthodox in the following remarks, the same problem does not arise. It is absolutely impossible to be an orthodox Jew and not to consider one's every action in the light of God's will. The orthodox Jew has to be careful about what he eats and drinks; about when he sleeps and how long; about his prayers several times a day; about his Sabbath and festivals; about his fast-days. He has to say blessings when he gets up in the morning, before and after meals, on taking a glass of water, on smelling an odorous plant, on seeing a beautiful tree or animal, on seeing a deformed person, after relieving nature ('Blessed art thou, O Lord our God, King of the Universe, who hast formed man in wisdom and created in him many orifices and vessels; it is revealed and known before the throne of thy glory that if one of these be opened, or one of these be closed, it would be impossible to exist and stand before thee; blessed art thou, O Lord, who healest all flesh and doest wondrously'),[1] on going to bed and so on. The slightest deviation from truth is a desecration of God's name; he must set aside a certain time

---

1. I am quoting this blessing in full since in some modern prayer books it is omitted from a misconceived sense of propriety.

every day for the study of his religion; however poor he may be, he must give a minimum percentage of any earnings for charity; he must visit the sick, he must wash and dress the dead (an office never left to paid servants). This list could be extended *ad libitum*. The orthodox Jew cannot move a finger without thinking of the religious implications.

III. This does not mean that orthodox Judaism is a system of mere forms, with no emphasis on higher ideals and faith. Can anyone imagine that orthodox Jews have been practising all those tremendously inconvenient rules throughout thousands of years, and are still practising them, for the fun of it? Admittedly, it is quite conceivable that an individual person might abandon his ideals and faith and yet go on, from habit or other motives, observing the traditional forms of orthodoxy. But why should generation after generation shoulder that burden if it were not for a profound trust in God? The true reason why there is comparatively little discussion in orthodox writings of faith and the wider aims is not that these are lacking, but, on the contrary, that they are taken for granted. They are so firmly established that no laborious teaching is needed: without them, the whole edifice, Sabbath and dietary rules and blessings and all, would fall to the ground. In other words, the orthodox Jew attaches so much importance to the forms because, the goal being clear, 'an ever-fixed mark', what matters on this earth is the way to the goal: and the Law, in his eyes, is the guidance that God has given him. For him, the higher ideals and faith constitute the unshakeable basis of all religion, as evident as the fact of life itself. But as it is not sufficient to recognize or pay lip-service to them, his main object on earth must be to bear witness to his faith and to stand for his ideals. In this, he believes, the forms support him, by making him mindful of God's will in everything he does. No man is free of sin. But the Law, in the orthodox view, at least helps man not to forget about his task. This is the significance of the forms: they are the means, pointed out by God, of making life at least as holy as possible.

IV. Two passages may here by adduced (countless others would be equally good), both going back to the age before Constantine. The first is from the Talmud.[2] 'Rabbi Simlai said, 613 commandments were given to Moses...Then came Micah and reduced them to three: And what doth the Lord

2. Babylonian Makkoth 23b - 24a.

require of thee, but to do justly, and to love mercy, and to walk humbly with thy God?'. This Rabbi at any rate looks upon the forms as the means by which a man may carry into practice the eternal ideals of justice and mercy, and express his faith in one omnipotent God. The other quotation is from Josephus.[3] He describes as the great, distinctive feature of the law that 'it did not make piety one of the virtues, but it made all virtues — such as justice, wisdom, constancy, complete harmony between all citizens — parts of piety; for, with us, all actions, pursuits and statements have reference to piety towards God'. The fear of God is the only source from which any good deeds may spring; and all our good deeds, all our observances of the Law, must rest on that.

V. As is well known, Christianity at a fairly early stage ceased practising the Law. Of the causes that led to this attitude, suffice it to mention four: first, the attacks on dissemblers in the gospels; second, the necessity of smoothing the way for pagan converts; third, the doctrine of Jesus as replacing the Law; and fourth, the setting up of the new faith as an absolute criterion. First, the gospels contain a good many condemnations of hypocrites who, while saying their prescribed prayers, keeping the Sabbath and observing the dietary rules, do not hesitate to cheat or slander a neighbour (nor is it maintained by the present writer that there were not such hypocrites at the time of Jesus or that there are not such now). From these passages, a large number of early readers must have gained the impression, as even modern readers quite often do, that Jesus disapproved of the forms as such, that he objected to saying the prescribed prayers, keeping the Sabbath and observing the dietary rules as such. The result was that the followers of Jesus thought it their duty to discard the forms. Secondly, the followers of Jesus, under the influence of Paul, decided that it was essential not to confine the new religion to the Jews but to throw it open to pagans as well. Of pagans, however, it was too much to expect that they would submit to the Law: the very form by which alone male pagans could join the community under the Law, circumcision, was quite unacceptable to most. If the pagans were to be included, therefore, the only thing to do was to dispense with the Law — and this was done. The third point also is associated with the name of Paul. He worked out the doctrine that

3. Contra Apionem 2.16.170.

Jesus replaced the Law; that the Law had been necessary, as a 'schoolmaster', before the arrival of Jesus; but that henceforth the duty of man was to live, not under the Law, but in Jesus. Logically, this doctrine ought perhaps to have made for a Christian life even more dominated by religion (if that were possible) than the orthodox Jewish. For, logically, what it implied was not that the Christian should be satisfied with less practice but that no amount of practice should satisfy him at all; he should dispense with blessings on certain occasions, for example, not because there was any secular department in life, but because the whole life — not only certain occasions — was to be uniformly permeated by Jesus. As a matter of fact, however, the doctrine had the opposite consequence. As is only natural, few have been able to live up to it (Francis of Assisi comes to one's mind as one of them). Generally speaking, people found it easier to embrace the negative part of the doctrine, the rejection of the Law, than the positive, the substitution for the Law of an equally exacting task. Fourthly and finally, there is a point which the writer has not come across in the literature on the subject but which, he believes, played a considerable part in bringing about the difference here under notice between Judaism and Christianity. It has been argued above that, for the orthodox Jew, faith is the obvious basis for all action, requiring no demonstration; it is only the way in which faith can best be expressed, the Law, that calls for constant and closest examination. The followers of Jesus, however, introduced a dogma that was anything but obvious, the dogma of Jesus as Messiah and Son of God. In fact, the vast majority of Jews refused to recognize this dogma. Small wonder that those who stuck to it made of it the very touchstone of their community. The acceptance of the dogma became the principal demand of the new religion and thus, whereas in orthodox Judaism faith is the unquestioned element and to practice it man's chief duty, in Christianity practice lost a great deal of its importance and faith came to be deemed the chief aim.

VI. Needless to say, there has remained a high standard of behaviour which the Christian is expected to attain. Yet in the absence of any definite rules giving definite guidance that standard grows vaguer and vaguer. Indeed, the current view is that to some of the most important provinces of modern life, such as politics or science, it need not be applied at all. The movement of 'The Nails' is intended to remedy the situation;

and to see to it that the Christian religion is not only professed but also practised, practised not only on Sundays but also during the week, practised not only in private life but also in business, politics, science. The founders have expressed the hope that the movement will be supported by orthodox Judaism, with its long experience of scrupulously practised religion. Let it be said at once: since the movement takes as its basis the Christian religion, and as its symbol a cross made of four nails, obviously, Jews cannot join as members. But this is a minor matter compared with what they can do. They can take part in any measures designed to raise the social, moral, cultural and religious standard of the nation and, in particular, the lower classes.

VII. It has been frequently observed that 'the Hebrew term for to give charity is to do justice'.[4] In the orthodox Jewish view, that one man should be wealthy and another destitute constitutes a wrong which to redress is no more than simple justice: we are not bestowing favours, we are administering simple justice when we fight poverty. Any action undertaken by the new movement to abolish want will be welcomed by Jewish orthodóxy. As for education, little need be added to the bidding of the Talmud,[5] 'Be heedful of the children of the poor, for from them the Torah shall go forth'; or to quote a text with no specific reference to the poor, Josephus says[6] that 'of all things we seek our glory in these, the education of children and the observance of the rules and the piety handed down through the latter'. Jewish orthodoxy will welcome any action undertaken by the new movement to improve education and render it more generally accessible. There is no need here to go through the various items of the new movement's programme one by one and to show how they all suit the orthodox Jewish notion of the duty of man. In fact, it would be surprising if there were any actions contemplated in a genuine Christian programme that orthodox Jews could not support. For Jewish ideals and Christian ideals are so much alike, 'two young roes that are twins which feed among the lilies', the common heritage of the two religions and developed further on similar lines throughout the Middle Ages and the modern era, that few differences should exist when it comes to real, practical tasks like building better houses for the poor, mak-

4. Proudhon, *Qu'est-ce que la propriété?*, 2nd ed., vol. 1 p. 202.
5. Babylonian Nedarim 81a.
6. Contra Apionem 1.12.60.

ing the life of a miner worth living, securing peace within the nation and in the world, and so on. This is not saying that every orthodox Jew must necessarily agree with every detail of the Code of 'The Nails'; nor would the authors of the Code themselves maintain (if the present writer interprets them correctly) that none of their points could possibly be disputed by any Christian. When the Code, for instance, in chapter 3, advocates 'equal educational opportunities for all children', nobody will deny that this is the ultimate object for which to strive. But surely, it may well be argued even by a most sincerely religious person that, in an imperfect world, one cannot achieve one's ideals by a stroke of a pen; and that, indeed, more might be destroyed than gained by over-hasty reforms. In short, if the new movement, which is not content with a purely theoretical Christianity, is itself to avoid becoming theoretical, it must carefully consider, in each matter that it deals with, what are the measures most likely to prove of real benefit to society. However, these are questions of detail which will be solved as the movement takes its course. The success of the new movement as a whole will depend entirely on the spirit of its Christian members and Jewish friends; they must be resolved, in a world that is growing ever more materialistic, to give an example of humble, unselfish work in the interest of their fellow-beings. Maybe the very fact of Christians and Jews joining in such an effort will mark a step towards the great goal, the fulfilment of the Psalmist's word: 'Behold, how good and how pleasant it is for brethren to dwell together in unity'.

THUS FAR 1942. I apologize for unfortunate concepts typical of the period; for example, 'the lower classes' at the end of section VI. I took this over from the programme and I do not remember finding anything wrong with it at the time. Well before the end of the war, the designation 'the underprivileged' came to the fore; and, beyond terminology, we have grown more aware of the strong dose of self-satisfaction and narrowness which went into that entire way of seeing things. (No doubt the present one has its own flaws). Again, in section II, I should have included a few more immediately appealing instances of law's beneficent power. Take the old teaching that the Day of Atonement, while procuring forgiveness to the penitent for sins against God, does not erase a wrong against your fellow unless you have done your best to pacify him.[7] Certain definite practices ensued. Here is one of them: in our small orthodox congregation at Freiburg, on the eve of this Day, members who had had a falling-out in the course of the year called on one another to make it up. To be sure, some quarrels would flare up again; but most did not and even the others had a new chance the following year — as, in a fallible world, but for the ritualism they might not have.

However, what I propose to have a closer look at is the prayer set forth in section II.[8] Nothing like it seems to exist in any other religion. Whereas in Judaism, far from representing some fringe element, it is part of the central tradition. My eldest son was still brought up like me to recite it every time he had been to the toilet; more precisely, to recite it after another, shorter blessing, 'Blessed art thou, O Lord our God, King of the Universe, who hast sanctified us by thy commandments and commanded us concerning the washing (raising) of the hands' — for this washing also belongs to the ceremony. (It is attested for the Essenes at least already by Josephus.[9] Note, by the way, how this standard phrase in benedictions over performance of a duty, 'who hast sanctified us by thy commandments and commanded us so-and-so', will never allow you to lose sight of the fundamental meaning underlying all the minutiae of the system: sanctification.) In fact, at a fairly early date, the two pieces were made the opening of the regular morning service, to be followed by one having regard to a Jew's main task, 'Blessed art thou...who hast commanded us to occupy ourselves with the words of the Torah'. That, then, is how each day starts.

Significantly, the blessing under review conceives of divine care as absolutely universal, speaking of *adham*, the most inclusive word for 'man', and *kol bašar*, 'all flesh'. This is a feature of many Jewish prayers to do with basic bodily needs. The primary portion of grace after a meal celebrates God as provider for 'the entire

7. Based on Leviticus 16.30 by Eleazar ben Azariah: Siphra ad loc., Mishnah Yoma 8.9.
8. To be found in Hebrew and English in *Authorized Daily Prayer Book*, transl. S.Singer, 9th ed., 1912, p. 4.
9. Jewish War 2.8.9. 149.

world', 'all flesh', 'all his creatures' — covering even animals; similarly a briefer thanksgiving for food, to 'the creator of many living beings and their wants'.[10] The roots of this trend reach back deep into the Old Testament.[11]

As for the genesis of the blessing, to begin with, some crude data. The bulk of it, i.e. all except the concluding benediction 'blessed art thou, O Lord, who healest all flesh and doest wondrously' is due to Abaye, around A.D. 300.[12] The conclusion is in a sense older. Apparently Rab, of the first half of the third century, had advised that, after easing oneself, one give thanks: 'Blessed art thou, O Lord, who healest the sick'. His contemporary Samuel objected that this was to turn everybody into a patient and substituted 'who healest all flesh'. Samuel's disciple Shesheth found even this too reminiscent of sickness and suggested 'who doest wondrously'.[13] Finally, Papa, disciple of Abaye and Abaye's friend and rival Raba, favoured a combination of Samuel's and Shesheth's texts — by now in the role of a coda to Abaye's lengthier and more specific prayer.[14] His became the authoritative version.

To go on to the background of the prayer — forty-five years ago, I despised the 'progressives' who purged it from their worship. By now, while still admiring it no end, I am just a little less furious, for three reasons. First, it has become clearer to me that part of the blame attaches not to those reformers but to the surrounding culture which would treat them and their faith as uncivilized if sponsoring such coarseness. It was, of course, hopeless to put up a rational defence — say, to point out the hygiene bound up with this blessing. (It is widely held that if the Black Death struck Jewry somewhat less severely than gentiles, ritual washing

10. *Authorized Prayer Book*, pp. 280, 290.
11. E.g. Psalms 104.11 ff. On its use in the Sabbath afternoon service between Tabernacles and Passover, see I. Abrahams, *Annotated Edition of the Authorized Daily Prayer Book*, 1914, pp. CLXXIf. An impressive yet neglected illustration is met in Genesis 45.5, 50.20: Joseph's sale was providential in preserving Egyptian lives in a famine as well as in what it did for the Hebrews. In a Boalt Hall lecture *Appeasing or Resisting the Oppressor*, to appear shortly, I argue that Caiaphas's prophecy of salvation beyond the nation in John 11.52 harks back to these verses.
12. Babylonian Berakoth 60b.
13. Cp. e.g. Enoch 36.4.
14. L. Goldschmidt, *Der Babylonische Talmud*, vol. 1, 1897, p. 223, in the margin calls attention to another such conciliatory decision of Papa's in Berakoth 59a.

before a meal, after relief and on numerous other occasions was a factor.[15]) This is not an area governed by sober discourse. Part of the blame only, since they ought to have stood their ground. Still...Second, developments since then in certain societies in certain periods have caused me to think harder about the price paid for overthrowing shame. (Or guilt; but this does not come in here.) It is a tremendous plus, I am convinced, that in many regions of the U.S.A. a paper will not lose its bourgeois readers if it counsels teenagers who are worried about the look of their genitals. But a university course on masturbation? Or, less heavy: was it antiquated brainwashing alone that produced a mild discomfort in some when President Johnson displayed the scar from his hernia operation in public? I well remember my late gentle, wise colleague David Louisell in the sixties questioning the slogan 'to let it all hang out'. Third, feelings were divided even in Abaye's age.

That he himself — rightly — places excretion below other activities is inferable, paradoxically, from the style reverential to an extraordinary degree, which takes doing considering the intensely worshipful tone of even the standard supplications. As if to make up for the subject, or better, so as to lift it into a sphere where nothing of its baser aspect remains. 'It is revealed and known before the throne of thy glory': not simply 'before thee'. (First occurrence of 'the throne of thy glory' is in a prayer of Jeremiah.[16]) 'To endure and stand before thee': existence depends on the functions in question but its sole purpose is heavenward. (First occurrence of 'to stand before God' is in the story of Abraham, when he undertook to plead for any righteous citizens that might dwell in Sodom.[17]) He has broken through, that is, to a rare balance: certain refinements, however valuable in social intercourse, are absurd *vis-à-vis* the power and understanding that

15. See G. Herlitz, art, Black Death, in *Universal Jewish Encyclopedia*, vol. 2, 1969, p. 368. Alas, the boon misfired. Perhaps precisely because suffering less from the epidemic, the Jews were deemed to cause it by poisoning the wells, and incomparably more were slaughtered in revenge than could have been by the plague at its worst. My Freiburg behaved badly.
16. 14.21.
17. Genesis 18.22.

encompasses everything.

We have indeed direct evidence of the profound and daring spirit which went into his introduction of this blessing. The Talmudic report of it is preceded by a controversy between him and Aha, another sage of that era. The latter taught that, when entering the privy, one ought to ask one's guardian angels to wait outside. Abaye protested that they might take this seriously, suspending their service just while it was least dispensable — the last thing really wanted. In other words, communication with heaven had no use for polite dishonesties. The appropriate petition to the angels was: 'Guard me, guard me, help me, help me, support me, support me, throughout my entering and leaving'. No point, he added, in hiding from them our earthly make-up: 'for such is the way of the sons of man'. (Josephus, in his sketch of the Essenes adverted to above,[18] characterizes excretions as 'natural'.) It is at this juncture that we are told of his prayer after relieving nature which, in contrast to the earlier ones ('Blessed art thou who healest the sick', 'healest all flesh', 'doest wondrously'), calls a spade a spade. A devout address to the Lord can be open, should be open.

Plainly the dissension about this prayer is only a dramatic illustration of the problem coming up in countless shapes: where to place the lowlier bodily functions in terms of sacred and profane. Thus, R. Huna — third century — greatly admired a pupil of his, R. Hisda, who had himself become an authority. Yet Rabbah, Huna's son, flagrantly did not cultivate contact with Hisda, so Huna questioned him. Rabbah explained that he had visited Hisda in the past — to be treated, however, not to matters concerning heaven, but to mundane ones such as how to avoid hurting oneself when going to stool. Huna[19] demolished this evalu-

18. Text with footnote 9.
19. Babylonian Shabbath 82a. In Jerusalemite Berakoth 11b, he once again reproves his son, and here also for being too narrow - though in a quite different area. Huna, his son Rabbah and his pupil Zeira, by then an accomplished scholar, dined together. Zeira got up to wait on the others (a first-century parallel is recorded in Babylonian Qiddushin 32b and quoted in connection with Matthew 20.26 by H.L. Strack and P. Billerbeck, *Kommentar zum Neuen Testament aus Talmud und Midrasch*, vol. 1, 1926, repr. 1969, p. 838). He brought wine and oil for the end-of-Sabbath ceremony. Now according to the School of Shammai, you had to carry the wine in the right

ation: 'He is engaged in preserving the lives of God's creatures and you call it mundane matters'. Here it may be appropriate to remember the fourteenth-century anchoress Julian of Norwich. 'Food is shut in our bodies' she writes, 'as in a very beautiful purse. When necessity calls, the purse opens and then shuts again in the most fitting way. And it is God who does this because I was shown that the goodness of God permeates us even in our humblest needs'.[20]

At least three more old-established prayers are disapproved by Abaye on basically the same grounds. One:[21] the customary acceptance by a mourner of his loss, in the course of which he confesses 'I have sinned and thou hast not collected from me a thousandth part of my debt'. Too theatrical for a genuine offer to undergo an endless series of such blows; if God acted on it, as he might, it would not be welcome. The text substituted by Abaye is not recorded. Perhaps he simply cuts out the florid 'and thou has not collected....' It might be rewarding to compare, and contrast, Old Testament precursors.[22]

The other two disputes — as to how to pray when visiting a bath-house and when visiting a doctor for blood-letting — are preserved in the immediate vicinity of that about going to the toilet. [23] By tradition, a visitor of the baths begs God to keep him

hand, the oil in the left, according to the School of Hillel, the other way round. Zeira carried both in one hand. Which caused Rabbah to ask: 'What is your other hand carrying?'. His father was enraged by this fault-finding with one doing a selfless act - indeed, remarkably selfless seeing that Zeira was of priestly descent. He ordered Zeira to return to his place and his son to do the serving. On Huna's allergy to self-importance and hypocrisy, see H. Loewe, in C.G. Montefiore and H. Loewe, *A Rabbinic Anthology*, 1938, repr. 1974 with a prolegomenon by R. Loewe, p. LXXIX.

20. See B. Doyle, *Meditations with Julian of Norwich*, 1983, p. 28. I am indebted for this reference to my colleague Lawrence A. Sullivan. - A thought. 'The purse opening and shutting' in Julian's meditation is very close to 'one of the orifices opening and shutting' in Abaye's thanksgiving; and we have three options. 1) In all probability, there is no historical tie. 2) It is possible that the two formulations go back, ultimately, to a common source, Galen or the like. 3) Norwich had an important Jewish community prior to the expulsion in 1290. Just conceivably, the Jewish prayer, or fragments of it, reached Julian over half a century later. I could offer parallels from Europe 1925-1985.

21. Babylonian Berakoth 19a. It looks as if Joseph, his predecessor as head of the School of Pum Beditha, had contributed to this criticism. Cp. W. Bacher, *Die Agada der Babylonischen Amoräer*, 1878, pp. 109f.

22. Such as Psalms 103.10: 'He has not dealt with us after our sins...'.

23. Babylonian Berakoth 60a. In the case of the bath-house, once again, Abaye seems to be

from sinning and, should he sin, to count his death an atonement. Abaye here too finds the self-condemnation exaggerated, the man does not truly wish to be taken at his word — to be slain, by way of atonement, for a lapse. Here too no substitute prayer by him is quoted. There is a strong indication that Aha adheres to the conservative line. He, we learn, counsels that, on exiting from a bath-house, one give thanks for being 'saved from the fire' — sounds distinctly extremist. The conflict regarding blood-letting, once more between Aha and Abaye, brings out further facets of the problem. Aha's prayer emphasizes that God alone heals and men have no part in it — not even the physician to whom, following convention, one is turning. For Abaye, this is yet another cover-up, almost an attempt to fool the All-knowing. The doctor does promote the cure, under authority from God. The School of Ishmael (second century), Abaye points out, actually discovered a snippet in the Law itself sanctioning this office.[24] I suppose the prayer he prefers would conform to the old one, except for omitting the, to him, spurious alibi. Some five hundred years before, Ben-Sira staked out the general position.[25] 'Cultivate the physician, for him God hath ordained. God hath created medicines out of the earth and let not a discerning man reject them'. Like Abaye, he felt constrained to supply Scriptural proof — so even there was a 'Jewish Science' sect; indeed, as early as in Chronicles it savagely denounces King Asah for taking the other route.[26] However, in Ben-Sira's period such proof might still consist in a respected example and need not yet come from the Law proper.[27] Hence he

influenced by Joseph. The major modern translators fail to appreciate the clash of opposing principles informing all this material, hence are driven to mispunctuate and even mutilate the prevalent reading: see L. Goldschmidt l.c. and M. Simon, *Berakoth*, in Hebrew-English Edition of the Babylonian Talmud, ed. I. Epstein, vol. 1, 1960, 60a towards the end, esp. footnote da. A detailed discussion would add little to my thesis.

24. Exodus 21.19.
25. Ecclesiasticus 38.1 ff. See G.H. Box and W.O.E. Oesterley, The Book of Sirach, in *The Apocrypha and Pseudepigrapha of the Old Testament*, ed. R.H. Charles, 1913, vol. 1, pp. 448f.
26. II Chronicles 16.12.
27. See my *The New Testament and Rabbinic Judaism*, 1956, repr. 1973, pp. 67 ff., Zukunftsmusik, in *Bulletin of the John Rylands Library Manchester*, vol. 68, 1985, pp. 56 f., and From Sirach to R. Ishmael, in a forthcoming volume in honour of E. Earle Ellis, ed. G.F. Hawthorne.

could invoke the episode [28] when God instructed Moses how to sweeten the bitter waters with the help of a wood: a model cooperation of a beneficient plant, an enlightened human and Ultimate Source — 'I am the Lord that healeth thee'. It may be worth mentioning Aha's benediction when taking leave of the phlebotomist: 'Blessed is he who healeth gratis'. Impossible to miss the barb: the Lord, sole agent of the recovery, unlike the good-for-nothing bleeder, charges no fee. Ben-Sira looked on an opulent reward as a feather in a doctor's cap. To be sure, it takes the form not of vulgar pay but of a honorarium: 'From God he getteth his wisdom and from the king gifts'.[29]

It will come as no surprise that, with the Rabbis forming two camps, one purist, the other realist,[30] Abaye is altogether a member of the latter. Here is a striking statement of his.[31] Ishmael, a realist (which, needless to say, does not detract from piety: he died a martyr under Hadrian), had contended that the exhortation 'this book of Torah shall not depart out of your mouth day and night'[32] was to be taken with a grain of salt, adjusted to the condition of mortals. For Simeon ben Johai, purist, it meant that you must renounce all worldly occupation and care for livelihood, trusting that God would respond by his saving might. Abaye comments: 'Many acted in accordance with Ishmael and succeeded and many in accordance with Simeon and did not succeed'.

28. Exodus 15.23 ff.
29. A doctor might act for free, of course, even in Talmudic times. That such services were invariably despised by no means follows, as is often held, from the quip or proverb put into the mouth of an injured person in a very particular situation in Babylonian Baba Qamma 85a. For a proper exploration of the subject, other noble vocations would have to be compared: teaching, preaching, judging and so forth. Scripture is rich in material, much of it highly complicated. Think, for example, of Elisha's propagandist motives when refusing the presents of the Syrian general he had rid of his leprosy (II Kings 5). The same prophet's acceptance of hospitality from a wealthy couple (II Kings 4.8 ff.) is remembered by the Rabbis when dealing with etiquette (Babylonian Berakoth 10b). Of New Testament passages, it suffices to name Matthew 10.10, Luke 10.7, I Corinthians 9.14, I Timothy 5.18, plus Didache 13.1. On a special aspect of a prophet's honorarium, see my remarks in *Zeitschrift der Savigny-Stiftung*, vol. 96, 1979, Rom. Abt., pp. 5 f.
30. Just a useful simplification. See my contribution to *Aufstieg and Niedergang*, pp. 2329 ff. As may be seen from the title of this portion of my essay, Encomium Prudentiae, I am breaking a lance for the realists - in defiance of my instinctive sympathies.
31. Babylonian Berakoth 35b.
32. Joshua 1.8.

(It may be recalled that he relies on a down-to-earth exegesis of the School of Ishmael in the more circumscribed debate as to the physician's role.) Again, when we compare his mottos with those of his lifelong friend and rival Raba,[33] he is the harmonizer, striving 'to be beloved above and well liked below', Raba the stringent, proclaiming that if you follow out the Law from selfish motives, 'it were better for you not to have been created.[34] Admittedly, there are utterances by the latter in the realist direction: maybe he relaxed once he had his own academy. [35] Abaye's affinity with Wisdom is significant — the motto just cited obviously echoes the ideal of 'finding favour in the eyes of God and man'[36] — and so is Raba's with mysticism, *à la* Simeon ben Johai. It should be borne in mind, too, that the former descends from an exceptionally old and distinguished lineage.[37]

I wonder, in fact, whether an anecdote from the adolesence of this pair may not adumbrate this very divergence.[38] A youngster, though he has not yet reached full puberty, counts toward the quorum for ceremonial grace provided he understands the nature of the addressee. When Abaye and Raba were, say, twelve-and-a-half, they were studying under the same master, the former's uncle, Rabba bar Nahmani. He tested them, asking first to whom grace was directed; both replied 'To the All-merciful'. Next he asked where the All-merciful resided, and at this they parted company: Raba pointed to the ceiling. Abaye stepped into the open and pointed to the sky. Whereupon their examiner called out: 'You are both of you Rabbis already', i.e. far above the requisite standard for communal grace. The Talmud then appends the proverb: 'Any pumpkin's quality is predictable from its stalk'.

33. Babylonian Berakoth 17a. I adverted to the two above, text with footnote 14.
34. A moving prayer ascribed to him further up in Babylonian Berakoth 17a and found in *Authorized Prayer Book*, p. 263, fits the perfectionist picture.
35. Another possibility is that we have been too quick in crediting him with these realist opinions. For instance, the one in Babylonian Pesahim 50b (quoted by me in *Aufstieg und Niedergang*, p. 2331) which makes use of Psalms 57.11, 108.5 and goes back to Rab may not have been accepted by him at all.
36. Proverbs 3.4.
37. See *Aufstieg und Niedergang*, pp. 2331 f. Caiaphas, whose realism I am calling attention to in the lecture cited above, footnote 11, belongs to an eminent high-priestly family.
38. Babylonian Berakoth 48a.

Up to not long ago, I shared the prevalent interpretation of the tale as a glorification of Raba. That he outshone Abaye in dialectical agility is beyond doubt;[39] and this incident is universally believed to be transmitted as demonstrating his overall, innate superiority: even in boyhood, a more or less majestic environment made no difference to his recognition of the One-on-high, while Abaye did welcome a prop. I still take off my hat — or should I say, put on my skullcap — to him. But by now I also sense a trace of the overrational, a lack of vitality, an estrangement from the concrete universe. Abaye is more natural, has a place for the senses, does not totally give over to logic. Interestingly, the story itself contains no evaluation of their respective stands. I have already quoted their teacher's eulogy, indiscriminately extended to both. If he had a preference, he was considerate enough to keep it to himself. The actions of the two are arranged in the sequence I have reproduced: first Raba's pointing to the ceiling, then Abaye's to the sky. Which implies no assessment, at least none ascertainable by us.[40] W. Bacher turns them around and adds two loaded details, whereby Raba emerges triumphant: 'Abaye steps outside and points to the sky whereas Raba remains seated (not in the original) and, undeflected (not in the original), points to the ceiling.[41] It is conceivable, then, that the legend is trying to do justice to Abaye no less than to Raba. After all, the former's victory over the latter in being made President of the academy of Pum Beditha shows that his qualities were appreciated. (This is not to exclude his aristocratic provenance as a factor.) Indeed, the terse, riddling account of his election[42] could be hinting at his restraint and tolerance as decisive considerations: his pronouncements, we are told, were less open to refutation than those of Raba and other candidates.

In conclusion, two philological points and one perhaps falling under ethnology. In conformity with English usage, I have put the

---

39. See W. Bacher op. cit., pp. 109, 115.
40. I should love setting out my findings about the upward or downward or neutral order chosen by authors - including myself and acquaintances of mine.
41. Op. cit., p., 109: *Geht Abaji hinaus und zeigt zum Himmel, während Raba sitzen bleibt und unbeirrt zur Zimmerdecke hinaufweist.*
42. Babylonian Horayoth 14a.

second person in the 'who'-stretch of benedictions: e.g. 'Blessed are thou who hast sanctified us'. The Hebrew consistently puts the third, 'Blessed are thou who hath sanctified us'. As has been seen for some time,[43] this is no small matter. In the Hebrew, the bold, direct approach to the Lord, 'Blessed are thou', is followed by an awed retreat, 'who hath sanctified us'.

Abaye is conscious that it would be fatal if one of the artfully constructed ducts 'be opened or closed' — meaning 'be opened or closed through malfunctioning in a troublesome, dangerous way'. The use of a verb to single out an extraordinary instance of what it commonly denotes is a widespread phenomenon; the extraordinary element may be of a negative hue — as here — or positive. To explain it, one would have to compare many related data and, in fact, probe into the mainsprings of speech. It must suffice, therefore, to offer the simplest parallels from English. A schoolmaster who announces that any pupil 'talking during class' will be punished means 'talking out of order'; he does not mean one who answers when he calls on him, maybe not even one who asks an intelligent question. For a positive variant, we may think of a committee member who in the course of a long meeting gets a previously hostile majority to vote for his side, a follower of his, on returning home, reports to his wife: 'I tell you, that guy talks', meaning 'talks without giving up, breaking down all resistance'.

The ethnical item is not, I bet, recorded anywhere and, but for this little plaque, would soon be forgotten for good. In the first third of this century, among the rank and file of practising South-German Jews, toilet-paper (often consisting of old newspapers) was known as *asher yotsar Papier*. *Papier* is German for 'paper'. *Asher yotsar,*[44] 'who hast formed', are the two words with which, following the general introductory formula 'Blessed art thou' up to 'King of the Universe', the prayer after relieving nature commences: 'who hast formed man in wisdom and created in him' and so on. 'Who-hast-formed-paper', then. I have no idea how far back

43. At least I think so, but I cannot remember my source.
44. I write *yotsar*: that is how it was pronounced - and with the accent on the first syllable. Official Israeli pronunciation agrees with the academic one: yatsar, and accent on the second syllable.

the designation goes nor how far it extended beyond South-Germany.[45] As for its social setting, I doubt that my mother's brothers, doctors of some eminence at a time when that profession was pretty clannish, employed it — though they never objected. There was not the slightest disrespect or irony or scruple attaching to this usage. Evidently, one sought to avoid a crude reference to defecation: the same motive that led to 'toilet paper'. No one from age four or thereabouts was not familiar with the thanksgiving recited so often, day in, day out, by everybody. Its distinctive opening provided a ready-made civilized, indeed, religious, term.

45. Reuven Yaron, to whom I showed the typescript, informs me that it was part of the Yiddish vocabulary in Austria-Hungary at least.

Alexander Goehr

Concerning my 'Sonata about Jerusalem'

I WANT TO TAKE this opportunity to record the circumstances of the commissioning and realization of my *Sonata about Jerusalem*. More than an account of my piece (which has been discussed elsewhere, in a moving, if slightly fanciful article by Melanie Daiken*), or of my compositional or theatrical ideas of that time, it deals with a friendship with a great, almost legendary lady and serves to add a marginal anecdote to other, more authoritative accounts which must be available in Israel. The lady was Mrs. Recha Freier; the commission she gave me was for a composition to be performed as part of her *Testimonium* project.

I was in Israel for one week in June 1968 to visit my friend, the conductor Gary Bertini. I had been given a Churchill Scholarship and was on my way to Japan to study the Noh Theatre, and had recently composed and performed *Naboth's Vineyard*, the first *music theatre* piece written in this country. Bertini, at that time conductor of the Israel Chamber Orchestra, was doing a concert of new works, which took place outside David's Tower in the old city of Jerusalem, for *Testimonium*. The astonishing setting of this concert under the walls remains with me; when I came to write my own contribution for *Testimonium*, it was my hope that it too might be performed there. It wasn't, but it doesn't matter.

At that concert Bertini introduced me to Mrs. Freier. She was not a particularly large lady, but I was instantly impressed, if not

---

* Melanie Daiken, 'Notes on Goehr's Triptych' in *The Music of Alexander Goehr* ed. Bayan Northcott, London, 1980 overwhelmed by what radiated from her. At that time perhaps in her early seventies, she had the powerful features often found in German Jews, beautiful and strong, indicating determination and serenity. She was dressed then, as always, in a sacklike, colourless dress which hung loosely down to her ankles. It was explained to me that she was a poetess, had founded and operated the *Youth Alijah* from Germany right into the Nazi period and had herself only come out of Germany at the very last moment. In Israel she had worked on behalf of deprived children, making opportunities for their education and their absorption. Later she had become interested in the idea of creating a repertoire of musical works based on texts to do with the City of Jerusalem. She explained that as Rome was celebrated in music (I don't quite know what she meant) Jerusalem provided the focus for an immense number of stories, historic episodes and poems — Christian, Jewish and Moslem. The idea of *Testimonium* was to take a particular collection of texts, ask composers to set them, and to perform them as a cycle. This she was able to do a number of times. I agreed to participate in the next *Testimonium* which was planned for 1971.

My own credentials vis-a-vis Jewish culture are not great. Brought up in a totally non-religious environment, I had little opportunity, or, for that matter, interest in reading any Jewish books other than a *History of the Jews* which fell into my hands at some point. After leaving school, I worked at a music publisher's in London, while preparing to appear before a Tribunal for Conscientious Objectors, as I had registered myself as such. It was at this time quite by chance, that I was drawn into a meeting at Broadhurst Gardens, of the Socialist Zionist (MaPaM) Party. In the months that I spent in London I went there quite often. The people there shared many of my interests (not so much music, as literature and politics), so that when I was ordered to do landwork, they proposed that I might do this at Hatfield Heath in Essex, where at that time the Hashomer Hatzair had a training (*Hachshara*) farm. Their idea and purpose was to recruit me for the Kibbutz movement in Israel. I never made it, but the time I spent with them at the farm, and later in Manchester, constituted a valuable education — the first 'university of my life'. Socialist

Zionist culture consisted of readings from Russian Jewish theorists such as Borochov and Ahad Ha'am as well as more generally from Marx and Engels, Lenin, Stalin on the National question, Trotsky. These rubbed shoulders with Freud and Reich. Among the more intellectual colleagues, Koestler, Malraux, Orwell were read, as were Kafka, Joyce and Thomas Mann. 'Left Wing' painting was influenced by the work of Picasso, Diego Riviera and Siqueiros. These enthusiasms were reflected in our own endless discussions and little sketches and plays put on to mark various Jewish Festivals. In the Hashomer Hatzair at that time, *Succoth* was presented in such a way that the Bible and Bialik were easily combined with Brecht and Braque. In fact it was for an event or festival of this kind that I wrote my first attempt at a *music theatre* — a pageant of some kind based on poems by Yehuda Halevi, and performed in Cheetham Hill Town Hall: 'My heart is in the East, and I in the uttermost West...'

The members of Hashomer Hatzair were drawn from all over Europe and further afield. Overtly the farm was run by Israelis with some authority: there was meant to be some mixture of socialist and youth movement codes of behaviour linked to an attempt to instil Jewish culture and Hebrew language into us. Prohibition against drink or cigarettes, strict collectivism, a certain amount of folklorism and some party-line talks were easily ignored in local pubs, and I received a valuable lesson quite early in life that whatever my theoretical beliefs, too much can easily turn into boredom and oppression. What this, albeit temporary, system of life demonstrated was that the membership, aged from eighteen to twenty five, divided quite clearly into potential solid citizens and rogues.

In general the intellectuals, not to mention those of us with artistic aspirations, sided with the rogues. This was a playing out in practice of what I read in *Felix Krull* by Thomas Mann, or in Brecht, and to some extent vitiated any serious attempt to master the Hebrew language and Zionist literature.

I visited Israel in 1952, but after that the growing avant-garde movements in the music of this time fully absorbed me.

Recha Freier started corresponding with me in 1969 about the

proposed piece. (I was in the United States in those years). Her
first letter to me on 21.5.69 described her idea:

*The theme I chose refers to Obadia the Proselyte and this is the
background: in the beginning of the 12th century the monk Johannes from a monastery in Apulia became Jew, left monastery and
Europe and went to the Orient, to those countries where at that
time the Jews were hated, persecuted and outcast (which did not
occur in Italy at that period). He changed his name into Obadia.
Little is known about him, there are some pages of his handwritten
autobiography (found in Cambridge); nota bene; these fragments
gave to the musicologist the possibility to identify some other pages
of the first-known notation of a Hebrew melody as written by him
and all this is known to you I am sure.* (Naturally it wasn't).

*But not his story did I choose. There is one point, never cleared
up nor by him nor by the historians (or in a very superficial way);
what caused him to join the Jews as a Jew? As this point cannot
be dealed on the historic basis, I had to write a saga of Obadia and
even this point is the very subject of that saga. Each of the creations
for Middle Ages are thought to be written for about 12 minutes. I
made a libretto which could serve music for 12 minutes.*
It is divided in 4 parts:

    (1) The monastery
    (2) Jews
    (3) The shame of the sandals (Baghdad)
    (4) The hope for Messiah

*The conversion of Obadia as to this conception — is based on the
burning love to Jesus (he goes to his people) and at the same time
in his way, to the hated, the persecuted and cast out. The text is
short, some phrases in every of the 4 points, in prose though not in
'historical style'.*

I must have made encouraging noises, because a few days later,
Mrs. Freier writes of *a fine perspective of cooperation* opening
before her. At this point she sent a bibliography adding, *we shall
work on the texts together (the composer decides!) even by letter.*
The whole plan of the work is described in a letter of 29th

September, 1969 when I also received the first version of my text.

It consisted of 7 parts:

L. Dallapiccola,	Jerusaleme
G. Rochberg,	Apokalypse
L. Foss,	Without Text
A. Goehr,	Obadia the Proselyte
R. Haubenstock-Ramati.	Text from *More-Nebuchim*
	(Minnesänger)
Andre Heydu,	Totentanz
	(Medieval children's game)
Benzion Orgad,	Crusades.

The first text of Johannes Obadjah was in five sections and written in German. The first, slightly imitative of the beginning of Goethe's *Faust*, was a montage of voices: the echo from the Mount of Olives, the Black voices of those who carried the Crucifix, a chorus of Jews of Jerusalem, a chorus of Bishops. Obadjah puts off his habit, takes the Crucifix from the wall and speaks: 'I go now with you, Jesus, son of Israel to your people, to the East. I am not moved by the wounds of your flesh but by your living being. Your word not the bells call me. See, my name is now Obadjah and I too am become a son of Israel. The 'Black voice' adds threateningly, 'Go traitor, rage, hate and curse upon you too'.

The second piece plays in Baghdad and deals with the persecution of the Jews there. The third is a short dialogue between Obadjah and Schlomo Alroy who, to Obadjah's consternation, announces the coming of the Messiah. The remainder of the text deals with the proclamation of this prophecy and the nocturnal flight of the Jews to Jerusalem. The text ends with brutal laughter at the discomfiture of the Jews: 'The Jews wanted to fly to Jerusalem, but their wings didn't want to grow'.

The way the text was presented and the style of the language clearly derived from German expressionist writing. I observed to Mrs. Freier that on the one hand the treatment, with its contrasting choirs evoked the scale of Mahler's VIII Symphony, or *Jakobsleiter*, on the other the expressionist elimination of connection made it look unbalanced in size, and potentially incomprehensible. Like many poets who loved music, Mrs. Freier clearly visualized a work of far greater scope than the practical possibilities of her scheme allowed.

She answered my objections in a long letter of the 8th November 1969, writing now in German. In this letter she describes again the plan for all seven pieces and how the particular text intended for me fitted into the scheme. She explains how she has *juxtaposed the Church in the symbol of the Crucifix and Jesus' Word of love and consolation*, expressed through the New Testament texts, opposed to the black voices. In this way Obadjah's actions became comprehensible, and his story *is the other side of the picture*, of the accounts in the *Totentanz* and *Crusades* episodes, of the presentation of Jews in Worms, Speyer and Mainz.

In the letter, Mrs, Freier refers to the great Jewish historian of Christianity, David Flusser, whose encouragement she acknowledges, and adds significantly, in answer to my objections *If you want, we might develop the text for a larger work. I'd be very interested to do this. But it would have to be separate from this miniature creation. Don't let me down because of the brevity of the texts!!*.

The next version of her text, which came a month later, expanded the earlier version by the addition of a narrating speaker at the beginning and some additions to the scenes as previously presented. Again she mentioned the possibility of a further expanded treatment of these texts, repeating, *Don't let me down this time!*.

At this point I realized that I was in a fairly difficult position. I certainly liked the material that Mrs. Freier had provided, but I did not see how I could possibly compose the text she had provided. So I asked her to send me copies of the documents upon which she had based her version. This produced a little bit of substantially more useful information. It seems from my own papers that I must have worked in the Judaica Library at Yale and found other references to the events in Baghdad described in our texts, or analogous accounts elsewhere. In any case, I very quickly composed a text of my own, eliminating Obadjah as a presence and focusing the treatment entirely on the story of the Jews who wanted to fly to Jerusalem. In general it seems to me that a story told in concrete images — the colours of shoes worn by the Jews in Baghdad, the green of the robes symbolizing the journey to Paradise, the attempt to fly from the rooftops of Baghdad, the subsequent humiliation, is inspiring for a composer. I bound the various short episodes of my text together with repetitions of the apocalyptic sentence, taken from the Book of Joel, 'Sol convertitur in tenebras et luna in sanguinem antequam veniat dies Domini magnus et horribilis'. Obadjah, it appears, had himself transcribed this text in the Latin, but written in Hebrew characters. I created a kind of Rondo form, where the Latin text formed the refrain, and the dramatic scenes the episodes, and I called this, *Sonata about Jerusalem*, in imitation of Monteverdi's *Sonata Sopra Sancta Maria*, from the *Vespers* (1610).

This seems to me an example of the ruthless and fairly philistine way in which artists work. At one stroke I had savaged Mrs. Freier's whole idea and reassembled some part of her words together with others into a new synthesis. Being herself a creative person, she took this well, translated my text into Hebrew; and I set it in Hebrew, with the help of a transliteration.

The performance took place in Tel Aviv and Jerusalem in January 1971. The whole plan of the seven pieces had to be divided into two, and as far as I recall, Abel Ehrlich replaced Haubenstock Ramati. My work was well played, and partially staged with two mimes playing the roles of the wise Jews of Baghdad. The image of flight — the Jews in their imagination on the way to Paradise, was particularly effectively realized. This image, together with the fact that the final jeering words (spoken in my version by a child: 'The Jews wanted to fly to Jerusalem but they had no wings' were ambivalent in Modern Hebrew — wings being a colloquial usage meaning testicles, gave the composition a secondary, almost Freudian aspect.

It was well received and has been frequently performed in many countries since.

While I was in Jerusalem, Mrs. Freier talked enthusiastically about the expansion of the work discussed in earlier letters, but was also intrigued by the way I had put fragments of different documents together to make the text of the *Sonata*. I saw her again a number of times in London in the following year and we continued to talk about her ideas. At the same time (and I mention this because it casts an interesting light on the way she operated) she was paying me my commission fees in tiny instalments. For not only was *Testimonium* her brainchild, but she fed it with contributions from friends and well-wishers all over the world. I was quite ashamed to take the money from her, but needed it badly at the time....

In the years that followed she sent me her poetry and short prose fragments (sometimes inspired by Kafka) as well as a series of documents to do with Shabbatai Zewi. For a time I thought to write a work on this material, but a reading of the English translation of Gershon Scholem's study convinced me of the impossibility of the undertaking, in the way I might have visualized it. At the same time I remembered Hans Eisler's laconic remark, when a young composer told him he wanted to do an opera on the *Dybbuk*; 'Can you imagine Windgassen in *paies*?'.

But Mrs. Freier had struck a chord in me and in the years that followed I became fascinated by the history of medieval Jewry. The Messianic movements and the literature that went with these, were my way to something, some feeling or understanding for the things Jewish that I had not previously experienced. Through the work of Norman Cohn (*The Pursuit of the Millenium*) and the great classics of Gershon Scholem and Ernst Block (*Münzer* and *Das Prinzip Hoffnung*), I came finally to the Anabaptists in Münster. My opera, with large choruses, *Behold the Sun*, is in fact the 'child' of the *Sonata about Jerusalem*, the expanded version of which Mrs. Freier and I talked. In Jerusalem in 1978, I played her the recording of the four polyphonic Choruses from this work, performed separately as *Babylon the Great is Fallen*. Next day she sent me a strange object, some dark thick paper on which she had painted in gold. She told me this expressed her reaction to hearing my music. She was now a very old lady, but still full of ideas, and above all of the enthusiasm, the passion, the indifference to trivialities which had made her lead her life the way she had. It's well known how much a great good she did for the German Jewish children she helped to rescue. To more than this one of the composers whom she enthused by her schemes, I suspect, she gave something special of her own. One of her short poems reads:

> Ich fühle mich
> wie reifes Korn.–
> Nun mahle mich,
> Und iss mich,
> Herr!

(I feel I am like ripe corn. Now grind me, and eat me, Lord!)

Elaine Feinstein

New Year

Blue velvet, white satin, bone horn: once again
We are summoned to-day to consider mistakes and failures
into the shabby synagogue on Thompson's Lane.
Shopkeepers, scholars, children and middleaged strangers
are gathering to mumble the ancient prayers,

because this is Rosh Hashonah, the New Year,
we have all come in out of the Cambridge streets
to look around and recognize the faces
of friends we almost think of as relations
and lost relations who never lived anywhere near.

How are we Jewish, and what brings us together
in this most puritan of protestant centres?
Are the others talking to God, or do they remember
filial duties, or are they puzzled
themselves at the nature of being displaced?

I sit and think of the love between brothers,
my sons, who never took to festivals
happily seated round a family table;
I remember their laughter rising up to my bedroom,
late at night, playing music and cards together.

And as I look back on too many surprises
and face up to next year's uncertainties,
somehow I find it easier and easier
to pray. And this September, hope at least for
perfumes rising from a scrubby hedge
if not from flowering Birds of Paradise.

Renee Winegarten

Simone de Beauvoir's Encounter with the Jews

F OR YEARS THE signature of Simone de Beauvoir, novelist, feminist pioneer, tireless traveller and fellow-traveller, was to be found near the head of any protest against injustice. And that included injustice to Jews, whether it took the form of UNESCO declarations hostile to the state of Israel or the wrongful imprisonment of Jewish dissidents in the Soviet Union, long regarded by her as the hope of the world. This notable stance helped to earn her the Jerusalem prize in 1975. How this fidelity came about is a complex story of an inner revolution and awakening. It is dependent not only upon terrible historical circumstances but also upon private shocks and associations.

In January 1940, Jean-Paul Sartre and Simone de Beauvoir, who discussed everything together (people, literary technique, philosophical ideas), came around to the vexed subject of the Jews. Their free union — always particularly free on Sartre's part — dated from 1929. At the time they were separated by the phoney war; he had been mobilized and was stationed in Alsace; she was still teaching in Paris. Unlike her companion, whose novel, *La Nausée (The Diary of Antoine Roquentin)*, appeared in 1938, she had as yet published nothing.

In a letter to her, Sartre challenged what she had stated in a recent missive to him: 'You write: in that case (if to take responsibility for oneself as a Jew was to claim rights for the Jews as Jews) to take responsibility for oneself as a Frenchman would be to become a chauvinist'. As he envisaged it, in existentialist terminology, Simone de Beauvoir was suggesting that for a Jew to recognize in himself a specific Jewish identity and authenticity was to imply a form of nationalism. Certainly, neither of them was in favour of that.

Sartre went on to try to clarify his meaning for Simone de Beauvoir. The problem in his view was whether, for the Jew, responsibility for oneself as a Jew meant to aim for the suppression of 'the Jewish race' (just as Sartre thought that the bourgeois Marxist was aiming to put an end to the bourgeoisie); or whether it could possible signify the recognition of a cultural and human value in Judaism itself. 'In which case,' Sartre observed, 'the principle to inspire one in fighting against antisemitism would not be because the Jew is a human being but rather because the Jew is a Jew'. Here there can be found the germ of Sartre's *Réflexions sur la question juive*, published in 1946, a work which was to arouse so much controversy and to exert a wide influence on the treatment of Jewish identity (and not only by Francophone writers). When he was writing *La Nausée*, Sartre had met a Jew named Mendel who had convinced him of the cultural and religious 'specific character' of the Jewish situation which required special rights.

Sartre's words presumably struck a chord in Simone de Beauvoir. She herself, in the years before the outbreak of the Second World War, had firmly believed that there was no such thing as Jews, there were simply human beings. This rather abstract 'liberal' attitude, inherited from one strain in the eighteenth-century French Enlightenment, had been somewhat shaken by the detailed account of savage Nazi persecution of the Jews as Jews which she had heard around 1938-39 from one of her Jewish pupils, who had family connections in Austria. Yet it seems clear from her words as quoted by Sartre in 1940 — her own letters to him have not been published — that her attitude still retained something of the abstract 'liberalism' she had supposedly abandoned by then.

As for nationalism, there was good reason for her profound suspicion of it, in any form. She had been in revolt as an adolescent against her father, a Parisian dilettante and man-about-town whose sole religion was nationalism. Thoroughly convinced of the guilt of Captain Dreyfus, he had passed on to his daughter in her most vulnerable years many of his Right-Wing opinions, including the racial theories of Gobineau. When she became emancipated from her father and from her bourgeois upbringing, she saw him as the symbol of the *bien-pensant* Right Wing nationalism that she had come to loathe.

In her account of her Catholic education in her autobiography- — and she was extremely devout up to the age of fourteen, when she lost her faith — Simone de Beauvoir makes no mention of Jews. Perhaps she had not met any until she went to study at the Ecole Normale Supérieure, where her fellow students included such future luminaries as the religious thinker, Simone Weil; the political philosopher, Raymond Aron; and the social anthropologist Claude Lévi-Strauss. Sartre thought that Raymond Aron (a close friend of his there until his meeting with Simone de Beauvoir) betrayed the common fault of Jewish intellectuals: 'lack of authenticity'. This was a grave shortcoming in Sartre's philosophy, 'authenticity' being the supreme virtue. He spoke of the 'unauthentic Jews' of his acquaintance.

Sartre had followed Raymond Aron to the French Institute in Berlin in 1933-34. Simone de Beauvoir visited him there on two occasions. It seems plain from her account, written long after the event, that they were not too bothered by the rise of Hitler and its implications. Of course, they grew indignant at the burning of books and at the hounding of Jewish artists and intellectuals. They felt extremely sorry for the Jewish refugees who were not permitted to land anywhere. All the same, they remained comparatively sanguine, involved as they were in their own intense personal affairs. Like so many of her compatriots, Simone de Beavoir was deeply pacifist after the staggering losses sustained by the French in the 1914-18 War; and she went so far as to say that any injustice, however cruel, was preferable to another conflict. Here, Sartre could not bring himself to agree with her.

He had taken to visiting the Jewish district in Paris around the rue des Rosiers, just before the outbreak of war in 1939, in the company of Simone de Beauvoir, Wanda Kosakiewicz (a current mistress), and other friends. He found there a kind of poetry that appealed to him, and of which she makes no mention. The whole subject of the Jews seemed to be exerting a fascination for him around 1939-40, which she apparently did not share. About that time, he could write to the Jewish girl she calls 'Louis Védrine', one of her pupils with whom he was besotted, ironically making antisemitic remarks about a 'base' Jewish lawyer he had met, 'fort juif (au sens classique et antisémite du terme)'. This objectionable fellow was the 'sort who needed a kick up the backside'. Soon, he was much taken with fellow conscript, Pieter, a rather 'vulgar' Jew, seen as naturally inclined to self-interest (as he told Simone de Beauvoir). Since her own letters are missing, we do not know what tone she herself adopted, or if it differed from his.

With the humiliating defeat of France in May 1940, Sartre was taken prisoner, and Simone de Beauvoir was left to fend for herself in Occupied Paris, to which she returned after having fled the capital in the general chaotic exodus. In order to live, she had to work. To work required the permission of the German authorities. So it was that she signed the declaration that she was neither a freemason nor a Jew, and thus she was allowed to continue teaching. When Sartre returned from prison camp in 1941, he was extremely annoyed to learn what she had done — though presumably he himself was obliged to make the same declaration when he resumed his teaching post.

At first, the situation of Jews in Occupied Paris seems to have been relatively fluid. The future film actress, the young half-Jewish Simone Signoret, could work briefly in the office of the collaborator, Jean Luchaire, who tried to protect her. The unspeakable Maurice Sachs engaged in the black-market and lived with a German officer. Some took extraordinary chances, like the girls (mentioned in Simone de Beauvoir's autobiography) who frequented the Café de Flore and who were finally denounced to the Gestapo. The risk of denunciation was always great. Leading lights in the collaborationist press — and these Simone de Beauvoir would never forgive — were in the business of denouncing Jews publicly. Lesser lights would give the names of their Jewish fellow citizens on the quiet.

The strange thing is that certain Jews felt themselves to be invulnerable. (One Parisian Jewish lady I have met actually went to Gestapo headquarters to make inquiries, and was fortunate to address herself to a decent officer who advised her to beat a hasty retreat). Among those who felt that nothing could touch them was Jean-Pierre Bourla, a budding poet and one of Sartre's pupils at the Lyceé Pasteur. Bourla's father, a wealthy businessman, thought he was safe because of his connection. Supposing the Germans win the war, Simone de Beauvoir suggested to young Bourla: 'A German victory does not fit in with my plans,' he replied. He became attached to one of Simone de Beauvoir's pupils and protégés, Nathalie Sorokine (called 'Lise' in *La Force de l'âge*), and they moved in together. Simone de Beauvoir did not discourage them.

Madame Sorokine, who wanted her daughter to make 'a good marriage', was not at all pleased at this liaison. She took her complaint to the school authorities and, as a result, Simone de Beauvoir was dismissed for the 'abduction of a minor'. This meant that she was not permitted to teach anywhere. How was she to subsist? She took to writing scripts for Radio Vichy on anodyne historical themes. This was in 1943, a few months before the successful publication of her novel, *L'Invitée*. However 'anodyne' the subject-matter, the fact that she was prepared to contribute in any way at all to the instrument of Vichy propaganda, whose stress on fatherland and family she loathed, seems strange. It is worth remembering, also, the Pétain régime's over-zealous collaboration in anti-Jewish measures especially from 1942. She passes rapidly over this equivocal episode of her contribution to Radio Vichy in her autobiography, and that seems highly significant.

The fate of Bourla in the last days of the Nazi Occupation is one of the most moving passages of *La Force de l'âge*. Simone de Beauvoir was attached to the young man, who seemed to her to be so full of life and promise. One night, he decided to sleep at his father's house. At that moment father and son were denounced, taken to the prison at Drancy, deported and killed. And this happened while Sartre and Simone de Beauvoir, along with

Camus and the rest of the literati, were enjoying themselves in high style at pre-Liberation parties, their belated commitment to clandestine literacy resistance activity — after an earlier failure — being of recent date, in the final months of the war.

The death of Bourla would haunt the pages of Simone de Beauvoir's most impressive novel, *Les Mandarins*, published in 1954, in the person of Diégo, the dead Jewish lover of the heroine's daughter, Nadine. He stands as the symbol of the Jewish friends who perished, half-forgotten and yet never-to-be-forgotten, the image of those whose life has been, as it were, usurped by the survivors. With the fearful pictures of the human remnants in the liberated extermination camps, with the return of deportees, Simone de Beauvoir could speak of her 'shame' at being alive.

The manner of Bourla's death marks a turning-point in Simone de Beauvoir's attitude to the Jews. But there was an earlier episode which left its mark on her sensibility and which, together with Bourla's fate, would ultimately turn her into an indefatigable supporter of numerous Jewish causes. This was the series of *rafles* or raids carried out largely by the French *milice*, and culminating in the 'grande rafle du Vel d'Hiv' in July 1942, when Jews and their families were herded into the stadium for deportation. In her autobiography, Simone de Beauvoir does not allude to these *rafles*, when children could be separated from their parents. But in her novel, *Le Sang des autres*, begun in 1941 and completed in 1943, she has the self-centred apolitical Hélène witness such a raid. A distraught woman runs after her small daughter who is being bundled into a bus with the rest of the Jewish children.

Hélène and the other people in the street stand there in a state of shock but they make no move to try to rescue the little girl and her companions. Why is this so? Hélène wonders. When she lies dying, after having accomplished a mission for the Resistance, she is still obsessed with the terrible episode. It would seem from *Le Sand des autres* that Simone de Beauvoir herself may well have witnessed such a raid. In her autobiography she alludes to the trains that carried deportees (the politically committed as well as Jews) in the direction of Germany. No longer was any distinction being made between foreign-born Jews and French Jews. There were suicides. 'The horror of these fates obsessed us. This obsession was mild in comparison with the horror itself, as thousands of men and women lived it...their misfortune remained foreign to us; but it is also true that it poisoned the air we breathed'. Always haunted by fear of mortality as she was, she blends these individual deaths into the enduring theme of the mystery of chance and destiny.

Scarcely surprising, then, that in the years after the end of the War, having followed Sartre along the path of *littérature engagée* or politically committed literature, she joined him in sympathizing with the effort to establish the state of Israel, and afterwards with justifying its right to exist. In 1948 the matter seemed clear-cut enough. Only later would it appear more complex and difficult. As Simone de Beauvoir, along with Sartre, chose to support the extremist and terrorist wing of the Algerian movement for liberation from France, they acquired numerous friends and associates who favoured the Palestinian cause. Besides, as committed Leftists, they were both opposed to colonialism and imperialism on principle, and this theme of Palestinian propaganda warred with their feelings of shame and guilt vis-à-vis the Jews who suffered at the hands of the Nazis and their active or passive supporters. Sartre was possibly more torn than she was in trying to keep an even hand. She herself would refuse to accept the notion of Israel as colonialist in tendency. Once again, there was a personal cause for her particular stance.

In 1952, the young Jewish Marxist journalist, Claude Lanzmann, moved into her studio flat just as her stormy on-off liaison with the American novelist, Nelson Algren, who was part Jewish himself, was reaching one of its recurrent crises. Best known today for his documentary film, *Shoah*, Claude Lanzmann was a good deal younger than Simone de Beauvoir. (He was not yet thirty, she was in her early forties). As a youth he had joined the *maquis* — his father was an early member of the Resistance in Clermont-Ferrand. Young Lanzmann emerged from his war experiences with that acute and aggressive self-conscious pride in his Jewish inheritance which seems so characteristic of French or Francophone Jews who have been forced by circumstance to probe their identity. Simone de Beauvoir could write that through Lanzmann she discovered 'Jewish reality' (whatever that might be).

Their liaison lasted some six years, until the latter part of 1958. During that period, they travelled abroad together, or in the company of Sartre and Michelle Vian, his current lady friend. After the liaison was over, Simone de Beauvoir and Claude Lanzmann remained friends, continuing to work together on the editorial board of *Les Temps Modernes*. In 1967, just before the outbreak of the 6-Day War, it was Lanzmann who accompanied Sartre and Simone de Beauvoir on their visit to Egypt and Israel. Severe in her condemnation of the poor treatment of women in Egypt, she was particularly interested in the status of Israeli women.

In the previous year, 1966, she produced two works which reveal the mark of her close association with Lanzmann. One of these is her preface to Jean-François Steiner's documentary novel, *Treblinka*. There, along with Steiner, she lays stress on the nature and importance of Jewish resistance to the Nazis. The other is her novel, *Les Belles Images*, dedicated to Lanzmann, which treats of the response to suffering and, in particular, to Jewish suffering.

The protagonist of *Les Belles Images*, Françoise, who works successfully in advertising, appears to share the meretricious values of her well-to-do circle. Her young daughter, Catharine, becomes devoted to a slightly older Jewish girl, Brigitte, who has known suffering. Shattered by what Brigitte has revealed to her, Catharine cannot put it out of her mind. Everyone, apart from her mother, would like to separate the two children. However, Françoise finds the courage to defy her husband and her family, and to ensure that the friendship between the girls can continue. The theme of Jewish suffering is central to the novel. 'Jewish reality', as conveyed to her by Lanzmann, joins with the theme of Jewish fate as portrayed in *Le Sang des autres* to present a leading motive of moral regeneration and commitment to one's fellow creatures. In these fictional works, the Jewish aspect is united with the assumption of the burden of suffering in general which is one of the deepest Catholic obsessions of this atheist existentialist. Unless they recognize that burden, that obligation, human beings have no chance of improvement, suggests Simone de Beauvoir.

It was unfortunate for her that in his long decline Sartre fell under the influence of his Maoist Cairo-born Jewish secretary, Pierre Victor, who real name was Benny Lévy. She found him arrogant, and she felt that he distorted the philosopher's true opinions. It seemed to her that Sartre, blind, dependent on others, not always in control, now sounded like Lévy after the young man returned to the God of his fathers. She had a blazing row with the interloper, and they never spoke to each other again, whereas Sartre continued to view him with favour. What was worse, Lévy had the support of Arlette Elkaïm, a young Algerian-born Jewess and one-time mistress of Sartre's whom the philosopher had legally adopted as his daughter. Simone de Beauvoir's keen resentment against this pair became manifest after Sartre's death.

Nothing, however, could make her deviate in her last years from the pro-Jewish stance she adopted immediately after the Liberation. Her enduring recollection of the tragedy that had overtaken her Jewish friends during the Occupation; her feelings of impotence, guilt and shame; her private awareness that her own conduct had not always been above reproach; her determination never to have to reprove herself again for failing to take a high moral stand — all these combined to preserve her loyalty. Perhaps she would always be trying to make amends for what she conceived to be sins of omission.

Alice Shalvi

The View from the Distaff Side

L OOKING BACK AT my life in a women's college, I am amazed at the paradoxical combination of intellectual stimulus and excitement — the long, strenuous, heated, complex arguments on abstract and academic issues, the sense of widening horizons — with an even then outmoded maze of stringent rules governing our movements, curbing our freedom, specifically so far as this related to being in the company of the opposite sex.

'Out-books', 'Pink Slips' (in no way directly to do with lingerie), 'Gate-fees', the need to escort one's (previously registered) male guests to and from the Porter's Lodge if they were so rash as to agree to visit of an evening — all these were presumably based on the premise that men were predators, women vulnerable to attack, and our (almost without exception unmarried) tutors, in *loco parentis*, responsible for the protection of that virginity which was virtually a *conditio sine qua non* for attaining the bourgeois *Ultima Thule* of marriage and family. Bohemians we were emphatically not. Though we were, at least in theory, free spirits, our bodies were bound in respectability. Extra-marital sex was, significantly, termed 'living in sin'. We were the men's equals academically (almost, not quite; in my time, women were still denied the gowned glory of a graduation ceremony), but we were distinctly unequal as far as the body was concerned.

Coming to Israel in 1949 after a two-year transition at L.S.E., where I discovered that the English faculty at Cambridge had been a veritable swarm of drones compared to the busy hive of earnest socialists I now encountered, was to travel to another stratosphere. All was youth and energy. A great, inspiring sense of partnership in a pioneering adventure bound us all together. Questions of gender were irrelevant and never posed. Women had fought alongside men in the very recently ended War of Liberation. They were perceived as having an equal part in the redemption of the land, as contributing equally to the economic development which was just commencing.

When I began my teaching career on January 1, 1950, as many women as men filled the packed rooms of Terra Sancta and other church properties recruited by the Hebrew University in its exile from Mount Scopus. Women constituted a significant proportion of the teaching staff, recruited — like their male colleagues — from the senior ranks of the major secondary schools, Gymnasia Rehavia and Beth-Hakerem. Excellent kindergartens and cheap, reliable home-based child-care made it possible for mothers to be gainfully employed outside their homes. Israeli women were, by and large, the envy of their European and American contemporaries; despite food shortages and an almost total lack of labour-saving gadgetry, we were undoubtedly — as a later generation termed it — 'liberated.'

Shades of the prison-house began to close upon us as the years passed. In 1975, when Israel marked International Women's Year by establishing a Commission on the Status of Women, the data collected (based on systematic research and enquiry never before undertaken, because not considered relevant or of interest) revealed a surprising and sorry state of underprivilege, disadvantage, non-representation. We had had a noted woman Prime Minister, but Thatcher's Britain like Indira Gandhi's India have since taught us all that this is in itself no indication of true equality of the sexes. Though women Members of Knesset constitute 8% of our legislators, while in the U.S. Congress women are only 4%, this is little consolation in view of our constituting over 51% of the total population. Israel has not a single woman mayor or head of local authority, very few women executives in business or industry and only a comparatively small number of female senior civil servants.

The Jewish tradition of a clear division of spheres of activity restricts woman to house- and home-bound functions. While recognizing and respecting the importance of those functions, it denies them a public role in prayer and, even more important, by extension and extrapolation, denies them equal opportunities of *Torah* study. Israel has neither women rabbis nor (with one or two very rare exceptions) *Talmidot Hakhamim*, women sages.

We are legitimately proud of having been in the vanguard of egalitarian legislation: equality of status, like equal pay, has been on the books since the 1950's. For a long time, we were also proud of that legislation which gave certain discriminatory advantages to women fulfilling their biologically unique role of motherhood: fully-paid maternity leave for 12 weeks, sick-leave to care for a child who falls ill — these were only two of the privileges we enjoyed, privileges which are still denied to working mothers even in many western countries, to say nothing of the Third World.

These privileges are now increasingly seen as in fact militating against equality of opportunity. The Kibbutz experience has opened our eyes to the fact that, so long as it is women only who are perceived as responsible for child-care, child-rearing and allied services, and so long as this home-making remains, as it perforce must, an occupation that is neither financially rewarded nor remunerative and, in consequence, enjoys no concomitant social status, there will be no true equality between women and men.

Those of us who, in the late 1960's and early 1970's, perceived that the Women's Liberation Movement then sweeping the U.S. was as relevant politically and socially to Israel as to other countries, were at that time dismissed for 'Importing (our) Western complexes' into the Israeli Utopia.

The legitimacy of our critical contentions is at last being recognized and not only because this particular 'western' concept, like so many other ideologies, fashions and fads, has seeped into the Israeli mass-conscious. The Knesset and local elections of 1984 had their own native impact on the growing number of academically trained, politically involved, middle-class women in Israel: seeing women politicians swept aside, rejected or demoted as candidates for high rank on party lists, denied a position in a cabinet of unprecedented size, reproached for raising 'irrelevant' issues of equal opportunity and equal reward, more and more Israeli-born and Israeli-educated women have become avowed feminists. Indeed, feminism has almost — though not quite — ceased to be a dirty word: even a number of male politicians have ventured to describe themselves as such. The ten women M.K.'s have, in an unprecedented gesture of unity in itself astonishing on our splintered political scene, allowed themselves to be persuaded to act as one, irrespective of party differences, where legislation on women-related issues is concerned.

For twenty years and more, Israeli feminists (of whom I am one very largely because of my Newnham education) feel like passengers on a stationary train: as we sat in our carriages poised for travel, we watched the trains alongside us move out of the station and were overwhelmed by the illusion of actually moving backwards. Now our own train has begun to move. Bearing many eager women and not a few supportive men, it launches us on our journey into the 21st century — or rather, most encouragingly, into the 59th.

Part Four

Reports, Lists
and Indexes

CAMBRIDGE HEBREW CONGREGATION

זמירות ושירות

לשיר ביום חנוכת בית הכנסת של

ק"ק קאנטאבריגיא

אור לי"ז מרחשון שנת בְּשֵׁם הֹ' נִקְרֹא לפ"ק

ORDER OF SERVICE

on the occasion of the

OPENING OF THE NEW SYNAGOGUE

by

Mr. LIONEL de ROTHSCHILD, O.B.E., M.A.

AND ITS CONSECRATION

by

The Very Reverend THE CHIEF RABBI

On THURSDAY, 21st OCTOBER, 1937-5698

The Reverend D. BUENO de MESQUITA, B.A., and The
Reverend L. I. EDGAR, M.A., *will take part in the Service*

Invitation to Meeting to discuss the formation of CUJS

Cambridge Hebrew Congregation*

Consecration of New Synagogue

Distinguished University Gathering

The new Synagogue of the Cambridge Hebrew Congregation was opened on Thursday in last week by Mr. Lionel de Rothschild, and consecrated by the Chief Rabbi, in the presence of the Vice-Chancellor of Cambridge University (Professor H. R. Dean, Master of Trinity Hall) and a distinguished congregation. The Rev. D. Bueno de Mesquita, the Rev. L.I. Edgar, and Mr. Nelson Berkoff (Trinity Hall) conducted the service. Mr. de Rothschild was presented with a golden key by Mr. R.J. Hersch, one of the architects, and he declared the Synagogue open. Those who took part in the procession of scrolls were the officiating ministers, Mr. de Rothschild, Mr. Hersch, Sir Robert Waley Cohen, Mr. H. Dagut, Dr. Redcliffe N. Salaman, F.R.S., Mr. Augustus Kahn, Mr. Ernest Cohen, and Mr. A.S. Eban (Queens'). The Ark was opened during the service by Dr. Charles S. Myers, F.R.S., Mr. I.H. Hersch and Mr. A. B.......

ERRATA

The caption on page 150 should read:

Order of Service of Consecration, 21st October 1937

The caption on page 157 should read:

Programme for Michaelmas term, 1937

The caption on page 158 should read:

Front cover, programme for Michaelmas term, 1985

* ... report appeared in the Jewish Chronicle on October 29th 1937, and is reprinted with the kind permission of the Editor.

As a House of Prayer the Synagogue was an everlasting Witness to God in the Jew's universe, and gave birth to the noblest of liturgies. Scripture reading and Scripture exposition always retained the central position of the Sabbath or Festival Service. The House of Prayer was thus also a Beth Hamedrash, a House of Religious Study. In Israel, study of the Torah was, alongside the direct communion with God in prayer, the way of closest approach to Him. Such study constituted Divine Worship, and may be said to be the Rabbinic form of the Beatific Vision. That religious study saved the Jews from the degradation which rightlessness and obloquy and hideous suffering brought in their train. Bialik, the great poet of the New Judea, with good reason hailed the Beth Hamedrash as the source of Jewish idealism and death-defying heroism throughout the days of martyrdom and hate.

Rousing the indifferent Jew

That new Cambridge Synagogue would have failed in its duty to the present and future, if it did little to rouse the indifferent Jew from his soul-slumber, change his whole attitude towards the Jewish sanctities and cause him to exclaim with the Patriarch, 'Surely the Lord is in this place; and I knew it not.'

It was not an impossible task, continued Dr. Hertz, that he was proposing to the members of the Cambridge Hebrew Congregation. Laudable efforts in the direction indicated had for years been made by the Schechter and kindred societies; and it would be ingratitude to the *genius loci* if there were any relaxation in those efforts. Their University was the first seat of Higher Learning in the world to have 'emancipated' Jewish Studies—that is, given them academic recognition and appointed an eminent Jewish scholar on the University staff to expound the specifically Jewish disciplines! That was nearly seventy years ago. Thanks to Cambridge men like Joseph Jacobs, Solomon Schechter, and Israel Abrahams, and their colleagues of other Universities, a large portion of the new Jewish learning was now accessible to the cultured layman.

Speaking of the antecedents of the congregation, the Chief Rabbi said they all should remember for good the names of John Sylvester, Numa Hartog, and Arthur Cohen, who by refusing to proceed to their degree at the expense of their Judaism, laid the spiritual foundations of that Synagogue. It was, however, only in 1888 that his revered predecessor, Hermann Adler, went to Cambridge to confer with the Jewish members of the University how to create something like *organised* congregational life among them. One of them, Mr. Augustus Kahn, was, happily, with them that night; and the other survivor, the Rev. A.P. Bender, had just completed more than four decades of notable service to South African Jewry. Seven Sabbaths of years had passed since that day. In this fiftieth year, and thereafter, let everyone regain the religious inheritance which was inalienably his. Let that Synagogue become the spiritual home of *all* the Jewish students of the University.

The architects of the Synagogue are Mr. R.J.Hersch, M.A., A.R.I.B.A. (Gonville and Caius), and Mr. C. J. Eprile, F.R.I.B.A. The Synagogue stands in Thompson's Lane on what was formerly Ellis Court. A pleasant turfed forecourt leads up to the new building, which is faced with a warm multi-coloured brick. The small entrance-hall gives on to the main hall, which is hexagonal with two short sides containing a recess for the Ark (which is stated to be one of the most beautiful in England) and a recess for the women's seats. There are a dining-hall a and kitchen.

The First Jew to enter the University

Before the ceremony tea was taken in the Hall of Magdalene College. Arthur Cohen, Q.C., the first Jew to enter the University, was a member of this college, and by special permission of its Master and Fellows, the tea was held there.

Among those present in a congregation of about 300 were:
The Master of Peterhouse (Field-Marshal Sir William B. Birdwood, Bart.), the Master of Jesus (Mr. A. Gray), the Master of Pembroke (Sir Montague S.D. Butler), the President of Queens'

(Dr. J.A. Venn), the Master of St. Catharine's (the Rev. Dr. J.A. Chaytor), the Master of Magdalene (Mr. A.R. Ramsay), the Master of St, John's (Mr. E.A. Benians), the Censor of Fitzwilliam (Mr. W.S. Thatcher), the Mistress of Girton (Miss H.M. Wodehouse), the Principal of Newnham (Miss J.P. Strachey), the Rev. Principal W.A.L. Elmslie, the Rev. Principal and Mrs. R. Newton Flew, the Regius Professor of Divinity (Canon C.E. Raven) and Mrs. Raven, the Regius Professor of Hebrew (Dr. Stanley A. Cook) and Mrs. Cook, the Regius Professor of Civil Law, the Reader in Rabbinics and Mrs. Loewe, Mr. Charles Fox, the Headmaster of the Perse School, the Rev. Dr. H.F. Stewart, the Rev. J.S. Boys Smith, the Rev. Dr. R.F. Rattray, Mrs. Salaman, Dr. S. Goldstein, F.R.S., and Mrs. Goldstein, Lord and Lady Rothschild, Miss Hannah F. Cohen, Mr. H.M. Adler, Mrs. Israel Abrahams, Mrs. L.D. Barnett, Mrs. Magnus, Mrs. R.J. Hersch, Miss Hertz, Dr. L.V. Snowman, Dr. L.J. and Mrs. Harris, Dr. and Mrs. H. Richards, Dr. and Mrs. S. Greenburgh, Mrs. H. Dagut, the Hon. Mrs. R.M. Sebag-Montefiore, Mr. and Mrs. O. Sebag-Montefiore, Mr. Hugh Harris, Mr. A.I. Polack, Mr. and Mrs. J. Sebag-Montefiore, Mrs. Walter Cohen, Dr. Phyllis Abrahams, Mr. and Mrs. Augustus Kahn, the President of the Union, Mr. Harold Soref, President of the Oxford University Jewish Society, Mr. G. Kitson Clark, Mr. E. Royalton Kisch, Mrs. Kennett, and Mr. R.F. Kahn.

Paul Ellerman

Address of Welcome

by the President of CUJS to the Celebration Jubilee Dinner
on September 13th 1987 at the Guildhall, Cambridge

I T IS BOTH an honour and a pleasure for me to welcome you
all to this Dinner to celebrate 50 years of the Cambridge
University Jewish Society. It is, perhaps, appropriate that as the
current co-President of the Society I can extend a very warm
greeting to Mr. Abba Eban, the first President of the Society. I
would like to thank both Mr. and Mrs. Eban for coming over from
Israel to be present at this most important occasion for the Society
and I am certain that I speak for us all when I say how much I am
looking forward to hearing Mr. Eban's address later this evening.

In the fifty years between our terms of office, generations of
Jewish students, having left the comfort and convenience of their
homes and local Jewish communities, have come to Cambridge
and have been fortunate enough to have enjoyed the very special
atmosphere belonging to the Jewish Society. Through the doors of
the Thompson's Lane Synagogue have passed many students,
many of whom have gone on to reach prominence in their chosen
careers, active in both public and communal life, particularly
providing religious and lay leadership for the Jewish Community.
There can be few Societies in Cambridge able to boast of having
a President of Israel, several national and foreign cabinet ministers, politicians, the occasional Peer, numerous professors, judges
and artists among its rank and file.

The Cambridge University Jewish Society Constitution begins
thus: 'The aim of the CUJS shall be to advance the Jewish religion,
and to this end it shall assist and encourage all Jewish students
in Cambridge to take part in all aspects of Jewish communal life,
and shall provide them with opportunities for common worship,

for studying Judaism, Jewish history, literature and general culture, and for discussing matters of Jewish interest and in many ways the Society has tried, and continues to try to live up to this ideal. Perhaps the finest feature of the Society is its toleration of all views. On a Friday evening it is no uncommon sight to see a Yeshiva-trained student sitting next to someone who has never attended a Synagogue service before. The weekly Shiurim, the important SEED study program, the campaigns for Israel and Soviet Jewry and the regular speaker meetings are all important ways in which students, of whatever degree of religiosity or knowledge, are welcomed into the Jewish Society. There are countless people who have been introduced to Jewish culture and their heritage through coming along to the Jewish Society. It is a Society that aims to provide something for everyone. It is more than just somewhere to have a kosher meal or to attend the occasional Service. It simply is the focal point of all Jewish life in Cambridge. It provides communal, educational and social facilities for all Jews in Cambridge, as it has done for fifty years and as, we hope, it will continue to do for another fifty. While it is sad that many Jewish students choose to hide away from their Jewish background, it is encouraging that the past decade has seen a continued growth in the size and scope of the Society.

Your presence here tonight demonstrates that you too have a great feeling of affinity with the Jewish Society, where perhaps you made friends for life or spent much of your 'valuable' student time. On behalf of the 50th Anniversary Building Committee and the Cambridge University Jewish Society I would like to welcome you to this celebratory dinner, to ask you to enjoy yourselves by renewing old acquaintenceships and recalling old memories, but, most importantly, to remember how important the Cambridge University Jewish Society was to you individually and still is to the University, the local community and, especially, to the Jewish students of Cambridge.

The Life and Work of Isaac Abravanel

This year is the five hundredth anniversary of the birth of ISAAC ABRAVANEL. The attention of the Society is drawn to the course of lectures announced by the Professor of Spanish and the Reader in Rabbinics to be delivered in Christ's College (lecture-room 1, Third Court) at 5.45 p.m., and to the Abravanel Service arranged by the Society.

October 30. Introduction and Life, by P. Goodman, F.R.Hist.Soc.

November 6. Abravanel's Portuguese and Spanish Environment, by I. Gonzalez Llubera, Professor of Spanish in the Queen's University of Belfast.

November 13. Abravanel's Literary Works, by Dr. M. Gaster, late Ilchester Lecturer in the University of Oxford.

November 20. Abravanel's Biblical Exegesis, by Dr. L. Rabinowitz.

November 27. Abravanel's Political Theories, by Dr. L. Strauss, Sidney Sussex College.

Dec. 4. Leone Ebreo and the Renaissance, by A. R. Milburn, King's College.

Cambridge University Jewish Society

Michaelmas Term 1937

President :
A. S. EBAN, B.A. (Queens')

Senior Treasurer :
R. F. KAHN, M.A. (King's)

Hon. Auditor :
DR. S. GOLDSTEIN, F.R.S. (St. John's)

Junior Treasurer :
N. A. BERKOFF (Trinity Hall)

Hon. Secretary :
A. BAUM (Trinity)

Hon. Assistant Secretaries :
H. C. SCHWAB (Trinity), Cambridge Hebrew Congregation.
G. SILMAN (Sidney), Zionist Society.
B. M. CASPER (Trinity), Anglo-Jewish Association.

The Synagogue, Ellis Court, Thompson's Lane.

13th October.
Reception at the Dorothy Cafe.

17th October.
"The earliest Hebrew Literature : the Ras Shamra texts."
Mr. THEODOR H. GASTER.

21st October.
The new Synagogue will be opened by Mr. Lionel de Rothschild, O.B.E., M.A., and consecrated by the Very Reverend the Chief Rabbi. The Rev. D. Bueno de Mesquita, B.A. and the Rev. L. I. Edgar, M.A., will take part in the Service.

7th November.
Mr. ARTHUR LOURIE, M.A., LL.B.,
Secretary, Political Department, World Zionist Organisation

14th November.
ABRAVANEL SERVICE.
The Sermon will be preached by The Reverend the Haham, Dr. MOSES GASTER.

18th November.
"Palestine and Partition."
The Rev. M. L. PERLZWEIG, M.A.
Hon. Secretary, Zionist Federation.

20th November.
Rabbi Dr. L. RABINOWITZ will preach in the Synagogue.

3rd December.
"Traditional Judaism and Modern Problems."
Rabbi E. W. KIRZNER, Ph.D., M.A., M.Sc.,
Barrister-at-Law, Lincoln's Inn.

4th December.
Sabbath Chanukah.
Rabbi Dr. KIRZNER will preach in the Synagogue.

Services are held throughout the term in the Synagogue on Friday evenings at 6.30 and on Saturday mornings at 10.30, and Communal Suppers on Friday evenings at Thurston's Cafe, opposite Emmanuel College.

Order of Service of Consecration, 21st October 1937

C.U JEWISH SOCIETY

MICHAELMAS TERM
1985

Programme for Michaelmas term, 1937

Preface to the Book of Memorial[*]

BEFORE THE CAMBRIDGE HEBREW CONGREGATION left the last of the four temporary buildings in which it had worshipped, and before the occupation of the new and permanent Synagogue, a Committee was appointed

'To edit the list of deceased members of the C.H.C. and prepare it for printing: to recover, where possible, the Hebrew names; to arrange the Hebrew and English names in proper order for use on days appointed for the Commemoration of Benefactors and the Memorial of the Departed: to include, either in footnotes or in special, differentiating type, such biographical or historical detail as it was desirable to record but which need not be read aloud during public worship: to preserve, in Hebrew and English, the traditional order of service in use, for many years, in the Cambridge Hebrew Congregation on these occasions, together with the Prayer for the Sovereign: to raise the amount needed for the printing of this book so that the expense should in no wise become a charge upon the Congregational Funds but that a special account be opened, to be maintained out of the proceeds of the sale of the book, so that the money thus obtained could be saved for future editions when the present one is exhausted.'

The Committee consisted of Mr. H. Loewe, M.A. (Queens'), Mr. H. Schwab (Trinity) and Mr. C. Feather (St John's), with power to co-opt others: Miss Ismay Levy (Newnham), President of the Cambridge Hebrew Congregation (Cambridge University Jewish Society) in the Easter Term 1939, and Mr. H. Goodman (Downing), President in the Michaelmas Term of 1939, have been so co-opted. Owing to the heavy burdens which the Refugee problem has imposed, the Committee's work has, inevitably and excusably, been delayed; it was felt that the needs of the living and suffering

[*]The Book of Memerial was never published and only corrected proofs remain.

were paramount. Nevertheless, the important duty which had been assigned to the Committee has never been overlooked and at last the task has been completed.

The Committee had, as a basis, the manuscript lists which have been in use for so many years, certainly since the Synagogue was situated 'over Barrett's', in St. Mary's Passage. The following circular was then issued:

CAMBRIDGE HEBREW CONGREGATION

'BOOK OF MEMORIAL'

It has long been the custom in Cambridge to recall, at certain proper periods, the names of the deceased members of the Congregation. Usually, in accordance with Jewish tradition, this has taken place on the Eighth Day of Solemn Assembly, and on Pentecost, which appropriately coincide with the beginning and end of the Academic year, or, if these Feasts fall in vacation, on the nearest convenient Sabbaths (Passover and the Day of Atonement do not usually fall in Term). The University and Colleges similarly hold their Commemorations early in the Michaelmas Term.

Our Memorial Roll comprises three divisions:

1. Names of scholars like Abendana, who were famous in ancient days.

2. Immediate predecessors of the present Congregation, such as Arthur Cohen, Numa Hartog, J. Sylvester: founders of the present Congregation, benefactors and scholars, such as David Israel, Schiller-Szinessy, Schechter and Israel Abrahams.

3. Those who fell in the War.

It is our duty and desire to recall and to honour the memory of our predecessors. The list, moreover, is of considerable historical interest, but in the course of time the number of those acquainted with the details is decreasing and the younger generation is unacquainted with them. It is, therefore, desirable to draw up a proper, permanent roll. This will be printed, so that each worshipper may have a copy. One will be worthily bound and preserved on a lectern, always available to visitors and members.

Some of our predecessors are, by the generosity of their families, already commemorated by ritual objects in the Synagogue; but 'some there be, which have no memorial'. This defect we wish to repair. As the roll will be prefaced by one of the usual formulas of memorial (*Hazkoroh or Hashkabah*), the Hebrew names are required. The object of this notice is to obtain them. The whole, i.e. roll and names, will be in Hebrew and English and the English side will contain such detailed information as is appropriate in each case.

The response received to the circular was very encouraging. The project was warmly welcomed alike by the kinsfolk of those whose names are recorded and by the present and former members, who were glad to see historical information about the Cambridge Hebrew Congregation preserved and made accessible. It is a source of regret that some of the Hebrew names have not been traced.

The highly laborious work of preparing the Roll of Honour was undertaken by Mr. H. Schwab: by a careful collation of the University War Register with the Jewish Roll of Honour compiled by the Reverend M. Adler, D.S.O., he recovered many names. But the method was largely empirical: it could not, by the size of the undertaking, be carried out with mathematical accuracy. The University Register naturally does not mention the religion of anyone included in its pages, and Mr. Adler, just as naturally, does not state how many of the Jewish names which he records belong to Cambridge men. By a happy flair and by unremitting diligence, Mr Schwab has produced a substantial list. But it cannot claim to be complete. He interviewed College Deans and Clerks, seeking thus to find out how many Jews were mentioned on the College War Memorials. He wrote letters to relatives, inquiring whether their kinsfolk were entitled, as Cambridge Jews, to be included in our list, and he endeavoured to elicit the Hebrew names of those so entitled. But we feel that there may well be omissions and we hope that the publicity accorded by the appearance of this book may bring to notice missing names for incorporation in subsequent editions.

In the historical sections, certain omissions will be remarked. We naturally regret that the distinguished name of Elias Levita could not be added to the list of Cambridge Jewish notables. It is not generally known that, but for his death, Levita would probably have been the first Regius Professor of Hebrew in the University. He had declined the offer, made by Francis I, of a similar post in Paris, because Jews were not permitted to reside in that city. In the meanwhile, Levita's friend and collaborator, Paulus Fagius, had arrived in Cambridge with Martin Bucer and had proposed that Levita be invited to initiate the teaching of Hebrew. The negotiations were interrupted by the sudden death of Fagius, in Corpus Christi College, on 13 November 1549: Levita himself died in Venice less than a month later.

An examination of the documents relating to these negotiations would be a useful piece of investigation.

Other names have been excluded for a different reason. In a list of Jewish notables, there is no place for those who changed their faith. For this reason no mention is made of Moses Scialitti (1663) and of a certain scholar called Michael, both of whom were in residence in Cambridge. Definite proof of conversion must, however, be forthcoming before a name is omitted. Mere inclusion in the roll of inmates of the *Domus Conversorum* is not adequate evidence: it may, by itself, be no more than a form analogous to registration of aliens or passport procedure. On such grounds alone one would not reject Philip Ferdinand, who was born in Poland about 1555 and who matriculated in Cambridge in 1596. He may then, it would seem have still been a Jew. He taught Hebrew in the University. Three years later he entered the *Domus* but he must have embraced Christianity in 1597, for in that year he published the Latin Version of Abraham b. Kattan's *Six hundred and thirteen commandments*, under the title *Haec sunt verba Dei*. On folio E, 4, *verso*, there is a sentence which no Jew could have penned but it is the only sentence in the book which is incompatible with Judaism, as far as a somewhat cursory inspection would reveal.

Jonah ben Jacob Xeres is connected with Cambridge only by reason of his connection with Dr Peter Allix, of Swaffham Prior, who baptised him. John Xeres, as he was then called, was the author of *An Address to the Jews* (London, 1710) a work which gives him a title to scholarship. With regard to the story of his conversion, see Mr C.P. Allix's paper in the *Proceedings of the Cambridge Antiquarian Society* for 1909 (3 May to 31 May: No. LIV, pp.224 foll.).

By the loss of these names our roll of scholars is the poorer. On the other hand, we have felt justified in including Isaac Cardenas, since there is no evidence that he abandoned the faith of his fathers. His matriculation and election to a Fellowship, being sponsored by Royal Authority, may well have been accomplished without the normal subscription to a profession of the Christian religion.

The Congregation asked the Committee also to include the Prayers for the Sovereign and for the University. About this a few words must be said. It was felt desirable to safeguard the old and cherished Congregational traditions when the Congregation entered the new building and the years of transition were ended. These traditions were to be perpetuated in the main. They were based on the two associated principles of religious and academic freedom. By religious freedom is meant the fact that this Congregation occupies a unique position: it meets for worship only for two dozen Sabbaths in the year and its membership is composed of constantly changing elements. The majority may, in one given term, belong to the Orthodox section of Jewry and in the next term to the Liberal section. Jews come to Cambridge from different parts of the Old and New Worlds. Their religious outlooks may diverge widely. Some accommodation is therefore necessary in order to prevent the domination of extreme factions on either side, with the inevitable consequence of violent and successive changes of ritual. To secure stability and a form of service that will be suitable for the average Jew, a well-balanced mean is essential. The Synagogue is 'under the jurisdiction of no spiritual authority' and it is therefore able and eager to welcome visitors from all Jewish bodies. But the Synagogue is entirely free and the form of service is determined solely by the prevailing majority. Two methods of securing this democratic supremacy of the majority, combined with consideration for the wishes not only of the minority but even of the individual, prevailed. In Market Hill and Park Terrace, it was usually the custom for the Reader to follow the pronunciation and formulas of his own home Congregation in regard to the Prayer for the Royal Family, the blessings and tunes for the *Haftaroth*, etc. Then, in Sidney Street, the custom grew up of stabilizing the formulas term by term. Sometimes the Sephardic Prayer for the Royal Family was read throughout one term and changed for the next: sometimes that of the Liberal Jewish Synagogue. Sometimes portions of the service would be read in Hebrew, sometimes in English. But whatever system was followed, the principle which prevailed was that no single rite was to predominate exclusively and perpetually. It is in order to preserve this fundamental tradition that all forms are here given, so that Sabbath by Sabbath not only shall the Reader be able to select the formula which is most familiar to him but the worshippers will be directed to the page on which that formula is to be found. In this way the Congregational traditions will be safeguarded.

So much for religious freedom. The term academic freedom, mentioned above, is no less important. It means that the government of the Congregation is exclusively in the hands of undergraduates. In 1899 this principle was adopted as a result of a series of incidents which led to a vote of censure on the Senior Members of the University and Townsmen who were then holding office in the Cambridge Hebrew Congregation, to the resignation of the officers and to the resolutions passed by the Congregation that in future no graduates or townsfolk were eligible for office, for voting or for attendance at meetings unless specially invited to be present for some definite purpose. This resolution was found to be so valuable that it was followed, in 1903, at Oxford, but at first only partially. Originally there were, at Oxford, under this arrangement, two co-wardens, one representing the town and one the University. But gradually the Cambridge system was adopted completely.

In yet another matter is Oxford indebted to Cambridge. The Cambridge Hebrew Congregation had followed the precedents of Baer and Singer and adapted the ancient Academic prayer, *Yekum Purkan*, to present needs of the University and had approximated it to the Cambridge University official 'Bidding' prayer. This used to be read in English on Friday night, instead of *Bammeh Madlikin*, and in Aramaic on Sabbath morning instead of the first *Yekum Purkan*. In 1920, or later, Oxford took our prayer but changed it to conform to the Oxford 'Bidding' prayer.

In its present wording, the Cambridge formula is composite. The former portion incorporates and adapts an ancient petition on behalf of the Exilarchs, the heads of Academies, the teachers, Rabbis and students in the Colleges of Babylonia. For this reason, it is in Aramaic, the vernacular of the Babylonian Jews: in this language parts of the Bible (certain chapters in Daniel and Ezra, etc.) and the Liturgy (for example the *Kaddish*) are composed. The date of the prayer is uncertain, but it is at least as old as the third century of the civil era.

The latter portion is based on the ancient prayer recited at the conclusion of a lecture or the completion of the study of a Talmudical tractate. According to a *Baraitha* in the Babylonian Talmud (*Ber*.28b), certain sentences, which are included in our version, were formulated by R. Nehunya b. hak-Kanah, a famous teacher and logician, and used by him daily at the termination of his lectures; being a contemporary of R. Johanan b. Zakkai, he must have lived during the existence of the Temple, the fall of which he survived. It seems almost certain that the words were known to the editor of Luke's Gospel, who misunderstood them. He makes the Pharisee say 'I thank God that Thou hast not made me as other men' (xviii. II) in a spirit of pride. But it is in deep humility and in a sense of thanksgiving that the prayer is offered. It is a confession of unworthiness of special opportunities. This is clear from the remaining portions, some of which are omitted in Luke. In the present form, which includes sentences from other parts of the Liturgy, there can be no room for misunderstanding. These old prayers help to carry on in Cambridge the traditions of the great Colleges where Jewish learning flourished.

It is to be hoped that as a result of this book the traditions of the Cambridge Hebrew Congregation will neither decay nor become standardized. Each generation has a right to determine the ritual it desires but no generation has a right to withhold from its successor the heritage which it has received from the past. When this edition is exhausted, the next may well be increased in bulk by such additions as the future may produce. It is the hope, prayer and belief of the Committee that the provision of a permanent home will increase the spiritual life of the Congregation so that 'there may never be wanting a living or abiding succession of scholars who will not depart from truth or prove heedless of the words of the Torah'.

H. LOEWE
H. SCHWAB
C. FEATHER
I. LEVY
H. GOODMAN

APPENDIX TO
Cambridge Jewry
Jewish Graduates etc, of
Cambridge deceased by December 1987

It is important that the terms of reference of the following list should be understood.

1. No one has been included unless in some way connected with the University or one of its colleges, either as a student (irrespective of whether or not a degree course was completed) or as a member of the teaching body. This explains why such familiar figures in the Cambridge Jewish scene as Harry Dagut (housemaster at the Perse School), or Rabbi Dr S. Margulies, a refugee in Cambridge from the second World War until his death, are not to be found in the list. Numerous refugee scholars and scientists spent some time at Cambridge on emigrating from Germany, being granted laboratory facilities etc; but unless formally connected with the University, e.g. by taking a Ph.D. (as did E.B. Chain) they are omitted.

2. The list, of those by now deceased, cannot claim to be complete, but it is believed to be substantially so. Leaving aside the 102 individuals marked [ ] or ? (for whom see below, 3), it comprises — subject to any last-minute additions — the names of 324 persons (262 men, 62 women), with the appropriate cross-references for changes of surname. No one has been included unless there is firm evidence of death or the person concerned would, if untraced, now be aged over 100. In assembling the material, I have noticed in the early tripos-lists for the present century a number of other Jewish names, and have doubtless overlooked others that have been anglicized beyond spot-recognition; and since anyone who graduated before, say 1926, would if still living be by now aged 82 or more, I would surmise that the substantive number of 324 here stated might need to be increased by something over 15%.

3. In addition to these 324 another 102 individuals are listed within [ ] or marked with a ?. Those bracketed were, despite in many cases bearing distinctive Jewish names, certainly not to be reckoned as Jewish. Either there is direct evidence of their apostasy, or they were children or very near descendants of parents who had converted to Christianity. Naturally, those of remoter Jewish ancestry have been ignored. A few women are included who also married a Cambridge Jewish graduate, and circumspection has here been requisite if the maiden name is obviously a non-Jewish one. If it is shown without brackets, a form of conversion (not necessarily an orthodox one) was undergone, e.g. in the case of Lucy Cohen *née* Cobb. In cases where there must be a strong presumption that the person concerned was not of Jewish birth and that there was no conversional ceremony, the name is prefixed by ? e.g. Ethel Chotzner, *née* Lan-Davis. ? is likewise prefixed to a substantial number of bearers of Jewish-sounding surnames about whose status evidence is not to hand; when, however, in such cases the parents bore forenames strongly suggestive of their being Jewish, no question-mark has been prefixed to the name of their issue.

4. The list, by almost any criterion, is a distinguished one. The following statistics — which relate exclusively to those about whose Jewish status there can be no question — are revealing; not least, the fact that something like 10% of such entries qualified for inclusion in the *Dictionary of National Biography*. Where two figures are given the first refers to those themselves educated at Cambridge, the second, in ( ) to those educated elsewhere who joined the Cambridge teaching faculties; the two are then aggregated.

	Men	Women	Total	
Nobel Laureates	2		2	
Fellows of the Royal Society	8 (1)=9	*	9	*H. Ayrton was debarred by her sex from election; R. Franklin, who died young, would probably have been elected later
Fellows of the British Academy	5 (4)=9		9	
Members of Parliament (UK and Dominions)	10 *		10	*2 members of a British Cabinet
Senior local government office (chairman or deputy, LCC, etc.)	4	1	5	
Judges (UK and Dominions, including recorders, masters in chambers)	7 (1*)=8		8	*Includes 1 member of The Hague International Court; 1 colonial Chief Justice
Senior civil servants (under-secretary, etc)	4		4	
Entries in the Dictionary National Biography	28 (2)=30	1	31*	*Up to 1980; a few of later demise will probably be included in the 1980-90 volume

Prominent Service to the Jewish Community (UK, Dominions, Palestine)

(This list is probably misleading, in that distinguished service is not necessarily spectacular. Reference to the numerous obituary notices in the Jewish Chronicle to which references are included would no doubt redress the balance)

	Men	Women	Total	
Synagogue				
Senior lay office in United synagogue, Reform Synagogue, etc.	7		7	
Local synagogue wardens	7		7	
Ministers etc	6		6	
Education				
Teachers (including teachers of Hebrew at University)	7 (8)=15		15	
Lay administration, inspection, etc.	4	3	7	
Welfare	1	3	4	
Jewish Journalism	4*	1	5	*Includes 1 editor of *Jewish Chronicle* and 1 literary editor
Communal Lay Office				
President, Treasurer etc. of Board of Deputies, AJA, Board of Guardians etc. (UK and Dominions)	9		9	
Palestine and Zionism (including *Aliyah*)	9	2	11	
Entries in (English) *Encyclopaedia Judaica* and/or *Jewish Encyclopaedia*	37 (4)=41	1	42	

Sources

A. University

J. & J.A. Venn *Alumni Cantabrigienses*. Part I (to 1751), vols 1-4, Cambridge, 1922-27; Part II (1752-1900), vols 1-6, Cambridge, 1940-54

The Book of Matriculations and Degrees. 1544-1659, Cambridge, 1913; 1851-1900 (anon), Cambridge, 1902; 1901-12, Cambridge, 1915

C.H. & T. Cooper *Athenae Cantabrigienses*. 1. 1500-85, Cambridge, 1858; 2.1586-1609, Cambridge, 1861; 3. 1609-11 and index, Cambridge, 1913

J.R. Tanner *The Historical Register of the University of Cambridge ......to....1910*. Cambridge, 1917 (tripos results etc); *Index to Tripos lists 1748-1910*. by C.W. Previté-Orton, Cambridge, 1923; *Supplements to Historical Register* (indexed), *1911-20*, Cambridge, 1922; *1921-30*, Cambridge 1932; *1931-40*, Cambridge, 1942; *1941-50*, Cambridge, 1952; subsequently in 5-year periods to 1971-75, Cambridge, 1977 etc.

H.P. Stokes. *Studies in Anglo-Jewish History*, Edinburgh, 1913 (from p. 103 concerns Jews of Cambridge, from the middle ages to the 19th century)

H. Loewe et al. *The Book of Memorial*. Cambridge Hebrew Congregation. [Not published, but printed from proof in a small edition, 1939. Includes 75 names of those connected with the University, amongst them 38 of those who fell in the 1st World War]

B. Colleges*

Christ's College Biographical Register. J. Peile. i. 1448-1665. ii.1666-1905. Cambridge, 1910, 1913

Clare College *Notes on the Masters, Fellows, Scholars and Exhibitioners of Clare College, Cambridge*. W.J. Harrison and A.H. Lloyd, Cambridge, 1953

Corpus Christi College. A History 1822 to 1952. Patrick Bury, Cambridge, 1952

Girton College Register 1869-1946. K.T. Butler and H.I. McMorran, Cambridge, 1948

Gonville & Caius College *Biographical History of Gonville and Caius College*. J. Venn. i. 1349-1713. Cambridge, 1897; ii. 1713-1897. Cambridge, 1898; iii (masters. etc). Cambridge, 1901; iv. 1899—. E.S. Roberts. Cambridge, 1912; v. 1911-32. F.E.A. Trayes. 1948; vi. 1933-56. F.J. Stratton. Cambridge, 1958; vii. 1957-72. M.J. Pritchard and J.B. Skemp. Cambridge, 1978

King's College *A Register of Admissions to King's College Cambridge, 1797-1925*. J.J. Withers, London, 1903 (2nd ed.. 1929); 1919-58. R.A.Bulmer and L.P. Wilkinson. London 1963; 1945-70, London. 1973; *King's College Annual Report*

Newnham College Register. A.B. White, Cambridge, 1963 (most references are to this edition); 2nd ed. M.E. Grimshaw. i. 1871-1923. ii. 1924-50, Cambridge, 1981

Peterhouse *A Biographical Register of Peterhouse Men* i. 1284-1574. T.A.Walker, Cambridge, 1927; ii. 1574-1616, Cambridge, 1930; *Admissions to Peterhouse, A Biographical Register, 1615-1887* (with abstract to 1911), Cambridge, 1912; 1911-30, E. Ansell, Cambridge, 1939; 1931-50, Cambridge 1971

St John's College *Admissions to the College of St John the Evangelist*. J.E.B.Mayor. i. ii. 1629/30-1715, Cambridge, 1882; iii. R.F. Scott.1715-67, Cambridge, 1903; iv. 1767-1802, Cambridge 1931

Trinity College *Admissions to Trinity College Cambridge*. W.W. Rouse Ball and J.A. Venn. i. (introduction. index). London, 1916; ii. 1546-1700. London, 1913; iii. 1701-1800. London, 1911; iv. 1801-1850. London, 1911; v. 1851-1900. London, 1913

---

*I am grateful to archivists and records clerks in many of the colleges for responses to my requests for supplementary information.

Abbreviations

In addition to abbreviations in common use and some others that will be readily intelligible, the following are employed:

adm   admitted (to college: refers to entry of MAs etc., or of junior members proceeding to the womens' colleges prior to the constitutional incorporation of those colleges in the University in 1948)

BA   Bachelor of Arts

DNB   *Dictionary of National Biography*

EJ   *Encyclopaedia Judaica* (English), Jerusalem, 1972

FBA   Fellow of the British Academy

FRS   Fellow of the Royal Society

Int. WW   *International Who's Who*

JC   *The Jewish Chronicle*

JE   *The Jewish Encyclopedia*. New York and London 1901-6 (not usually cited if there is also an article on the subject in EJ)

MA   Master of Arts

matr   matriculated (i.e. entered the University through a college, almost invariably in October)

sch   scholar (of the college; normally by competitive examination prior to entry, sometimes by promotion on university examination results. Note that information was not always forthcoming, and some not here so designated may have held college scholarships. College prizes, post-graduate studentships, etc. are in general omitted, major university prizes and scholarships being cited)

WW   *Who's Who* (followed by year)

WwW   *Who was Who* (decennial summaries)

| |, ?   See above, p.167, para 3.

List of Deceased Jewish Graduates

Abelson. Edward Gordon, ?-1916
> Emmanuel; matr 1914. Killed in 1st World War

Abendana. Isaac, c1640-1710
> Taught Hebrew at Cambridge (and Oxford); transl. the Mishnah into Latin (MS in Cambridge Univ. Library) (EJ)

Abrahams. Adolphe. 1883-1967
> Emmanuel; sch; matr 1903; Nat Sci (1st) 1906. Physician; Kt (WwW; JC 15.12.67)

Abrahams. Harold Maurice, 1899-1978
> Caius; matr 1919; Law I 1921, II 1923. Pres. Univ. Athletic Club; Barrist. and Olympic athlete. CBE (Caius Biographical Register 5 p200; DNB; WwW; EJ; JC 20.1.78)

Abrahams. Israel, 1858-1925
> Christ's; MA adm 1902. Reader in Rabbinic and Talmudic Literature in the Univ. 1902-25 (WwW; EJ; JC 9 & 16.10.25)

Abrahams. Sydney Solomon, 1885-1957
> Emmanuel; matr 1902; Law I 1904, II 1906. Olympic athlete. Barrist. Chief Justice of Ceylon. PC; Kt (WwW; EJ; JC 17.5.57)

Abrahamson. Isaac, see **Lubbock. Isaac**

Abrams. Lawrence Golding, 1882-1918
> Peterhouse; matr 1902; no coll. record of tripos. Killed in 1st World War (Peterhouse Admissions p652)

[Adler. August Ludwig Wilhelm, 1870-?
> Selwyn]

?Adler. Fritz Beaumann, ?-1964
> Clare; matr 1900 (Clare mortuary list, MS)

Adler. Hannah, see **French. Hannah**

Adler. Herbert Marcus, 1876-1940
> St John's; matr 1894; Classics (1st) 1897. Barrist. Collaborator in *The Service of the Synagogue*, ed. A. Davis. MBE (JC 30.8.40)

?Adler. Paul Sabel, 1915-44
> Christ's; matr 1933; Nat Sci I (med.) 1936. Killed in 2nd World War (Christ's Coll. Record Files)

Ahrons. Elizabeth Julia, 1869-1956
> Girton; sch; adm 1888; Classics I 1891. HM Schools Inspector. Public work (women, refugees) (Girton Register p48)

Alexander. (Alexander) Aaron, 1888-1945
> St John's; sch; matr 1908; Law II (1st) 1912; Geo. Long prize; Pres
> Schechter Soc; Barrist. practiced in Cairo (JC 21.9.45)

[Alexander. Alexander Benjamin, 1840-1905
> Christ's; matr 1859; Maths 1863. Christian clergyman]

Alexander. David Lindo, 1842-1922
> Trinity Hall; matr 1860; Maths (1st) 1864. Barrist. (KC); Pres Board of
> Deputies (WwW; JC 5.5.22)

Alexander. Eileen Helen, see **Ellenbogen. Eileen Helen**

[Alexander. George H. G., 1865-1934
> Clare]

Alexander. Morris, 1877-1946
> St John's; matr 1897; Law I (1st) 1899 (sch), II 1900. Barrist. (KC);
> Member Cape Town House of Assembly; championed rights of coloured and
> Indian communities. Pres. New Heb. Cong., Cape Town; Vice pres SA Jew.
> Board of Deputies (Int. WW 1938; EJ; JC 8.2.46)

Altschuler (*née* Persitz). Olga Hadasa, 1890-1969
> Newnham; adm 1912; Moral Sci. (did not take tripos) (Newnham Register
> p277)

Arakie. Ezra Aaron, 1876-1942
> Emmanuel; matr 1894; BA, no tripos, 1898. Jew comm. leader, Calcutta
> (E. D. Ezra, *Turning Back the Pages* 1986 p672)

Arnold (formerly Hoffmann). William Arnold, 1878-1945
> Christ's; sch; matr 1897; Nat Sci 1900. Schoolmaster (Christ's Biographical
> Register ii p815)

Aron. Eustace Mars, ?-1916
> Jesus; matr 1910; Med & Mod Lang. 1912 (1st), 1913 (1st). Killed in 1st
> World War (RN)

Aron. Frederick Adolph, 1888-1918
> Caius; matr 1906; Nat Sci I 1910. Killed in 1st World War (Caius
> Biographical Hist. 4 p67)

?Ashauer. Sonja, 1923-48
> Newnham; adm as research student 1944; Ph. D (Physics) 1948
> (Newnham Register ii p262)

Ashley (*née* Hayman). Doris, 1877-1941
> Newnham; adm 1895; Med & Mod Lang. (1st) 1898 (Newnham Register
> p129)

Ayrton (*née* Marks). Hertha Phoebe Sarah, 1854-1923
> Girton; adm 1876; Maths 1881 (but not in list). Physicist. Nominated FRS
> but disqualified by sex from election, 1902; Hughes medalist, Royal
> Society. Invented (1915) anti-gas fan, donated to govt. for duration of war.
> Science fellowship at Girton in her memory. (Girton Register p8; WwW; E.
> Sharp, *Hertha Ayrton, A Memoir*, 1926; JC 31.8.23)

Barnato. Jack Henry Wolf, ?-1918
    Trinity Hall; matr 1912. Killed in 1st World War (RFC)

Barnett. Lionel David, 1871-1960
    Trinity; matr 1892; sch 1893; 3 times Browne medalist; Classics I (1st)
    1894, II (1st) 1896. Indologist. Keeper of Orient. Books & MSS, Brit.
    Museum, CB; FBA (DNB; EJ; WwW; JC 5.2.60)

Barnett. Richard David, 1909-86
    Corpus; sch; matr 1927; Classics I (1st) 1929, II (1st) 1930. CBE; D. Litt.,
    FBA; Keeper Western Asiatic Antiquities, Brit. Museum (WW 1986; EJ; JC
    8.8.86)

Beer. Arthur Henry, ?- 1918
    Trinity; matr 1913. Killed in 1st World War. MC

?Behrens. Margaret Lundie, see Humphries. Margaret Lundie

Bein. Albert Baruch. 1892-1962
    King's; matr 1911; Classics I 1914. Solicitor & civil servant (Malay)
    (Withers p445; King's AR 1963 p21)

[Benamor. James (Haym),
    Magdalene; matr 1787]

Bender. Alfred Philipp, 1863-1937
    St John's; matr 1888; sch 1891; Semitic Lang. (1st) 1891; Tyrwhitt Scholar.
    Minister Cape Town Heb. Cong. and Professor of Hebrew, S. African Coll.
    JP; Bequeathed prize for Hebrew to Cambridge Univ. (WwW; JE; JC
    24.12.37)

Benjamin. John Alfred, ?-1916
    Clare; sch; matr 1911; Maths I (1st) 1912, Mech Sci 1914. Killed in 1st
    World War (Harrison-Lloyd; JC 14.7.16)

Benjamin. Louis Edmund, 1865-1935
    Peterhouse; matr 1885; Law 1888. KC; Judge of Supreme Court, S. Africa
    (Peterhouse Admissions p588; WwW; G. Saron & L Hotz, *The Jews in S.
    Africa*, 1955 p53)

Benjamin. Roy Neville,
    Clare; matr 1912 (Clare Admissions list, noted as dead)

Bennett (*née* Frankau). Joan, 1896-1986
    Girton; adm 1916; Mod & Med Lang. I 1918, English I (1st) 1919. Lecturer
    in English in the Univ. (Girton Register p274; WW 1986)

Bentwich. Hebe Rachel, see Mayer. Hebe Rachel

Bentwich. Joseph Solomon, 1902-82
    Trinity; sch; matr 1920; Maths I (1st) 1921, II (1st) 1923. Stewart of
    Rannoch scholar (Hebrew); Govt. of Palestine (education dept.)
    Headmaster Reali School, Haifa. Lecturer in Education, Heb. Univ (JC
    25.6.82)

Bentwich. Norman de Mattos, 1883-1971
Trinity; sch; matr 1901; Classics I 1903, II 1905. Whewell Scholar (Internat Law). Members' Essay and Yorke Prizes. Barrist. Attorney General, Palestine. Professor of Internat. Relations and chairman of Friends of Heb. Univ. MC; OBE (DNB; WwW; EJ; JC 16.4.71). The Bentwiches collectively donated the *menorah* in the Camb. Syn.

Bentwich. Rosalind Nita see **Lange. Rosalind Nita**

Berlyne. Daniel Ellis, 1924-76
Trinity; sch; matr 1941; Mod & Med Lang. I (1st) 1942, Moral Sci II (1st) 1947. Professor of Psychology, Toronto (JC 10.12.76)

[Bernal. Charles,
Clare; matr 1832]

[Bernal. Ralph, 1785-1854
Christ's]

[Bernal (-Osborne). Ralph, 1808-82
Trinity. Politician (DNB)]

[Bernard. Hermann Hedwig, 1785-1857
Taught Hebrew in Cambridge (JE)]

[Bernays. Adolphus Vaughan, 1857-1938?
Non-collegiate]

[Bernays. Albert Evan, 1874- ?
Trinity]

[Bernays. Leopold John,
incorp. MA from Oxford 1852. Non-collegiate]

Besicovitch. Abram Samoilovitch, 1891-1970
(Karaite); Trinity; Fellow 1930. Lecturer in Maths in the Univ., subsequently Rouse Ball Professor. FRS (DNB; WwW)

Besso. David, 1917?-86
St Catharine's; matr 1937; Maths I (1st) 1938, Nat Sci (Physics) II 1940.

Besso. Ruth, 1915-65
Newnham; sch; adm 1934; Nat Sci I (1st; out of 52 including 4 women) 1937. Science teacher S. Hampstead High Sch. (Newnham Register p545)

Billig. Levi, 1897-1936
Trinity; matr 1919; Orient. Lang. I & II (1st) 1922. Tyrwhitt Scholar; Wright Student. Lecturer (Arabic) at Heb. Univ. Killed in anti-Jew. riots in Palestine (EJ; JC 28.8.36)

Birnberg. Jonas, 1894-1970
Queens'; matr ?; Maths I (1st) 1914, II (1st) 1916. Schoolmaster & univ. lecturer.

174

Blackburn (formerly **Schwarzman**). **Rudolph Isaac, 1889-1973**
Queens'; matr 1908; Nat Sci 1911. Patent agent.

Blackman. Moses, 1908-83
Trinity; Ph.D 1938; Professor of Physics, Imperial Coll. Lond. FRS (WW 1983; *The Times* 10.6.83)

Bles. Edward Jeremiah, 1864-1926
King's; adm 1896; BA by theses 1898. Research scientist. Commemorated by endowment at Cambridge (Withers p271)

Bloch. Arnold, 1928-85
St. John's; matr 1945; Orient. Lang. I 1947, Law II (1st) 1948. Barrist. in Australia; Chairman, Victoria Board of Deputies (JC 1.3.85)

[Blumberg. Frederick William, ?-1882
Caius]

?Blumberg. Samuel Henry Gustav D'arnim 1869-1932
Peterhouse; matr 1887; went down 1888 (Peterhouse Admissions p594)

?Bolton (formerly **Sonnenschein**). **Susanna Frederica, 1873-1969**
Newnham; adm 1893; resided until 1895. Schoolteacher & coach (Newnham Register p128)

Bornstein. Harry, 1908-1943
Emmanuel; matr 1928; Hist I 1931, Orient Lang I (1st) 1932; Tyrwhitt Scholar; Anglo-Jew Minister. Died as milit. chaplain (JC 10.12.43)

Braudo. Charles Joseph, 1918-72
Kings'; matr 1938; Mech Sci 1941. Ph.D. Liverpool. Lieut.-Col., Israeli Air Force. Scientific adviser, Israel Water Authority. Returned to England. (Bulmer-Wilkinson, i, p187; King's AR 1985 p32)

?Braunholz. Eugen Gustav William 1859-1941
King's; adm MA 1886; Univ. lecturer in French (Withers p163; King's AR 1941 p11; WwW)

?Braunholz. Eugen Julius Karl, 1890-1969
King's; matr 1909; Classics I 1912. Schoolmaster (Withers p419; King's AR 1968 p66; 1969 p25)

Bridge (*née* **Makower**). **Ursula 1905-71**
Newnham; adm 1925; Maths I 1926, English I (1st; out of 14 including 6 women) 1928. English literary historian (Newnham Register p426)

Brodetsky. Israel, 1906-27
Caius; sch; matr 1924; Maths I (1st) 1925, II 1927. Killed in accident (Caius Biographical Hist. 5 p281; JC 17.6.27)

Brodetsky. Selig, 1888-1954
Trinity; sch; matr 1906; Maths (1st; bracketted Senior Wrangler) 1908. Professor of Maths, Leeds Univ. Pres. Board of Deputies; Pres. Heb. Univ. (DNB; WwW; EJ; JC 21.5.54)

Bronner. Lina, see **Kahn. Lina**

Bronowski. Jacob, 1908-74
> Jesus; matr 1927; Maths I (1st) 1928, II (1st) 1930; Ph. D 1933.
> Mathematician, author & broadcaster. Hon Fellow of Coll. (DNB; WwW;
> JC 30.8.74)

Burnham (formerly **Burnheim:** *née* **Nachbar). Henrietta 1871-1948**
> Girton; sch; adm 1891; Hist. 1894 (Girton Register p70)

Cahn (?Kahn). see Kahn. Lina

Chain. Ernst Boris, 1906-79
> Fitzwilliam House; Ph. D (Biochem.) 1935; Professor of Biochemistry,
> Imperial College London; Kt.; FRS; Nobel Laureate; (DNB; WwW; JC
> 17.8.79)

Chasanovitch. Leonita. 1919-67
> Newnham; adm 1938; Moral Sci. I 1940, II 1941. Civil servant (Board of
> Trade) (Newnham Register p 598)

Cherns. Albert Bernard, 1921-87
> Trinity; matr 1940; Moral Sci II (Psychology) 1947. Civil servant,
> subsequently Professor of Psychology, Loughborough Univ. (JC 5.6.87) see
> **also Members Roll**

Chotzner. Alfred James, 1873-1958
> St John's; sch; matr 1892; Classics 1895; Browne medalist 1895. Indian
> Civil Service, Judge of High Court, Calcutta; MP (WwW)

?Chotzner (*née* **[Lan] Davis). Ethel Kathleen, 1883-1925**
> Girton; adm 1901; Moral Sci. 1904 (Girton Register p135)

Churchill (*née* **Myers). Hannah Violet, 1875-1943**
> Girton; adm 1893; Med & Mod Lang. 1896. Concert singer; sec. Refugee
> Committee, Malvern (Girton Register p81)

Churchill (*née* **Myers). Stella, 1883-1954**
> Girton; adm 1902; Nat Sci (med) I 1905. Psychotherapist (Girton Register
> p144; WwW)

Cobb. Lucy Margaret, see **Cohen. Lucy Margaret**

Cohen. Abraham, 1887-1957
> Emmanuel; matr 1906; Orient. Lang. (1st) 1909; Tyrwhitt Scholar;
> Anglo-Jewish Minister (Birmingham); President of Board of Deputies; ed.
> Soncino Books of the Bible (EJ; JC 30.5.57)

Cohen. Alan Edward, 1910-36
> Peterhouse; sch; matr 1929; Nat. Sci. I (1st) 1932; MRCS, LRCP
> (Peterhouse Admissions p140)

Cohen. Alfred Henry, 1869-1906
> Christ's; matr 1889; ?Maths 1892; Law II 1893; Barrist. Bequeathed
> Spanish collection to the college library (Christ's Biographical Register ii
> p753)

Cohen. Arthur, 1829-1914
> Magdalene; matr. 1849 (fellow-commoner). Maths (1st) 1853; MA 1879;
> Pres. Cambridge Union Society 1853 (first Jewish president); Hon Fellow
> of college. Barrist. (QC); MP; PC (DNB; JE; JC 20.11.1914)

Cohen. Arthur Merton, 1875?-1966
> King's; matr 1895. History 1898; Mediaeval and Mod. Lang. 1899.
> Businessman (Withers p258; King's AR 1966; JC 18.2.66)

Cohen. David Lennard, 1882-?
> Christ's; matr 1900; BA 1903. Businessman (Christ's Biographical Register
> ii p843)

Cohen. Edward, ?-1914
> Queens'; matr 1914; Killed in 1st World War (MC)

Cohen. George Hubert, 1878-1915
> Christ's; matr 1896; Law I and II 1901; Barrist. Killed in 1st World War
> (Christ's Biographical Register ii p813; JC 28.5.15)

Cohen. Hannah Floretta, 1875-1946
> Newnham; adm 1894; Classics I 1897; Public worker (Jewish Board of
> Guardians etc); OBE; Member of council of Newnham and benefactor of
> college (Newnham Register p131; WwW; JC 29.11.46)

Cohen. Helen Olga, see **Taylor. Helen Olga**

Cohen. Herbert Benjamin (2nd Bart), 1874-1968
> King's; matr 1892; BA 1895; Barrist.; OBE (Withers p223; WwW; JC
> 26.4.68)

[Cohen. James, 1833-91
> Pembroke]

[Cohen. James Cecil, -?1955
> Emmanuel; matr 1903; BA (no tripos) 1906 missionary]

Cohen. John Icely, ?-1917
> Queens'; matr 1911; Classics 1 1914. Killed in 1st World War

?Cohen (*née* Hamill). Kathryn, 1905-60
> Newnham; adm 1943; Nat Sci I 1945; Fellow Roy Soc Med (dermatologist),
> 1st woman house physician St George's Hospital London 1948 (Newnham
> Register p667)

Cohen (*née* Cobb). Lucy Margaret, 1877-1942
> Newnham; adm 1896; Maths I 1899 (Newnham Register p145)

Cohen. Mary, (presumed deceased 1971)
> Newnham adm 1885; resided 1895-6, no tripos. Schoolteacher (Newnham
> Register p83)

Cohen. Nigel Benjamin, 1908-31
> King's; matr 1926; Maths I 1927, II 1929, subsequently medical student.
> Killed flying; Commemorated by bequest to College (Bulmer-Wilkinson
> p76)

Cohen. Oliver Henry Lionel, 1904-66
Peterhouse; matr 1925; History I 1927, II 1928 (Admissions to Peterhouse p101)

Cohen. Robert Waley, see **Waley Cohen. Robert**

Cohen. Samuel Hai, see **Craig, Seymour Ian Ralph**

Cohen. Solly Gabriel, 1920-84
Queens'; sch; matr ?; Nat Sci I (1st) 1941, II 1942; Ph.D. 1948. Professor of Experimental Physics, Hebrew University; member, Israel Academy of Sciences & Humanities. Awarded Weizmann Prize for Exact Sciences, 1984. (JC 16.3.84)

Cohen. Stephen Behrens, 1911-43
King's; matr 1929; History 1932, Law II 1933. Barrist. Killed in 2nd World War. Commemorated by studentship and travel exhibitions founded by Hannah Cohen (Bulmer-Wilkinson p102; Hannah Cohen, *Let Stephen Speak*, n. d.)

Cornforth (*née* Klugmann). Kitty Caroline, 1908-65
Girton; sch; adm 1926; Moral Sci. I and II (both 1st) 1928-9; Economics II 1930 (Girton Register p369)

[Cowen. C. H. G, (deceased by **1954**)
Christ's; matr 1910]

Craig. Seymour Ian Ralph (formerly **Samuel Hai Cohen**), **1904-83**
St Catharine's; matr ?; Hist I 1923, Law II 1925. Barrist. (E. D. Ezra, *Turning Back the Pages,* 1986 p315f)

?Cramer. Henry John, 1816-44
Trinity Hall and Peterhouse; matr 1835; (Peterhouse); 1839 Trinity Hall. BA 1843 (Peterhouse Admissions p452)

[?Crespin. Abraham John, 1771?-1850
Trinity]

[?Crespin. Elias David, Died **1795;**
Caius]

Crool. Joseph, -1829
Rabbi at Manchester and Nottingham, taught Hebrew Cambridge for Regius Professor; Controversialist writer (EJ; JC 30.6.1848)

Davis. Clement John Burton, 1894-1917
Caius; matr 1913; Killed in 1st World War. Commemorated together with his brother Herbert Nathaniel Davis by the *Ner Tamid* in the Cambridge Synagogue.

?Davis. Ethel Kathleen [Lan], see **Chotzner, Ethel Kathleen**

Davis, Felix Arthur, 1863-1916
St John's and Trinity Hall; matr 1882; Law (1st) 1886; Barrist. Treasurer of the United Synagogue (JC 27.10.16)

Davis. Herbert Nathaniel, 1891-1915
Emmanuel; matr 1909; Mech Sci 1912. Killed in 1st World War
(Commemorated in Cambridge Synagogue, see C. J. B. Davis)

Davis. Israel, 1847-1927
Christ's; sch; (first Jew elected to a college scholarship), matr 1866;
Classics (1st) 1870; Barrist.; editor *The Jewish Chronicle* (Christ's
Biographical Register ii p593; JC 28.1.27; 4. 2. 27 and 24. 6. 27)

Davis. Joyce Rachel Frances, 1905-58
Girton; adm 1923; Mod. Lang. 1925; Moral Sci. II 1926 (Girton Register p.
351)

De -,see **following surname**

Diamond. Arthur Sigismund, 1897-1978
Trinity; sch; matr 1916; Law I and II (1st) 1920, Ll. D. Barrist. Master of
the Supreme Court, Queen's Bench Division (WwW; JC 10.3.78)

Diringer. David, 1900-75
Pembroke, MA 1948; Univ. College (foundation fellow 1965); Reader in
Semitic Epigraphy, Cambridge; Established an Alphabet Museum in
Cambridge, subsequently transferred to Tel Aviv (EJ; JC 21.2.75)

Donnison (*née* Singer). Ruth Seruya, 1900-68
Newnham; adm 1920; Nat Sci I 1923; Welfare worker and magistrate
(Rangoon and Berks.); MBE (Newnham Register p361)

Edelman. Israel Maurice Moses, 1911-75
Trinity; matr 1929; Mod. & Mediaeval Lang I (1st) 1930, II 1932; MP and
author; Legion d'Honneur (officier); Medaille de Paris (DNB; WwW; JC
19.12.75)

[Edelman. William, 1794-1862
Queens']

[Edersheim. Alfred, 1825-89
Pembroke; Jewish historian and missionary (DNB; JE)]

Edgar. Leslie Isidore, 1905-84
Christ's; sch; matr 1924; History I (1st) 1926; Orient Lang. I (1st) 1928;
Rabbi, Liberal Jewish Synagogue London (JC 2.3.84)

?Ehrman. Sidney Hellman, 1905-30
King's; research student. Died during residence. Commemorated by
fellowship and studentship (King's AR 1930; Bulmer-Wilkinson p95)

Eichholz. Alfred, 1869-1933
Emmanuel; matr 1888; sch 1889; Nat Sci I 1891, II 1892 (both 1st); MD
BCh; Lecturer in Nat Sci in the Univ; schools inspector (pioneered school
medical inspections). First Jew to occupy a college fellowship in
Cambridge. Chairman Central Committee for Jewish Education (WwW;
JC 10.2.33)

Elkin. Charlotte Emily, see **Samuel. Charlotte Emily**

Ellenbogen (*née* **Alexander**). **Eileen Helen, 1917-86**
Girton; English II (1st) 1939; Translator (French and Italian literature); art collector; needlewoman and silversmith, made breastplate for Camb. Syn. College prize for English in her name founded by her parents 1943 (Girton Register p510; JC 5.12.86)

[Elton. Abraham 1755-1842
Christ's (also some descendants)]

Errera. Alfred Jacques Joseph Harold, 1886?-1960
King's; matr 1904. Took no degree. Professor of Maths and Physics, Brussels; Burgomaster of Uccle, Belgium (King's AR 1961 p30; Withers p364; JC 7.10.60)

?Eschwege. Fritz Salo, 1882- ?
Christ's; matr 1901; Nat Sci 1904. Engaged in medical practice (Christ's Biographical Register ii p852)

Ezra. David, 1884-1918
Trinity; matr 1902; BA 1905; No tripos. Killed in 1st World War

?Feigl. Hans Ernest John, 1926-54
Christ's; research student

[Ferdinand. Philip, c1555-98
matr 1596. Taught Hebrew at Cambridge (EJ)]

Finkelstein. Moses, see **Finley. Moses**

Finley (formerly **Finkelstein**). **Moses, 1912-86**
Jesus; adm fellow (Ph. D Columbia) 1957; Professor of Ancient History in the Univ; hon fellow of the college; Master of Darwin College Cambridge; Ancient economic historian. Kt; FBA (WW 1986; JC 12.12.86)

[?Fitz-Aucher (formerly Rappoport). Robert Alexis 1878-before 1954
Christ's; matr 1896; Med & Mod Lang. 1899. Schoolmaster. (Christ's Biographical Register ii p803)]

Fortes. Meyer, 1906-83
King's; adm MA 1950; William Wyse Professor of Social Anthropology in the Univ; hon fellow of the college; FBA (Bulmer-Wilkinson p321; King's AR 1983; WW 1983; JC 4.2.83)

Fox. Charles, 1876-1964
Christ's; sch; matr 1898; Nat Sci (1st) 1900; Moral Sci (1st) 1905. Principal Univ Training College for Schoolmasters (Christ's Biographical Register ii p829; JC 23.10.64)

Frankau. Joan see **Bennett, Joan**

Franklin. Rosalind Elsie, 1921-58
Newnham; sch; adm 1938; Nat Sci 1 (1st; one of 37 inc 8 women) 1940, II (Chemistry) (1st; one of 25 inc 6 women) 1941; Ph. D 1946 Research chemist (Newnham Register p600; JC 18.4.58)

Fraser (*née* **Harari). Esther, 1909-45**
> Girton; adm 1925; Mod. Lang I (1st) 1927; English 1928; Education Dept
> Tanganyika; Founder and principal European School, Lusoto (Girton
> Register p377)

French (*née* **Adler). Hannah, 1927-72**
> Newnham; adm 1945; Nat Sci I 1948; MRCS, LRCP. Psychiatrist
> (Newnham Register, 2nd ed p276; JC 24.11.72)

Freund. Ida, 1863-1914
> Girton (and Newnham); adm Girton 1882; Nat Sci (1st) 1885 and 86;
> Gamble Prize 1903 (devoted proceeds to science equipment, Girton and
> Balfour Laboratory); Demonstrator and lecturer at Newnham 1887-1903.
> Commemorated by prize at Girton; Research chemist, traveller and worker
> for womens' suffrage (Girton Register p21)

Fridlander. Ernest David,
> Emmanuel; matr 1893; did not graduate.

?Friedeberg, Elsie Louise, 1881-1967
> Newnham; adm 1904; Classics I 1907. Career in education (coaching)
> (Newnham Register, p201)

Friedman. Meyer, 1889-?
> Peterhouse; matr 1908; BA 1912. No tripos. Civil Service.

Gainsbrough (formerly **Ginsburg). (Hugh) Hyam Hirsch, 1893-1980**
> Downing; matr 1912; Nat Sci I (1st) 1914 Director of med. unit, St George's
> Hosp Med School (WwW; JC 23.1.81)

Galkoff. Leo, 1921-46
> Caius; sch; matr 1939; Classics I 1940; Law II 1941 (Caius Biographical
> History 6 p204; JC 22.3.46)

Gaster. Nellie Frances see **Ziman. Nellie Frances**

Gee, Nathan J., 1926-56
> St. Catharine's; matr. 1943; Nat. Sci. I 1946; M.M., B.Chir. 1952. Medical
> Officer, R.A.F., died in Singapore (JC 14.12.56 *death notice*)

Geiler. Lucy Elise, see **Winter. Lucy Elise**

[Ginsburg. Benedict William, 1859-1933
> St Catharine's; Lawyer and statistician (WwW)]

Ginsburg. Hyam Hirsch, see **Gainsbrough. (Hugh) Hyam Hirsch**

Gluckstein. Isidore Howard, 1903-33
> Caius; matr 1922; History I 1924; II 1925. Businessman (Caius
> Biographical History 5 p252)

Godinski. Leah, see **Marcus. Leah**

Golberg. Leon, 1915-87

Emmanuel; matr 1946; Nat Sci (1st) 1947; BA 1948; environmental chemist; Dir. Brit. Indust. Biolog. Research Assn, and Inst. Exper. Psychol. & Toxicology, North Carolina. (*The Times* 13.5.87)

Goldberg. Alan David, 1928-70

Christ's; matr 1945; History I (1st) 1947 (sch); Geography II 1948. Civil servant. (JC 27.2.70; 6. 3. 70)

[?Goldman. Peter, 1925-87

Pembroke; matr ?; English I 1945, History II (1st) 1946; Director, Conservative Political Centre; Director General, Consumers' Association. (WW; *The Times* 1.10 87)]

Gollancz. Emma, ?-1929

Newnham; adm 1889; resided 1889-91; took no tripos. Literary amanuensis to Israel Gollancz (Newnham Register p103; JC 20.9.29)

Gollancz. Israel, 1863-1930

Christ's; matr 1883; Med & Mod Lang. 1887; Lecturer in English in Univ; Professor of English, King's College London; Kt. FBA (founder member and sec.) (Christ's Biographical Register ii p700; DNB; EJ; WwW; JC 27.6.30)

Gollancz. Marguerite Eugenia Henriette Joyce, 1911-81

Girton; adm 1930; History I 1932, II 1933. Archivist and librarian (Girton Register p 435; JC 20.2.81)

[Gompertz. Henry Richard Barent,

Clare; matr 1846]

[Gompertz. Jack Frank Warden,

Non-collegiate, matr 1877]

[Gompertz. Solomon, 1805?-83

Peterhouse]

Goodhart. Arthur Lehman, 1891-1978

Trinity; matr 1912; Law II unclassified as advanced student, 1913; Lecturer in law in Univ. Sec. to Vice Chancellor 1921-3, Professor of Jurisprudence and Master of Univ. Coll., Oxford; (hon) KBE. FBA. hon fellow of Trinity, Corpus & Trinity Hall (DNB; WwW; JC 17.11.78)

?Goodhart. Eric John, ?-1914

Clare; matr 1913. Killed in 1st World War (Clare mortuary list MS)

Goodman (*née* Kay). Cissie Phyllis, 1907-52

Newnham; adm 1926; Nat Sci I 1928; II (Chemistry) 1929. Ophthalmic optician (Newnham Register p437; JC 2.5.52)

Gordon. Henry Herman, 1873-1939

Clare; matr 1893; Mech Sci I 1895. President Cambridge Hebrew Congregation; Engineer; Deputy Chairman London County Council (JC 15 and 22. 12. 39)

Gordon. Samuel, 1871-1927

Queens'; sch; matr 1890; Classics I 1893. Novelist (JE; JC 14 & 27. 1. 27)

?Gottschalck. Gustave James, 1878-1900
> Christ's; matr 1897; sch 1898. Died without graduation (Christ's Biographical Register ii p816)

Grabiner (*née* **Stanley). Estelle, 1923-69**
> Girton; adm 1941; History I 1943; Law II (1st) 1945. Barrist. (Girton Register p584)

Green. Brian M, 1894-1967
> Trinity; matr?; Nat Sci I 1920, II 1921.

Green. Stuart Montagu, 1889-1949
> St John's; matr 1907; Classics I 1910.

Greenberg. Bernard Morris see **Greenhill. Bernard Morris**

Greenhill (formerly **Greenberg). Bernard Morris, 1890-1959**
> Emmanuel; matr 1911; did not graduate.

Greenhill. Ethel Rachel see **Spencer-Smith. Ethel Rachel**

Greenwood (formerly **Grünbaum). Ida Florence, 1879-?**
> Newnham; adm 1899; resided 2 terms. Schoolteacher. No record of death up to 1971 (Newnham Register p166)

?Gregg (*née* **Schreiner). Frances Lyndall, 1887-1960**
> Newnham; adm 1907; Mod. Lang. 1910. First woman called to Bar in Cape Province, South Africa; biographer of Olive Schreiner (Newnham Register p228)

Grünbaum. Ida Florence, see **Greenwood. Ida Florence**
> ?Grüner. Alice, ?-1929
> Newnham; adm 1883; resided 1883-86. No tripos. Schoolteacher and social worker (founder, Women's Univ. Settlement) (Newnham Register p76)

Guiterman (*née* **Warburg). Elsie Lily, 1877-1948**
> Girton; adm 1894; Maths I 1897 (Girton Register p89)

Haes. Ruth Adele, 1907-61
> Newnham; adm 1926; Nat Sci I (med) 1929; Physician (Newnham Register, 2nd ed. p28)

Ha-Ezrahi-Brisker. Pepita, 1921-63
> Ph.D London; Newnham; Research fellow 1950-53 and 1955-58. Lecturer in Moral Sci in the Univ; Professor of Philosophy, Heb. Univ. Jerusalem 1962 (Newnham Register p44; JC 7.6.63)

Halsted. Edward Alex Michaelis, 1909-41
> Emmanuel; matr 1927; physician (chest specialist).

Halsted. Victor Michaelis, 1916-69
> Emmanuel; matr 1935; English I 1937, History II 1938

?Hamill. Kathryn, see **Cohen. Kathryn**

Harari. Esther, see **Fraser, Esther**

Harari. Ralph Andrew, (known to be dead)
Pembroke; matr 1910; Economics I (1st) 1912, II (1st) 1913

Harris. Hugh, 1897-1981
Emmanuel; matr 1924; M. Litt 1928; Anglo-Jew. literary journalist (JC 6.3.81)

Harris. Leslie Julius, 1898-1973
Emmanuel; Ph. D 1924. Sc. D; first director, Dunn Nutritional Laboratory in the Univ; Meldola medalist, Roy Inst Chem; Biochemist (nutrition) (WwW; JC 29.6.73)

Harris (*née* **Jacob). Nora Isabel, 1923-59**
Girton; adm 1941; Nat Sci I 1945, II 1946. Inst of Research, Liverpool Heart Hosp. (Girton Register p580)

Hartog. Marcus Manuel, 1851-1923
Trinity; matr 1870; sch 1872; Nat Sci (1st) 1873; D. Sc London. Botanist and zoologist. Assistant Director Royal Botanic Gardens, Ceylon; Professor of Zoology, Univ. Coll. Cork (WwW)

Hartog. Numa Edward, 1846-71
Trinity; sch; matr 1865; Maths (1st; the first Jew to be Senior Wrangler) 1869. His success finally led (1871) to the Act of Parliament abolishing remaining religious tests in Oxford and Cambridge (DNB JE)

Hayman. Doris, see **Ashley, Doris**

Hermann. Julius, ?-1916
Caius; matr 1914. Killed in 1st World War

Hermann. Leo, ? -1966
Clare; sch; matr 1913; Maths I (1st) 1914; II 1916 (Harrison-Lloyd)

Hersch (formerly **Herschkowitz). Israel Harris, 1869-1947**
Caius; sch; matr 1888; Maths I (1st) 1891. Schoolmaster, Perse School Cambridge, where he opened a Jewish boarding-house for pupils (Caius Biographical Hist. 2 p499; JC 29.8.47)

Hersch. Laurence Henry Joseph, 1899-1980
Caius; matr 1919; Mech Sci 1921. Petroleum engineer (Caius Biographical Hist. 5 p196)

[Herschell. John Francis Israel,
Queens'; matr 1838]

Herschkowitz. Israel Harris, see **Hersch. Israel Harris**

Hertz. Samuel Moses 1906-79
St Catharine's; matr 1925; Orient languages I 1928 (JC 10.8.79)

Herz. Flora, see **Levy. Flora**

?Hildesheim. Hannschen Gertrude, see **Hilton. Hannschen Gertrude**

?Hilton (formerly **Hildesheim**). **Hannschen Gertrude, 1873-1956**
Newnham; adm 1892; Nat Sci I 1895. Designer and craftswoman
(Newnham Register p120)

?Hirsch. J. G,
Clare; sch; matr 1902. (deceased by 1967/8?) (Harrison-Lloyd)

Hirschfield. Elizabeth, ?-1909
Newnham; adm 1891; resided 1891-2 Schoolteacher, USA (Newnham
Register p114)

Hoffmann. William Arnold, see **Arnold. William Arnold**

Hubback (*née* **Spielmann**). **Eva Marian, 1886-1949**
Newnham; adm 1905. Econom. I 1907, II (1st) 1908. Coll. Lecturer 1916-7.
Principal, Morley College for Working Men and Women: public worker
(family welfare etc) (Newnham Register p212; WwW; JC 22.7.49)

?Humphries (*née* **Behrens**). **Margaret Lundie, 1891-1927**
Newnham; adm 1910; History I 1912, II 1913. Civil servant; Nat. Council
of Women (Newnham Register p248)

Hyamson. Derek Joseph, 1914-71
St Catharine's; matr 1933; Law II (1st) 1936; Solicit. subsequently Barrist.
Master of the Supreme Court (WwW; JC 3.12.71)

Inf(i)eld. Harry, 1893-1968
King's; matr 1912; Nat Sci I 1914; Barrist. MC (Withers p455; King's AR
1968 p45)

Inf(i)eld. Louis, 1888-1951
Queens'; matr 1907; Maths I (1st) 1909, II (1st) 1910. Civil service (top of
list). Devised food ration-book in 2nd World War. OBE (JC 7.9.51)

[Isaacs. Albert Augustus, 1814-1903
Corpus; Missionary to Jews]

[?Isaacs. Hubert Headland, 1835-1900
Corpus]

[?Isaacs. Seymour, -1924
Cavendish Hostel and King's]

[?Isaacs. Wilfred Henry, -1937
King's]

Israel. Dennis David Gabriel, 1899-1959
Emmanuel; matr 1919; Law II 1921

Israel. Judah David, 1869-1928
Queens'; sch; matr 1888; Classics I 1891; Law II 1892; Ll.D.; Elder,
Spanish and Portuguese Congregation, London

Isserlis. Leon, 1881-after 1963
Christ's; sch; matr 1900; Maths I (1st) 1903. Head of Maths Dept. West
Ham Polytechnic (Christ's Biographical Register ii p838)

Jackson. Joseph, 1924-87
Queens'; matr ?; History I (1st) 1944, Law II 1945; Ll.B.; Barrist QC. (WW;
JC 22.5.87)

[Jacob.
Taught Hebrew at St John's, c1610 (Stokes, *Anglo-Jewish Hist.* p212)]

Jacob. Julius, 1873-1942
Caius; sch; matr 1891; Maths I (1st) 1894, II 1895. Civil servant, Special
Commissioner of Income Tax (JC 24.4.42)

Jacob. Lionel, 1858-1934
Trinity; matr 1876, resided 2 years; Vice-Principal, Working Mens College;
Vice Chairman Lib. Jew. Syn. Council (JC 28.9.34)

Jacob. Nora Isabel, see Harris. Nora Isabel

Jacob (*née* Kisch). Violet Henrietta, 1881-1965
Newnham; adm 1900; Mod Lang. 1903; Engaged in work for refugees
(Newnham Register p174)

Jacobs. Joseph, 1854-1916
St John's; matr 1873; Moral Sci (senior moralist) 1876. Historian and
folklorist; revising ed., *Jewish Encyclopedia*, and founder-member of Jew.
Hist. Soc. of England (WwW; Dict. Amer. Biography; EJ; JC 11.2.16)

Jaffe. Alfred Cecil, ?-?
Emmanuel; matr 1902; did not graduate.

Jaffe. Arthur Daniel 1880?-1954
King's; matr 1899; Mech Sci I (1st) 1902. Engineer and Barrist. (Withers
p306; King's AR 1955 p11)

[?Jaffe. Elspeth, 1889-1971
Girton; (Ph.D. Freiburg) engaged in research 1939-45; Medieval scholar
(Girton Register p690)]

Jaffe. William Edward Berthold, ?-?
Emmanuel; matr 1902; BA (no tripos) 1905

?Joachim. Maud Amalia Fanny, 1869-1947
Girton; adm 1890; Moral Sci I 1892. (Girton Register p62)

Joel. Dudley Jack Barnato, 1904-41
King's; matr 1922; Hist. I 1924. Diamond merchant. Killed in 2nd World
War (RN) (Withers p562; King's AR)

Jolowicz. Herbert Felix, 1890-1954
Trinity; sch; matr 1909; Classics I 1911; Law I (1st) 1913; Barrist.
Professor of Roman Law, Univ. Coll. London; Regius Professor Civil Law,
Oxford (DNB; WwW; JC 24.12.54)

Jolowicz. Marguerite Sarah, see **Wolff. Marguerite Sarah**

Joseph. Arthur Wolfe, 1905-74
Trinity; sch; matr 1923; Maths I (1st) 1924; II 1926. Actuary (Treasurer, Inst Actuaries) (JC 6.9.74)

Joseph. Jane Marian, 1894-1929
Girton; adm 1913; Classics I 1916. School-teacher (music) and composer. (Girton Register p246)

?Joseph (*née* **Myers). Matilda Louisa, ? -1961**
Newnham; adm 1876, resided 1876-78. Schoolteacher (South Africa). (Newnham Register p55)

Joseph. William Franklin George, 1882-1918
Christ's; matr 1901; BA 1904. Solicit. Killed in 1st World War (Christ's Biographical Register ii p854; JC 14.6.18)

?Josephy. Johanna, 1876-1934
Newnham; adm 1896; Hist. 1899; Mod Lang. (1st out of 5 incl 4 women), 1900 (Newnham Register p148)

Joshua. Catherine Marie, see **Vaughan-Morgan. Catherine Marie**

Jung. Leo, 1892-1987
Fitzwilliam House; Research student, 1920-21; MA 1927. Rabbi, Professor of Ethics, Yeshiva University, New York; writer, editor and orthodox Jewish apologist. (EJ; JC 25.12.87, 8.1.88)

Kahn. Augustus, 1868-1944
St John's; matr 1886. Maths I 1889. Headmaster and HM Schools Inspector (JC 29.9.44)

[Kahn. Charles Joseph, 1875-1938
St Catharine's]

[Kahn. Francis John, 1876- ?
St Catharine's]

[Kahn. Joseph, 1843-1923
St Catharine's]

Kahn (?Cahn). (*née* **Bronner) Lina, ?-1940**
Newnham; adm 1885; resided 1885-7 (Newnham Register p83)

[Katz. Wilhelm Peter Max, see **Walters. Wilhelm Peter Max]**

?Kaufmann. Bernhard, 1896-1942
Christ's; sch; matr 1919; BA 1920; Asiatic Petrol. Co. Killed in 2nd World War.

Kay. Cissie Phyllis, see **Goodman. Cissie Phyllis**

?Khayyatt. Robert Habib,
Clare; matr 1920; (noted as dead in admissions list)

[Kirby (formerly **Klein). Augusta, 1866-1943**
  Girton]

Kisch. Ernest Royalton, 1886-1967
  Clare; matr 1905; Hist. I 1907; MC (1st World War). Solicit. and communal
  worker (education aid). (Harrison-Lloyd; JC 21.7.67)

Kisch. Violet Henrietta, see **Jacob. Violet Henrietta**

[Klein. Augusta, see **Kirby. Augusta]**

?Klein. Marthe Camille Henrietta, 1885- ?
  Newnham; adm 1913, as graduate student (? alive in 1971). (Newnham
  Register p283)

Klugmann. Kitty Caroline, see **Cornforth. Kitty Caroline**

?Knight (*née* **Oppenheim,** subsequently **Osborne). Beatrice Joan,
1916-68**
  Newnham; adm 1934; Hist. I 1936, II 1937. Worked in Foreign Office
  during 2nd World War (Newnham Register p552)

Kohan. Robert Mendell, ?-1967
  Caius; matr 1901; Med & Mod Lang. 1904. Consul General in Buenos
  Aires (Caius Biographical Hist. 4 p23)

Kohn. Wilfred Arthur, ?-1916
  Caius; matr 1912; Law I 1914. Killed in 1st World War

Ko(h)nstam(m). Edwin Max, 1870-1956
  King's; sch; matr 1888; Indian Civil Service (Under-secretary, Government
  of Bengal 1896-98), KC; (County Court Judge); OBE; CBE. (Withers p185;
  WwW)

Korner. Asher, 1927-71
  Trinity; matr 1948; Nat Sci I (1st) 1950, II (Biochemistry) (1st) 1951.
  Professor of Biochemistry, Univ. Sussex. (JC 8.10.71)

Krebs, Hans Adolf, 1900-81;
  Research student in Biochemistry 1933-35. Professor of Biochemistry,
  Oxford. Nobel Laureate. Kt. FRS. (WW 1982 (*sic*); EJ; JC 27.11.81)

Ladenburg. Alfred Leopold, ?-?
  Clare; matr 1888; BA 1891, no tripos.

Ladenburg. Erich Robert. ? -1908
  King's; adm 1905 as advanced student (Ph. D Leipsig). Returned to
  Germany. (Withers p366)

? (Lan) Davies. Ethel Kathleen, see **Chotzner. Ethel Kathleen**

?Lange. Frederick William Theodore, 1866- ?
  Christ's; matr 1885. Librarian, Guildhall Library, Lond. (Christ's
  Biographical Register ii p718)

Lange. Michael Emil, 1873-1925
>Christ's; matr 1891; Semitics (1st) 1894; Tyrwhitt scholar, 1895. Barrist. Settled in Palestine. (Christ's Biographical Register ii p768; JC 11.8.25; M & N Bentwich, *Herbert Bentwich*, Jerusalem, 1940)

Lange (*née* Bentwich). Rosalind Nita, 1884-1922
>Girton; adm 1903; Hist. I 1905. Settled in Palestine. (Girton Register p149; JC 24.2.22)

Lauterpacht. Hersch, 1897-1960
>Trinity; adm MA 1938; Whewell Professor of Internat. Law; fellow of Coll. Judge at the Internat. Court of Justice, The Hague. Kt. (DNB; WwW; EJ; JC 13.5.60)

Leavis (*née* Roth). Queenie Dorothy, 1906-81
>Girton; adm 1925; English I 1927, II (1st) 1928. Research fellow; Ph. D 1932. Lit. critic (assisted F. R. Leavis ed. *Scrutiny*) (*The Times* 19. 3. 81)

Lehmann. Hermann, 1910-85
>Christ's; adm 1936; Ph. D (Biochemistry) 1938. Professor, Clinical Biochem. in the Univ. Fellow of Coll. CBE; FRS. (WwW; JC 16.8.85)

Lehmann. John Robert, ?
>Clare; matr 1909; BA 1912, no tripos. (Noted dead in admissions list)

[Lehmann. (Rudolph) John Frederick, 1907-87
>Trinity; matr 1926; author and editor. (WW)]

Leon. Edward Joseph, ? -1916
>Clare; matr 1914; Stewart of Rannoch sch. in Hebrew. Killed in 1st World War (Harrison-Lloyd; JC 29.6.17)

Leon. Henry Cecil, 1902-76
>King's; matr ?; Classics I 1921; Law II 1923. Barrist., County Court Judge, and author (Henry Cecil) MC (DNB; WwW)

Leon. Joseph Abraham. 1861-1934
>St. John's; matr 1882; Nat Sci I 1884, Maths I & II 1885, Nat. Sci II 1886.

Leon (*née* Soman), Marriette Eileen, 1889-1941
>Girton; sch; adm 1909; Mod Lang. I (1st) 1911, II 1912. Research student 1912-14. Sec. at Paris Peace Conference 1920. Univ. teacher (Girton Register p208)

Leon. Walter, 1900-87
>Clare; matr ?; Classics I 1921. Solicitor.

Levi. Anna Katharine, 1896-1980
>Newnham; sch; adm 1915; Hist. I 1917, II 1918. Fine art publisher (Newnham Register, 2nd ed. p265)

Levi. Felix Martin, 1876-1905
>Trinity; matr 1894; Maths I (1st) 1898. Killed in earthquake in India. Indian Civil Service.

[Levien. Edwin Goldsmid, ?-1973?
Emmanuel; matr 1898; Hist. I 1900, II 1901. Christian Clergyman]

?Levin. A. W. ? -1947
Clare; MA 1908. No tripos (Clare Mortuary List, MS)

?Levin. Emma Mabel, 1874-1941
Newnham; adm 1901; Maths 1904. Farmer (Newnham Register p182)

?Levin. Helen Minna, 1889-1925
Newnham; adm 1908; Mod Lang. I 1910, II 1911. Studied psychology at
Univ. Coll. Lond. Schoolteacher in England and Vienna where she founded
a Kinderheim (Newnham Register p233)

Levine. Abraham, 1870-1949
Jesus; matr 1889; Maths I (1st) 1891, II (1st) 1892. Fellow of Coll. Actuary.
(WwW; JC 18.2.49)

Levine. Ephraim, 1885-1966
Jesus; matr 1906; Orient. Lang. (1st) 1909; Theology II (1st) 1910,
Tyrwhitt Scholar. Anglo-Jewish minister (London) (JC 2.12.66)

Levinstein. Gerald Edward, 1887- 1916
Pembroke; matr 1905; Econom. I 1907, II 1908. Killed in 1st World War

?Levita. Claud Edward, 1869-1935
Trinity; matr 1886; did not graduate.

?Levita. Harry Plumridge, 1861- ?
Trinity; matr 1879; did not graduate.

Levy. Amy, 1861-89
Newnham; adm 1879; resided 1879-81 No tripos. Poet and novelist
(Newnham Register p 63; DNB; EJ; JC 13.9.89; *Trans., Jew. Hist. Soc.*, 11,
1927 p168)

Levy (*née* Herz). Flora, 1895-1962
Girton; adm affiliated student 1932. MRCS. LRCP 1940 (Girton Register
p462)

Levy. Isaac ?-1969
St Catharine's; sch; matr 1911; Maths I 1912, II 1914. Accountant. Settled
in Israel, later returned.

Levy. Leonard Angelo, 1885-1962
Clare; sch; matr 1904; Nat Sci I (1st) 1906, II (1st, one of 11) 1907.
Academic teacher of Chemistry. (Harrison-Lloyd; JC 21.7.62)

Levy. Reuben, 1891-1966
Christ's; (educ. Jesus Coll. Oxford) Litt.D; Professor of Persian in the Univ.
Fellow of Coll. (WwW; JC 16.9.66)

Levy. Stanley Isaac, 1890-1968
St John's; matr 1909; Nat Sci I (1st) 1911, II (1st) 1912. Consultant
Chemist and Barrist. QC. (WwW; JC 22.11.68)

Lewis. Harry Samuel, 1863-1940
> St John's; sch; matr 1881; Maths I, II (1st) 1884, Semitic Lang 1886. Social and communal worker. Co-author (with C. Russell), *The Jew in London* 1901 (JE; JC 3.5.40)

Libowitz. Olga, 1908-27
> Girton; adm 1926; Mod Lang. I 1927. Killed in accident and commemorated by college prize for mod. languages. (Girton Register p390; JC 17.6.27 (Brodetsky))

Lipkind. Goodman, ?-?
> St John's; matr 1901. Did not graduate. Rabbi in USA. Contributor to JE.

Lipschitz. Joshua Maurice, ?-?
> Clare; matr 1919; no tripos (Clare admissions list, noted deceased)

Lipschitz. Julius, ?-1966
> Clare; matr 1919 (Clare mortuary list MS)

Lipson. Daniel Leopold, 1886-1963
> Corpus; sch; matr 1905; Classics I 1908, Hist. I (1st) & II 1909. Schoolmaster, Mayor of Cheltenham, MP (Independent) (WwW; JC 19.4.63)

Lipson. Ephraim, 1888-1960
> Trinity; matr 1907; Hist. I & II (both 1st) 1909-1910. Reader in Econom. Hist., Oxford. Founder & editor, *Economic Hist. Review* (DNB; WwW; JC 29.4.60)

Littman. Louis Thomas Sidney, 1925-87
> Trinity; matr 1944(?); Law I 1946, II 1947. Solicitor, property developer, farmer, and publisher of Jewish books. (*The Times* 21.12.87, JC 11.12.87 and 25.12.87)

Lob. Hyman, ?-1941
> King's; matr 1905; Maths I 1908. Schoolmaster. Killed in 2nd World War (Air Raid Warden) (Withers p370; King's AR 1941 p8; JC 10.1.41)

Loewe. Herbert Martin James, 1882-1940
> Queens'; sch; matr 1901; Orient. Lang. (1st) 1904, Theology II (1st) 1905; Tyrwhitt scholar. Reader in Rabbinics in the Univ. Hon Fellow of Coll. (WwW; EJ; JC 18.10.40)

Loewe. Lionel Louis, 1891-1987
> Jesus; sch; matr 1911; classics I 1914; Stewart of Rannoch Scholar (Hebrew). Regular army (Royal Education Corps); Barrist.; member, *Shehitah* Board.

?Lowenstein. Minnie Louisa, 1869-1951
> Newnham; sch; adm 1888; Classics I 1891. Schoolteacher (Newnham Register p98)

Lubbock (formerly **Abrahamson**). **Isaac, ? -1962?**
> Clare; sch; matr 1910; Maths (1st) 1911, Mech Sci (1st, one of 4) 1913 (Harrison-Lloyd)

Lyon. Solomon, 1754-1820
 Teacher of Hebrew in Cambridge (JC 24.11.1871 and 6. 6. 1879)

Lyons. Israel, *c.*1700-1770
 Frankland Lecturer in Hebrew, Caius 1744 (DNB; EJ)

Lyons. Israel, 1739-75
 (b. in Cambridge) Astronomer, botanist and explorer (DNB; EJ)

Maccoby. Ephraim Myer, 1892-1956
 St John's; sch; matr 1910; Maths I (1st) 1911, II (1st) 1913; lecturer.

Makower. Dorothy Ida, see May. Dorothy Ida

Makower. Ursula, see Bridge. Ursula

Manasseh. Saleh David Ellis, 1921-44
 Christ's; matr 1939; Mech Sci 1941. Killed in 2nd World War

Marcus (*née* Godinski). Leah, 1894-1966
 Girton; adm 1941 as research student; M. Litt 1945. Teacher of French
 (school and univ.) Sec. to Vice- Chancellor, Bangor (Girton Register p586)

Marks. Hertha Phoebe Sarah, see Ayrton. Hertha Phoebe Sarah

Marmorstein. Emil, 1909-84
 St John's; matr 1929; Orient. Lang. I (1st) 1931, II 1933. Tyrwhitt Scholar.
 Linguist (BBC). Apologist for Orthodox Judaism.

May (*née* Makower). Dorothy Ida, 1906-61
 Newnham; adm 1926; Nat Sci I 1929. Schoolteacher and welfare worker
 (LCC, Red Cross) (Newnham Register p438)

Mayer (*née* Bentwich). Hebe Rachel, 1903-1973
 Girton; adm 1913; Med & Mod Lang. 1916. Settled in Palestine.
 Committee, Pales. Assoc. Univ. Women (Girton Register p241)

Melchett, Lord see Mond. Alfred Moritz

Mendel. Henry Leopold,
 Peterhouse; Fellow-commoner 1865

?Mendel. Vera Rosalind Wynn see Meynell. Vera Rosalind Wynn

Mere. Colin Leigh, 1888-1915
 Christ's; sch; matr 1907; Mech Sci 1910. Killed in 1st World War.

?Meyer. Philip C. F., 1806/7-29
 Peterhouse; matr 1824. (Admissions to Peterhouse p421)

?Meynell (*née* Mendel). Vera Rosalind Wynn, 1895-1947
 Girton; adm 1913; Mod Lang. 1916. Literary journalist and translator. Ed.,
 Vogue. County Councillor (Girton Register p247)

[Michael.
Taught Hebrew at Trinity, 1665 (Stokes, *Anglo-Jew. Hist.* p220)]

?Michaelis. Marie, 1873-1958
Girton; sch; adm 1893; Nat Sci I 1896. Teacher (geog. and science), school and training-coll. Vice-Principal, Froebel Educ. Inst London (Girton Register p81)

Michaelson. Samuel Morris Percy, 1888?-1957
King's; matr 1901; resided 1901-3. Timber-merchant and rancher, Canada (Withers p328; King's AR 1958 p50)

Miller. Emanuel, 1894-1970
St John's; sch; matr 1911; Nat Sci I 1913, Moral Sci II 1914. Lecturer in Psychol. in the Univ. 1924-5. Psychiatrist (WwW; JC 7.8.70)

Mindelsohn. Keith, 1908-83
Corpus; matr 1926; not in Tripos Lists.

Mond, Alfred Moritz, (1st Lord Melchett) 1868-1930
St John's; matr 1886; Nat Sci (failed). Barrist. Industrial Chemist. Chairman ICI; MP; PC. Zionist worker (DNB; WwW; EJ; JC 2.1.31)

Mond. Alfred William, 1901-28
Peterhouse; matr 1918/9; BA 1922. No Tripos. Businessman (Peterhouse Admissions 1911-30 p32)

Mond. Francis Leopold, 1895-1918
King's & Peterhouse; matr (King's) 1912; adm Peterhouse 1914. Killed in 1st World War (RFC). Chair of Aeronautical Engineering founded in his memory by his father (Withers p433; Peterhouse Admissions 1911-30 p16)

Mond. Robert Ludwig, 1867-1938
Peterhouse; matr 1885; Nat Sci 1888. Chemist, industrialist and archaeologist. FRS (Peterhouse Admissions p583; DNB; WwW; JC 28.10.38)

Montagu. Ewen Edward Samuel, 1901-85
Trinity; matr 1920; Econom. I 1922, Law II 1923. QC; Recorder of Southampton; Chairman Court of Quarter Sessions, London (Middlesex); Pres. Anglo-Jew. Ass., Pres. of United Syn. (WW 1985; JC 26.7.85)

Montagu. Edwin Samuel, 1879-1924
Trinity; matr 1898; Nat Sci I 1900, II 1902. Pres. Cambridge Union Soc. MP; PC; Sec. State for India (DNB; WwW; EJ; JC 21.11.24)

Montagu. Stuart Albert Samuel (3rd Lord Swaythling), 1898-1986
Trinity; matr 1919; JP; Master, Company of Farmers (WW 1986)

Montefiore see **also Sebag-Montefiore**

Montefiore (*née* Ward). Florence Fyfe Brereton, 1852-1938
Girton; teaching staff, Vice-Mistress (Girton Register p635; JC 16.12.38)

Montefiore (*née* **Schorstein**). **Therese Alice, 1864-89**
Girton; adm 1882; Moral Sci 1885. Coll. Memorial Prize founded by her husband (Girton Register p23)

Mordell. Louis Joel, 1888-1972
St John's; sch; Matr 1907; Maths I (1st) 1909, II (1st) 1910. Sadleirian Professor of Maths in the Univ. Fellow of Coll. FRS; Sylvester medalist (DNB; EJ; WwW; JC 24.3.72)

Morgan. Catherine Marie see **Vaughan-Morgan, Catherine Marie**

?Moritz Charles, 1863-87
Christ's and King's; matr (Christ's) 1884; resided 1 year only (Christ's Biographical Register ii p708; Withers p155)

?Mosley. Isaac Henry, 1883-before 1954
Christ's; matr 1901; Law I 1904. Solicit. (Christ's Biographical Register ii p851)

Mosseri. Felix Nezzim, ?-1986
Pembroke; matr 1912; BA (No tripos) 1915.

Mosseri. Lionel Nessim, 1891-1914
Pembroke; matr 1908; BA 1911. No tripos. President, Cambridge Heb. Cong., commemorated by inscription in Syn.

Moses. Vivian Sylvester, ?-1917
Emmanuel; matr 1916. Killed in 1st World War.

Myers. Charles Samuel, 1873-1946
Caius; matr 1891; Nat Sci I (1st) 1893, II (1st) 1895. Reader in Experimental Psychology in the Univ. and Professor, King's Coll. London. CBE; Hon Fellow of the Coll. (DNB; WwW; EJ; JC 18.10.46)

Myers. Hannah Violet, see **Churchill. Hannah Violet**

?Myers. Matilda Louisa, see **Joseph. Matilda Louisa**

Myers. Stella, see **Churchill. Stella**

Nachbar. Henrietta, see **Burnham. Henrietta**

Nahum. Effraim Alfred, 1918-42
Pembroke; matr 1936; Nat Sci I (1st) 1938, II (Physics) (1st) 1939. Physicist at Cavendish Lab. Killed in air raid on Cambridge in 2nd World War.

Nathan of Churt (*née* **Stettauer**). **Eleanor Joan Clara 1898-1972**
Girton; adm 1910; Maths I 1912; Econom II 1913. Local govt, educ. and social work. JP (juvenile court); Chairman LCC; Vice-Pres. Roy. Geograph. Soc.; on Governing Body of Coll. (Girton Register p 218; WwW; JC 9.6.72)

Nathan. Julian, ?-?
Clare; matr 1907; BA 1910. No tripos (Clare Admissions list, noted deceased)

Nathan. Leon, ? -1967/8
>Clare; sch; matr 1923; Classics I (1st) 1925, II (1st) 1926 (Clare Admissions list, noted deceased)

Nathan. Leopold Charles, ?-1916
>Trinity Hall; matr 1913. Killed in 1st World War.

Nathan, Robert, 1866-1921
>Peterhouse; matr 1885; Maths 1888. Barrist. Indian Civil Service; Private Sec. to Viceroy; Commissioner, Dacca Div; KCSI (Peterhouse Admissions p586; WwW; JC 1.7.21)

Neumann. Stephan Theodor see **Norman. Stephan Theodor**

Nissim. Joseph, 1882-1972
>St John's; matr 1912; Law I (1st) 1903, Hist II (1st) 1904. Barrist. (JC 11.8.72)

Norman (formerly **Neumann**). **Stephan Theodor, 1918-46**
>St John's; matr 1936?; Economics I 1937, Law II 1939 (Herzl's last descendant) (EJ, Herzl, end)

?Nunes. Francis 1842-?
>Christ's; matr 1861; BA 1865 (Christ's Biographical Register ii p570)

?Oppenheim. Beatrice Joan, see **Knight. Beatrice Joan**

Oppenheim. Lassa Francis Lawrence, 1858-1919
>Trinity; adm MA as Whewell Professor of Internat. Law 1908 (DNB; EJ; JC 17.10.19)

?Oppenheim. Mary Alix Rose, 1904-64
>Newnham; adm 1923; Hist I 1925, II 1926 (Newnham Register p397)

Oppenheimer. Frank Friedman, ?-1967/8?
>Clare; matr 1933; no tripos (Clare Admissions list, noted deceased)

Oppenheimer. J. Robert, 1904-67
>Christ's; matr 1925, resided 3 terms. Nuclear physicist; Professor, Calif. Inst Technol., Chairman, Advis. Committee to US Atomic Energy Commission; Hon. Fellow of Coll. (WwW; JC 24.2.67)

Ortweiler. Frederick John, 1899?-1922
>King's; matr 1919; Hist. II 1920. Businessman and air pilot. Killed in accident (Withers p504; JC 17.2.22)

?Osborne. Beatrice Joan *see* **Knight. Beatrice Joan**

[?Paiva. Henry de, 1827-46
>St John's]

Pass. Alfred Peter de, 1924-44
>King's; matr 1942. Killed in 2nd World War. (Bulmer-Wilkinson p223)

Pass. Crispin Asahel de, ?-1918
Trinity Hall; matr 1912. Killed in 1st World War. Commemorated by
Hebrew MSS collection in Fitzwilliam Museum.

[Pass. Herman Leonard, 1876-1938
St John's; matr 1894; Orient. Lang. 1898, Tyrwhitt Scholar. Christian
clergyman, converted at Cambridge (*The Times*, 19. 1. 38)]

Pearce (*née* Rosenhain) Mona Henrietta, 1903-31
Newnham; adm 1921; Hist I 1923, Econom. II 1924 (Newnham Register
p234)

Pereles (*née* Ulmann). Martha Wilhelmine, 1891-1944?
Newnham; adm 1909; resided 1909-10. Teacher in Jewish schools in
Czechoslovakia. Died in concentration camp (Newnham Register p246)

Perlzweig. Maurice L., 1895-1985
Christ's; matr ?; Orient Lang I 1924; Union cmtee; founder, Univ. Labour
Fed. of GB. Reform rabbi. Head of Internat. Affairs Dept, World Jew.
Congr. (EJ; JC 25.1.85)

Persitz. Olga Hadasa, see Altschuler. Olga Hadasa

Picciotto. Cyril Moses, 1888-1940
Trinity; sch; matr 1907; Classics I (1st) 1910, Law (1st) 1911. Whewell
Scholar (Internat. Law). Members' Latin Prize Essayist. Pres., Cambridge
Hebrew Cong., Member, Board of Deputies (JC 16.2.40)

?Pinto. Maurice Salvador, 1873- ?
Christ's; matr 1894; resided 2 terms. Civil servant (Ceylon) (Christ's
Biographical Register ii p790)

Polack. Albert Isaac, 1892-1982
St John's; matr 1911; Classics I 1914, II 1920. Housemaster, Jewish
House, Clifton Coll. Bristol (JC 9.7.82)

Polack. Benjamin James, ? -1916
King's; matr 1909; Med & Mod Lang. I 1911, II 1913. Killed in 1st World
War.

Polack. Ernest Emanuel, ?- 1916
St John's; sch; matr 1912. Stewart of Rannoch Scholar (Hebrew). Killed in
1st World War.

Pollak. Leslie Albert, 1888?-1934
King's; matr 1908; Mech Sci 1911. Emigrated to S. Africa (Withers p414;
King's AR 1934 p9)

?Posener. Edward Adrian, 1922-?
St Catharine's; matr 1940; Mod Lang I 1941. Killed in 2nd World War.

Postan. Michael Moissey, 1899-1981
Peterhouse; MA; adm Fellow 1935. Professor of Econom. Hist. in the Univ.
Kt; FBA; Hon Fellow of Coll. (WW 1982 *sic*).

Price. Harold Louis, 1917-86
>Sidney; sch; matr 1935; Maths II (1st) 1937, III 1938. Aerodynamicist.
>Professor of Maths, Leeds Univ. (WW 1986; JC 28.11.86)

Quastel. Juda Hirsch, 1899-1987
>Trinity; Ph.D. 1925. Fellow of Coll., lecturer in Biochem in Univ, Professor
>of Neurochemistry, Univ. Brit. Columbia, Vancouver; FRS. A founder of the
>Weizmann Institute, Rehovot. (JC 30.10.87)

Rabinowitch. Myer see **Rabson, Mear**

Rabson (formerly **Rabinowitch**). **Mear (Myer), 1892-1974**
>Corpus; matr 1911; Maths I 1912, II 1914.

Rappoport. John Gerald, 1914-43
>King's; matr 1933; Classics I 1935, II 1936. Colonial Service (Malay).
>Killed in 2nd World War (RAF) (Bulmer- Wilkinson p144)

[?Rappoport. Robert Alexis, see **Fitz-Aucher. Robert Alexis]**

Rashbass. Cyril, 1926-82
>Trinity; matr ? Nat Sci (med) I 1946, II 1947. Commemorated by college
>prize. (JC 23.7.82)

Reif. Arnold Eugen, ?-1967/8?
>Clare; matr 1942; Nat Sci 1944. (Clare Admissions list, noted deceased)

Reitlinger. Henry Scipio, 1866?-1950
>King's; matr 1906; Hist. I 1907, II 1908. Art historian (Withers p280;
>King's AR 1950 p16)

Reuben. Rebecca, 1889-1957
>?Non-collegiate. BA, Bombay; resided in Cambridge 2 yrs, *c.* 1910-12.
>Educationalist in India (Beney Israel) (JC 29.11.57)

[Reuter. George Julius de, 1863-1909
>Trinity]

Rosenhain. Mona Henrietta see **Pearce. Mona Henrietta**

Rosenhead. Louis, 1906-84
>St John's; adm as research student 1928. Ph. D (Maths) 1930. Professor of
>Applied Maths, Liverpool Univ. CBE; FRS (WW 1984; JC 16.11.84)

Rosenheim. Max Leonard, 1908-72
>St John's; sch; matr 1926; Nat Sci I (1st) 1929. Professor of Medicine,
>London Univ. Life Peer; KBE; Hon Fellow of Coll. (DNB; WwW; JC 8.12.72)

Rossdale. Frank Archibald, 1893-1967
>Magdalene; matr 1911; Law I (1st) 1916, II (1st) 1917. Treas. United Syn.

Rossdale. Ian Thomas Haines, ?- 1967/8?
>Clare; matr 1941; Econom. I 1942 (Clare Admissions list, noted deceased)

?Roth. George Kingsley, 1903-70
> Christ's; adm 1932 as research student. M. Sc 1937. Anthropologist (colon. service). (*Cambridge Daily News* 30. 6. 70)

Roth. Queenie Dorothy see **Leavis. Queenie Dorothy**

Rothschild. Alfred Charles de, 1842-1918
> Trinity; matr 1861; did not graduate. Director of Bank of England; Sheriff of London; Trustee, Nat. Gallery; CVO (WwW; JC 8.2.18)

Rothschild. Evelyn Achille de, 1884-1918
> Trinity; Matr 1902. No Tripos. Killed in 1st World War.

Rothschild. Leopold Lionel de, 1845-1917
> Trinity; matr 1863; BA 1867; Ph. D (Giessen). Patron of Turf. JP; Dep. Lieut; Treas. Jew. Board of Guardians; CVO (WwW; JE; JC 1.6.17 and 13.7.17)

Rothschild. Lionel Walter de (2nd Lord), 1868-1927
> Magdalene; matr 1887; no tripos. Zoologist. MP; Trustee of Brit. Museum; JP; Dep. Lieut; Addressee of Balfour Declaration (WwW; JE; JC 3.9.37)

Rothschild. Nathaniel Charles de, 1877-1923
> Trinity; matr 1895; Nat Sci 1898. Chairman, Alliance Insurance Co. Entomologist (WwW; JC 19.10.23)

Rothschild. Nathaniel Mayer de (1st Lord), 1840-1915
> Trinity; matr 1859; did not graduate. Hon Ll. D; MP; 1st Jewish peer and Lord Lieutenant; PC; GCVO (DNB; JE; JC 2.4.15)

Rothschild. Walter Alfred de, 1880-1909
> Trinity; matr 1899; BA 1903; no tripos.

?Rubens. Herbert Victor, 1879-1963
> King's; matr 1897; Mech Sci I 1900. Businessman (Withers p283; King's AR 1963 p39)

Rueff. A. Marcus,
> Trinity; matr ?; Mod & Med Lang. I 1934, English I 1936. Killed in 2nd World War.

?Rufford. Montague Jacobs, ?-?
> Clare; matr 1920; no tripos (Clare Admissions list; noted deceased)

?Sachs. Ida Beata, see **Saxby. Ida Beata**

Salaman. Arthur Gabriel, 1904-64
> Emmanuel; matr 1923; Econom. I 1925, Anthropology 1926 (JC 6.11.64)

Salaman. Elsie Esther, 1885-1953
> Girton; adm 1904; Hist. I 1906, II 1907. Welfare work (LCC, Min. of Pensions) (Girton Register p163)

Salaman. Louis Henry, 1882-1915
> Trinity; matr 1901; Mech Sci I 1904. Killed in 1st World War (RN)

Salaman. Redcliffe Nathan, 1874-1955
> Trinity Hall; sch; matr 1893; Nat Sci I (1st) 1896. Director, Potato Virus
> Research Inst., Cambridge; Trustee, Jews' Coll., Governor, Heb. Univ.,
> Pres., Jew. Hist. Soc. of England. JP; FRS; Hon. Fellow of Coll (DNB;
> WwW; EJ; JC 17.6.55)

Salamon. Montague William Henry, 1914-66
> Peterhouse; matr 1931; Law I 1934, II 1935. Barrister, later Solicitor;
> Under-Sheriff, County of London (Peterhouse Admissions 1931-50 p21)

Salomons. David Lionel (Goldsmid-Stern) (2nd Bart) 1851-1925
> Caius; matr 1870; Nat Sci 1874. Barrist., Pres. Inst Electrical Engineers;
> Dept. Lieut; Sheriff of Kent; Mayor of Tunbridge Wells; Motoring pioneer.
> Benefactor of Coll (Caius Biographical Hist 2 p391; WwW; JC 24.4.25)

Salomons. David Reginald Herman Philip Goldsmid-Stern, 1885-1915
> Caius; matr 1904; BA 1907; no tripos. Killed in 1st World War (Caius
> Biographical Hist. 4 p52, 5 p89)

Samuel. Cecil Harry, ? -1966
> Clare; matr 1910; BA 1913; no tripos (Clare Admissions list, noted
> deceased)

Samuel (*née* Elkin). Charlotte Emily, 1886-1963
> Newnham; adm 1905; Hist. I (1st, only woman out of 5) 1907, II (1st, only
> woman out of 8) 1908. Translator (ILO). Social work. Counsellor,
> Hampstead. MBE (Newnham Register p208)

Sassoon. Charles, ?-1916?
> Christ's; matr 1864, but left immediately (Christ's Biographical Register ii
> p586)

Sassoon. Michael Thorneycroft, ?-1966
> Clare; matr 1904; no tripos.

?Saxby (formerly Sachs). Ida Beata, 1883-*c*1914
> Newnham; sch; adm 1902; Maths I 1904, Hist. II 1905; D. Sc in
> Experimental Psychology; educationalist (school, training-coll. & research)
> (Newnham Register p189)

Schechter. Solomon, 1847-1915
> Christ's; adm MA 1890; Reader in Talmudic in the Univ.; Pres., Jew.
> Theological Seminary of America (EJ; N. Bentwich, *Solomon Schechter*,
> 1938; JC 26.11.15)

Schiff. Mortimer Edward Harold, 1888-1917
> Jesus; matr 1907; Hist. I (1st) 1909, Law II (1st) 1910. Solicitor. Killed in
> 1st World War.

Schiller-Szinessy. Alfred Solomon, 1863-?
> Christ's; matr 1882 and migrated to Fitzwilliam Hall; BA 1886, no tripos.
> (Christ's Biographical Register ii p693)

Schiller-Szinessy. Solomon Marcus, 1820-90
> Christ's; adm MA (*propter merita*) 1876; Reader in Talmudic & Rabbinic
> Lit. in the Univ. (Christ's Biographical Register ii p658; EJ; R. Loewe,
> *Trans. Jew. Hist. Soc. Engl.* 21, 1968; JC 14.3.1890)

Schloss. Arthur David, see Waley. Arthur David

Schorstein. Bertha Victoria, see **Shorstone. Bertha Victoria**

Schorstein. Therese Alice, see **Montefiore, Therese Alice**

?Schreiner. Frances Lyndall, see **Gregg. Frances Lyndall**

?Schreiner. Ursula Hester, see **Scott. Ursula Hester**

Schwab. Sigmund George, 1911-80
> Trinity; matr 1929; Mod & Med Lang. I 1930. Personnel Director.

?Schwabacher. Ottilie, see **Shaw Ottilie**

Schwarzman. Rudolph Isaac see **Blackburn. Rudolph Isaac**

[Scialetti. Moses Paul, 17th Cent.
> MA 1664; taught Hebrew at Trinity 1663-5 (Stokes, *Anglo-Jew. Hist.* p22)]

?Scott (*née* **Schreiner). Ursula Hester 1892-1963**
> Newnham; adm 1911; resided 1911-14, no tripos. Social work, S. Africa
> (Newnham Register p266)

Sebag-Montefiore see **also Montefiore**

Sebag-Montefiore. James Marcus, 1913-51
> King's; matr 1932; Econom. I 1933, II 1935. Businessman, horticulturist
> and yachtsman. Settled in New Zealand (Bulmer-Wilkinson p136; King's
> AR 1951)

Sebag-Montefiore. John, 1892-1972
> Pembroke; matr 1910; BA (no tripos) 1913. Insurance Broker. Nat. Council
> for Aged; Elder, Span & Port Congr; Ctee, Jew. Welfare Board (JC 14.1.72)

?[Sergel (*née* **Streiff). Hedwig 1882-1958**
> Newnham]

?Shaw (formerly **Schwabacher). Ottilie, 1881-1960**
> Girton; sch; adm 1900; Maths 1903. Schoolteacher (Girton Register p129)

Shorstone (formerly **Schorstein). Bertha Victoria 1868-***c***1925**
> Girton; adm 1887; resided 1887-90, no tripos (Girton Register p46)

?Silberrad. Charles Arthur, 1870-1937?
> Peterhouse; sch; matr 1888; Nat Sci (1st) 1892. Indian Civil Service (1st on
> list, 1893); Bhaunagar medalist 1894; Dep. Commissioner (Peterhouse
> Admissions p608)

Silkin. John Ernest, 1923-87
> Trinity Hall; matr ?; Law II 1942; Solicitor; MP; Govt. Chief Whip (Lab);
> Minister of Agriculture. (WW; JC 1.5.87)

Silverston. Bertram, 1871-1942?
> Caius; matr 1890; sch 1892; Maths I 1893. Solicit. (Caius Biographical Hist. 2 p516)

Singer. Ruth Seruya see Donnison. Ruth Seruya

Smouha. Ellis Hay, 1906-86
> St John's; matr 1925; BA 1928

Snowman. Leonard Victor, 1900-76
> Downing; matr 1918; Nat Sci I (1st) 1921. Physician; med. officer, Initiation Society; translator of modern Hebrew poetry. (JC 13.8.76)

Solomon. Elias Hilali, 1897-1960
> King's; sch; matr 1915; Econom. I (1st) 1917, II 1918. Briefly Lecturer (?later Prof) Econom. Rangoon. Religious eccentric (Withers p483; E. D. Ezra, *Turning Back the Pages* 1986 p377f.)

?Solomon. Martin Herbert Bernard, 1915-56
> Christ's; matr 1933; English 1936

[Solomon. Richard, 1850-1913
> Peterhouse; sch; matr 1871; Maths (1st) 1875. Barrist. Attorney Gen., Cape Province & Transvaal; High Commissioner of S. Africa; GCMG; Hon. Fellow of the Coll. (Peterhouse Admissions p538; WwW; L. Herrman, *Hist. of Jews in S. Africa*, 1935 p89]

[Solomon. William Henry, 1853-1930
> Peterhouse; sch; matr 1872; Maths 1876. Barrist. Senior Puisne Judge of Transvaal; Judge of Appelate Div., Supreme Court of S. Africa; KCMG; Hon. Fellow of the Coll. (Peterhouse Admissions p541; WwW; L. Herrman, see Solomon, Richard)]

Solomons. Maurice, ?-1916
> Jesus; matr 1915. Killed in 1st World War.

Soman. Marriette Eileen, see **Leon. Marriette Eileen**

?Sonnenschein. Susanna Frederica, see **Bolton. Susanna Frederica**

Sosnow. Norman Martyn, 1944-67
> Christ's; sch; matr 1962; Hist. I 1964, II 1965. Commemorated by coll. travel. studentships.

Spencer-Smith (*née* **Greenhill), Ethel Rachel 1898-1984**
> Girton; adm 1920 Hist I 1922, II 1923. Beds. CC Educ Ctee.

Spero. Leopold H, 1887-?
> Sidney and Downing; matr 1907; Law I 1916. Solicitor.

?Spielman. Roger Walter, 1928-74
> King's; matr 1948; Law II 1950. Solicit. (Bulmer-Wilkinson p 49)

Spielman(n). Claude Meyer,
> King's; matr 1907; Mech Sci 1910; AMICE (Withers p399)

Spielmann. Eva Marian, see **Hubback. Eva Marian**

Spielmann. Harold Lionel Isadore, ?-1915
Pembroke; matr 1911; Hist. I 1913, II 1914. Killed in 1st World War. Commemorated by ark in Cambridge Syn.

Spiers. Archibald Lionel Clive, 1885-1917
Trinity; matr 1903; Hist. I 1905, II 1906. Killed in 1st World War.

Spiers. Claude Hyman, 1895-1977
Emmanuel; sch; matr 1914; Nat Sci I (1st) 1916, II (1st) 1920, PhD 1925. Leather chemist (JC 8.4.77)

Spiers. Henry Michael, 1893-1968
Caius; sch; matr 1911; Nat Sci I (1st) 1913, II (1st) 1914. Research Chemist (oil fuels) (Caius Biographical Hist. 5 p129; JC 19.4.68)

Sraffa. Piero, 1898-1983
Trinity; adm fellow 1939; Reader in Economics in the Univ. FBA; (WW)

Stanley. Estelle, see **Grabiner. Estelle**

?Stein. Ronald Cambell, ?-?
Clare; matr 1938; not in tripos lists.

Stern. Leonard Herman, 1891-1915
Magdalene; matr 1910; Classics I (1st) 1913, Hist. II 1914. Killed in 1st World War. Commemorated by penitential *sepher* mantle in Cambridge Syn. fashioned from his masonic apron.

Stern. Sydney James (Lord Wandsworth). 1845-1912
Magdalene; matr 1870; no tripos. Barrist. Banker, MP; JP (WwW; JE; JC 16.2.12)

[Stiebel. Charles, 1876-1917
Trinity Hall; matr 1894; Medical missionary. Killed in 1st World War]

?[Streiff. Hedwig, see **Sergel. Hedwig]**

Swaythling. Lord, see **Montagu. Stuart Albert Samuel**

Sylvester. James Joseph, 1814-97
St John's; matr 1831; Maths (1st; 2nd Wrangler) 1837, but did not graduate until 1872. Savilian Professor of Maths at Oxford and founder of the Oxford Mathematical Soc. The first demonstrably professing Jew to be an undergraduate member of a Cambridge Coll., Hon Fellow of the Coll. FRS (DNB; EJ; JC 19.3 and 24. 12. 1897)

Tanburn. Walter Louis, ?- 1917
Clare; matr 1914. Killed in 1st World War (Clare Admissions list)

Taylor (*née* Cohen). Helen Olga, 1899-1969
Newnham; adm 1918; English, 1920, Mod Lang. 1921 (Newnham Register p329)

Teicher. Jacob Leib, 1904-81
> adm MA (non-collegiate) on appointment as Lecturer in Rabbinics, 1946; ed. *Journal of Jew. Studies*; Fellow, Wolfson, 1966 (JC 27.11.81)

Trachtenberg. Mendel Isidor, 1882-1918
> St John's; matr 1901; Maths I 1904. Statistician (Tariff Commission). Killed in 1st World War.

[Tremellius. John Emmanuel, 1510-80
> Acted as King's Reader (=Professor) of Hebrew, Cambridge from 1550 (DNB; EJ)]

?Trier. Norman Ernest, ?-1915
> Clare; matr 1907; BA 1911, no tripos. Killed in 1st World War (Clare Admissions list)

Tuck. Raphael Herman, 1910-82
> Trinity Hall; matr ?; Law II 1939. Barrist. Professor of Political Science, McGill Univ. MP (Westminister); Kt (WW 1982; JC 9.7.82)

Ulmann. Martha Wilhelmine, see **Pereles, Martha Wilhelmine**

Valentine. David Henriques, 1912-87
> St John's; matr 1930; Nat Sci I (1st) 1932, II (1st) 1933; Ph.D. 1937; research fellow of Coll; univ. curator of *Herbarium*; Professor of Botany, Manchester Univ. (WW)

Vaughan-Morgan (*née* **Joshua). Catherine Marie, 1896-1969**
> Newnham; adm 1917; Econom. I 1919, II 1920. Borough Councillor (Newnham Register p322)

Waldstein. Charles, see **Walston. Charles**

Waley (formerly **Schloss). Arthur David, 1889-1966**
> King's; sch; matr 1907; Classics I (1st) 1910. Civil Servant (Brit. Museum); translator of Chinese poetry. CH; Queen's Medal for Poetry; FBA; Hon. Fellow of Coll. (Withers p393; DNB; WwW; JC 1.7.66)

Waley. Frank Raphael, 1893-1987
> King's; matr 1912; no tripos. Horticulturalist, (founder, Alpine Garden Soc.); Chairman, Council of Westminster Syn.; communal worker (Board of Guardians); MC; OBE. (Withers p459; *The Times* 14.11.87; JC 20.11.87)

Waley Cohen. Robert, 1877-1952
> Emmanuel; sch; matr 1896; Nat Sci I 1898, II 1900. Industrialist and cellist. Pres., United Syn.; KBE (DNB; WwW; JC 5.12.52)

Walston (formerly **Waldstein). Charles, 1856-1927**
> King's; adm 1882; MA (*propter merita*). Litt. D. Reader in Classical Archaeology in the Univ., Slade Professor of Fine Art, Director, Fitzwilliam Museum; Fellow of Coll; Kt; Sheriff of Cambs. Originated Cambridge triennial Greek Play. Presented the wrought iron gate on King's Backs (Withers p132; WwW; JC 25.3.27)

[Walters (formerly **Katz). Wilhelm Peter Max, 1886-1962**
Fitzwilliam House; adm 1941; PhD 1945; Kaye prizeman. Lecturer, Divinity Faculty; Greek Bible scholar; Lutheran pastor.]

Wandsworth. Lord, see **Stern. Sidney James**

Warburg. Elsie Lily see **Guiterman. Elsie Lily**

Ward. Florence Fyfe Brereton, see **Montefiore. Florence Fyfe Brereton**

Wassey (formerly **Wassilevsky). Solomon, 1896-1951?**
Pembroke; matr ?; Hist. I 1919, II 1920. Teacher (in England), official JNF (Palestine); Solicit. Commemorated by English legal library at Heb. Univ. Jerusalem (JC 1951)

Wassilevsky. Solomon, see **Wassey. Solomon**

?Wayman. Myers, 1890-1959
Christ's; matr 1910; no tripos. Traveller. Mayor of Sunderland; JP; Dep. Lieut. (WwW)

Weiss. Helene, 1898-1951
Newnham; adm (Ph. D, Basle) as research student 1937; M. Litt (Classics) 1945. Univ. teacher of Classics (Cambridge, London, Glasgow) (Newnham Register p594)

Weizmann. Michael Oser, 1916-42
King's; matr 1934; Nat Sci I 1937. Killed in 2nd World War (RAF) (Bulmer-Wilkinson p156; JC 20.2.42)

Werner. Alice, 1859-1935
Newnham; sch; adm 1878; resided 1878-80. Research fellow 1913-18. D. Litt (Lond); Professor of Bantu Languages, School of Orient. Studies, London. CBE; Silver medalist, Africa Soc. (Newnham Register p32; WwW)

Werner. Charles Augustus, 1877-1915
King's; sch; matr 1896; Classics I (1st) 1898, Moral Sci II 1900. Schoolmaster. Killed in 1st World War (Withers p262)

Werner. Charles Henry, 1875-?
Clare; sch; matr 1894; Mech Sci I 1897, II 1898. Businessman (Harrison-Lloyd)

Whitehill. Geoffrey Harris, 1898-1971
Trinity; matr 1919; Classics I (1st) 1920, Econom II 1922. Stockbroker; adviser on investments to St John's College; Elder, Span & Port Congr (JC 21.5.71)

Wiener. Harold Marcus, 1875-1929
Caius; sch; matr 1894; Classics I (1st) 1897, Law I 1898. Whewell Scholar (Internat Law); Barrist. Elder and benefactor, Spanish & Portuguese Cong. London. Killed in anti-Jewish riots in Palestine (Caius Biographical Hist. ii p540, v p59; JC 30.8.29)

Wilk. Jack, 1903-40
Magdalene; matr ?; Law I 1923, II 1924. Barrist. Killed in 2nd World War.

Wilk. Lionel, 1907-82
Magdalene; matr 1925; Law I 1927, II (1st) 1928.

Wilmers (formerly **Wilmersdörffer**). John Geoffrey (H.M.) 1920-84
St John's; matr 1938; Law II 1941; Barrister (QC); Court of Appeal, Jersey & Guernsey. (WW 1986 *sic*)

Winter (*née* Geiler). Lucy Elise, 1882-1945
Newnham; adm 1901; Mod Lang. (1st) 1905 (Newnham Register p181)

Wirszubski. Chaim, 1915-77
King's; matr (research student) 1945; Ph. D 1946. Professor of Classics at Heb. Univ. (Bulmer-Wilkinson p268; King's AR 1978; EJ; JC 30.9.77)

Wittgenstein. Ludwig Josef Johann, 1889-1951
Trinity; matr 1912; Ph. D (Philosophy) 1929. Fellow of Coll. Professor of Philosophy in Univ (DNB; WwW)

Wolf. Charles George Lewis, 1872-1954
Christ's; matr 1917; Ph. D 1921 (1st Ph. D at Cambridge). Biochemist.

Wolfe. Joseph Alexander, 1896-after 1963
Christ's; matr 1915; Nat Sci 1920; Barrist.

Wolff (*née* Jolowicz). Marguerite Sarah, 1883-1964
Newnham; adm 1902; Mod Lang. (1st; of 9, 6 being women). Lecturer in English, Berlin, until 1933. Interpreter, Internat. Court, The Hague. Author and translator of legal works (Newnham Register p187)

Wolman. Lionel, 1920-69
Peterhouse; sch; matr 1937; Nat Sci I 1940, II (1st) 1941. Ph. D (Sheffield). Hon Lecturer (Neuropathology) Sheffield Univ. Founder Member of Coll. of Pathologists. (Peterhouse Admissions p92; JC 2.5.69)

?Woolf. John Lawrence, 1906-65
Peterhouse; matr 1925; BA 1928, no tripos. Regular army, then cotton-planter in Sudan (Peterhouse Admissions p106)

Woolf. Leonard Sidney, 1880-1969
Trinity; sch; matr 1899; Classics I (1st) 1902, II 1903. Author, publisher and political worker (DNB; WwW; JC 22.8.69)

Woolf. Walter Richard Mortimer 1886-1915
Christ's; matr 1903; Law I 1906, II 1907. Solicit. Killed in 1st World War (Christ's Biographical Register ii p70; JC 8.10.15)

Yates. George Algernon, 1908-49
St John's; sch; matr 1927; Orient. Lang. I (1st) 1929. Stewart of Rannoch Scholar (Hebrew)

Yellin. Avinoam, 1900-37
Christ's; sch; matr 1920; Orient. Lang I (1st) 1922, II (1st) 1923. Tyrwhitt Scholar, Wright Student. School inspector, govt. Palestine. MBE; killed in anti-Jew. riots in Palestine (EJ; JC 29.10.37)

Zaiman. Adolph, ?-?
King's; sch; matr 1913; Maths I (1st) 1914, II (1st) 1916. Indian civil service (Withers p466; reported deceased)

Zaiman. Barnet Abraham, ?-1959
Pembroke; matr 1911; Maths I (1st) 1912, II (1st) 1914, Econom. II 1915. Indian civil service; sessions judge (JC 9.10.59)

[Zangwill. Oliver Louis, 1913-87
King's; matr 1932; Nat Sci I 1934, Moral Sci II (1st) 1935. Lecturer in Psychology, Oxford; Professor of Experimental Psychology in the Univ; Fellow of the Coll. (Bulmer-Wilkinson p138; WW)]

Ziman (*née* Gaster). Nellie Frances 1899-1969
Newnham; adm 1919; Nat Sci I 1922. Pres., Nat Council for Women, New Zealand. Subsequently returned to England (Newnham Register p343)

Zissu. Theodore, 1916-42
Trinity; matr 1933; Law II 1936. Zionist activist; killed in 2nd World War. (EJ)

Back cover, programme for Michaelmas term, 1985

Roll of Members*

Aarons, Renee Cecile (Dr. Winegarten)
Girton, 1940-43, 45-46
Modern Languages

>Latin American section of the Foreign Office Research Department 1943-45. Returned to Cambridge in 1945 to begin studying for Ph.D. In 1946 married Asher Winegarten *q.v.* whom I met at CUJS. After teaching French and Spanish, became freelance writer, literary critic and biographer. Books include *French Lyric Poetry in the Age of Malherbe*; *Writers and Revolution*; *The Double Life of George Sand, Woman and Writer*; *Madame de Staël*. Contributed to *Commentary, The American Scholar, Midstream, French Studies, Modern Language Review, Encounter, The Jewish Quarterly*, etc.

Aaronson, Ian Anthony (Professor)
Downing, 1959-62
Medicine

>Qualified at St. Bartholomew's Hospital in 1965. After further studies in London I went to Cape Town as Head of Pediatric Urology at the University's Children's Hospital where I was appointed Associate Professor in 1985. I will shortly be taking up an appointment as Professor of Urology and Pediatrics at the Medical University of South Carolina in Charleston. Married 1978, one son.

>*To a freshman the CUJS provided a haven of familiarity in a strange world bursting with new experiences. I have particularly fond memories of the Friday evening service and dinner. I hope these both continue.*

Abrahams, Stanley
St. Catharine's, 1954-58
Mathematics

>Joined Medical Research Council 1958. Took M.A. in 1961 and moved to Wool Industries Research Association. Moved to Leeds Polytechnic 1969, am currently Senior Lecturer, Management Science, Leeds Polytechnic Business School. Fellow, Royal Statistical Society. Married, two children.

>*I have heard that a degree of polarization has occurred since the formation of the Israel Society (about 1957). I hope that the previous unity of interests within CUJS has not been too much affected.*

Abrams, Daniel
Sidney Sussex, 1975-78
Law

>Qualified as Barrister 1979; joined Arthur Andersen Co. and qualified as a chartered accountant 1983, becoming a tax manager in 1984; joined Guiness plc as senior corporate finance executive 1987. Deputy Chairman Professional Committee, Israel Bonds.

---

* The roll includes non-members of the University who participated in the activities of CUJS, such as members of London University during the 1939-45 World War.
The words 'After leaving Cambridge' are to be implied at the beginning of each entry.

Abrams, Hester
Newnham, 1982-86
Modern Languages
> Working as an account executive for an advertising agency.
> *J.Soc. had a fairly religious bias. Nice to come home to, but not the hot spot for extroverts. A highlight was the Cambridge Workshop Theatre play 'Hannah' — supported by J.Soc. — based on the life of Hannah Senesh, and improvised from her diary and other documents. I played the name part in Cambridge and on tour in July 1983.*

Abulafia, David S.H. (Dr.)
Kings, 1968-74
History
> Conducted research based in Rome 1972-74; Fellow of Caius since 1974 and now University lecturer in History, specializing in the medieval Mediterranean. Author of *The Two Italies*, of *Italy, Sicily & the Mediterranean* and of articles published in Europe, Israel and U.S.A. Sabbatical leave in Jerusalem in 1979. Married, two children.
> *I enjoyed eating lunch at the Jewish Society when I was an undergraduate. My great hope, as a Cambridge resident, is that the Society will retain the atmosphere of broadminded tolerance in which it was founded. At a time of growing extremism and fundamentalism we need some havens of religious pluralism to survive.*

Acker, Martin
Fitzwilliam, 1961-64
Economics
> Emigrated to Israel 1964. Internal Auditor of SONOL Ltd., an oil company. President of Nahariya Conservative (Masorti) Congregation.
> *CUJS should continue as an anchor and refuge for Jews of all persuasions.*

Alberman, K.B. (Dr.)
Trinity, 1944-47,49-51
Natural Sciences
> National Service with Ministry of Supply 1947-49. Postgraduate research at Cambridge 1949-51. Joined family firm, Innoxa Ltd., in 1951. Succeeded my father as chairman 1971. Married Eva Altmann *q.v.* in 1952.
> *Secretary CUJS in 1946. Met my wife and closest friends there. I hope that the Society will continue to act as a focal point of contact for all Cambridge Jewish students, whatever their level of orthodoxy.*

Albert, Stephen C.
Trinity, 1958-61
English
> Chairman and Managing Director of World Microfilms Publications Ltd.

Alexander, Anthony Victor
St. John's, 1949-53
Modern Languages, Law
> Went into City to become an insurance broker with the Sidjwick Group PLC; Chairman of the UK company 1968; have held a variety of Group Management appointments since then; Chairman of British Insurance Brokers Association 1983; appointed to Securities & Investments Board 1986; C.B.E. New Year 1987. Married, one child.

Alexander, Arthur Louis Lionel
St. John's, 1947-50
Law
> RAF 1943-47; B.A. 1949; Ll.B. 1951; Practising Barrister 1951-57; Civil Servant (Inland Revenue Solicitor's Office) 1957-86; now retired. Chairman, Inverness Social Security Appeal Tribunal. Married, three children, one grandchild.

Alexander, Eileen (Mrs. Ellenbogen)
Girton 1936-40
English
> War work in Army Welfare and then in Air Ministry; translated literature from French and Italian; lectured to W.E.A. classes and tutored for University entry; skilful jeweller and goldsmith. The Eileen Alexander Prize at Girton was founded by her parents in her honour. Married (Gershon Ellenbogen q.v.), one child. Died 1986.

Alexander, Nicholas P.B. (Aleksander)
Downing 1978-83
Engineering, Law
> Admitted Solicitor 1986; now in field of Corporate tax at Travers Smith Braithwaite, in City of London. National Treasure, British Youth Council 1983-84; currently Vice-chairman, Liberal Paty's Home Affairs Policy Panel and member, Law Policy Panel. Founder member of group attempting to establish a Reform Synagogue in Muswell Hill. Married.
>
> *Actively avoided the Jewish Society and the Israel Society until 1981/82, when I was President of the Cambridge Students Union. In that year there was an active campaign by certain students to 'twin' Cambridge University with Bir-Zeit University on the West Bank, and I became involved in the opposition campaign led by the Israel Society. Although I then had more contact with both societies, I rarely attended their functions, but became more involved in CUJS activities within the National Union of Students.*

Allen, Samuel
L.S.E. 1942-44
Banking, Currency and The Finance of International Trade
> Joined R.A.F. in 1944 and was present at the birth of Pakistan. Spent four years as professional economist at Commonwealth Secretariat and entered food import trade on decontrol in 1954; after twenty-five years building up an international group, retired as main Board Director; currently works as Finance Therapist. Married (Regina Nyman q.v.), one child.
>
> *Thompson's Lane was remarkable for the number of marriages it produced among our contemporaries, many of whom remain close friends to this day.*

Altmann, Eva (Professor Alberman)
Newnham, 1949-52
Medicine
> Left Cambridge, 1952, to do clinical medicine and specialized in Epidemiology. Have chair at London Hospital. Married Ken Alberman q.v.in 1952. Have four children and one grandchild.
>
> *I met my husband and many close friends at the J.Soc. It was clearly an important part of our lives.*

Amias, Jeremy Adrian
Churchill 1981-84
Classics

Trained with Salomon Brothers, Investment Bankers in New York; Since 1985 work as Bond dealer in London.

Atkin, Robert
Christ's, 1959-62
History

Joined family business manufacturing Baby Feeding products. 1964- 66 M.B.A. course at University of California at Berkeley. Married, three children.

Augenbraun, Barry S.
St. John's, 1960-62
History

Returned to USA to study at Harvard Law School, and practiced corporate Law in New York for ten years. Since 1975 have lived in Philadelphia as the general counsel of a large accounting and consulting firm. Married with two children. Active in the American Jewish Congress and Zionist activities, as well as both the American and Philadelphia Bar Associations.

'..the high point of the week was the Friday night service, followed by a hot dinner and an invited speaker. The speakers came from all points of the theological compass...an active member of the Communist Party... a Reconstructionist Rabbi... an Orthodox Rabbi from USA.'

Ayrton, Simon
Gonville & Caius, 1986-
Natural Sciences

Baker, Marion
Newnham, 1986-
Law

Despite its large membership there are vast numbers of Jewish undergraduates who never affiliate with the Jewish Society. I hope that by a wide variety of programmes to interest a diversity of people this can be changed.

Baker, Philip (Dr.)
Emmanuel, 1974-77
Law

From Cambridge to Oxford and then London University; taught for eight years at the School for Oriental and African Studies (Chinese Law); now practising at the Bar in London.

Memories: cleaning the Cholent pot after Shabbat; Clive Freedman's Yiddish version of the Law Reports; Rugby at the Landy's.

Balfour-Lynn, Lionel Peter (Dr.)
Christ's, 1946-49
Medicine

Qualified at Guy's Hospital in 1952, and spent two years in RAF as a medical officer. I specialized in Pediatrics, and still research at the Royal Postgraduate School, Hammersmith while practising privately in Harley Street. I have three adult children.

The Jewish Society was a haven on a Friday night where one could have a good Jewish meal and remember one's essential roots.

Ballheimer, Andrew Mark
Gonville & Caius, 1980-83
Law

Solicitors' Finals course at College of Law, Guilford. Travelled round the world for eight months, visiting USA, Tahiti, Australia, China, Hong Kong, Macao and Thailand. Currently under articles with D.J.Freeman, Solicitors.

I will always remember the hospitality shown to me over the High Holidays and wish the Society all the best for the future.

Baron, Raphael Raymond V. (Dr. Bar-On)
Trinity, 1944-48
Mathematics and Statistics

Worked at J.Lyons & Co. 1948-50; General Register Office 1950-51; Immigrated to Israel 1951; Israel Productivity Institute (Head, Research Division) 1951-55; Israel Central Bureau of Statistics (Director of Planning & Development) 1956-72; Israel Ministry of Tourism (Director of Research & Statistics) since 1972. Senior Lecturer at Hebrew University, Jerusalem, Technion, University of Haifa. Consultant to UN statistical Office, UNDP, Tourist Authority of Thailand, US Bureau of the Census and other organizations. Elected Fellow of Royal Statistical Society, International Institute of Statistics, International Association of Scientific Experts in Tourism, Time Series Analysis & Forecasting Society. Have published books and articles on statistics. Widowed, two children.

CUJS was of great importance to me in developing my Jewish and Zionist interests and my social life, and I hope it will serve many thousands more.

Baum, Debbie (Mrs. Kedar)
Clare, 1976-79
Engineering

1979 Married Steve Kedar (formerly Drake *q.v.*) and settled in Israel. 1979-82 studied Biomedical Engineering at Technion, Haifa. 1982 moved to Kfar Etzion; work in Kibbutz metal industry. Three children.

Baum, Naomi F.
New Hall, 1982-83
Social and Political Sciences

Completed B.A. at Wellesley College, Massachusetts in June 1984. Studied at Michlala College for Women, Jerusalem until June 1985. At present completing course for Masters degree in Public Administration at Harvard University.

I made many friends at the Society. I ate at Thompson's Lane daily and attended Shabbat services. I am especially grateful that the members made me feel so welcome during the one year I was in Cambridge. I hope that with renovated facilities the Society will continue to grow and serve the community.

Bell, Trevor Lewis
St. John's, 1964-67
Economics

Solicitor. Follower of Rabbi Nachman of Breslov. Married, two children.

A formative haven, occupying a central role during student years.

Ben-Israel, Hedva (Professor)
Girton, 1950-55
History

Returned home to Jerusalem. Joined History Department of Hebrew

University where I still am. Professor of Modern History and Ben- Eliezer
Chair for the Study of National Movements. Have published books and
articles, written television and radio programmes. Received Betty Miller
Award for book 'English Historians of the French Revolution'. Fellow of
National Humanities Center, North Carolina 1985-86. Have three sons.

Ben-Nathan, Colin Victor
Trinity, 1983-86
Natural Sciences
Have taken up articles with a firm of chartered accountants.
*I fondly recall Friday evenings at CUJS. There was always a healthy
attendance and a friendly atmosphere. I hope the Society continues to be
successful and to prosper in the future.*

Ben-Nathan, Martin
Trinity, 1955-58
Classics including Classical Archaeology
CUJS treasurer in 1958. Left Cambridge June 1958 for accountancy. Qualified in 1962 and specialized in UK and international taxation, as senior tax
partner in medium sized firm. Member of Board of Deputies. Married with
three children, *q.v.* the eldest, Colin.
*Many happy memories of J-Soc in my time, and wish it every success for
the future.*

Benady, Samuel
Jesus, 1922-25
Law
Joined Inner Temple and qualified as Barrister-at-Law in 1926. Practiced
in Gibraltar; Q.C. in 1955; O.B.E. in 1969; C.B.E. in 1986. Leader of the
Gibraltar Bar for 25 years. President of the Gibraltar Jewish Community
for 17 years.
*Attended Perse Grammar School 1919-22. Attended Saturday morning
services in small student synagogue. Regular Honorary Reader — Diamond,
later Senior Master of the High Court in England. My personal friend at
Cambridge was the late Arthur Lourie, afterwards Israeli Ambassador in
London.*

Benjamin, Jonathan C.
Pembroke,1973-77
English, Education
Taught at William Ellis School, Highgate for seven years, during which also
ran a cheder, was involved in the Jewish educational forum LIMMUD
(chairman, 1986) and taught adults and teenagers modern Jewish history.
In 1984 married, and was appointed Head of English at the Hasmonean
High Schools, London.
*Much of my attention was focussed on the task of providing food for the
Society across three terms. When the orthodox tended to favour Cambridge
over Oxford, this was an important facility. The Society seemed unique in
owning the Shul and in, generally, remaining aloof from the more trivial
pursuits of Jewish student politics. My fond and grateful memories of
hospitality — Landys, Reifs, Dombs et al. — must be far from unique.
'Manna' was launched at this time; editing the second issue preserved my
sanity in my Cert. Ed. year.*

Benn, Martin Jonathan
St. Catharine's, 1955-59
Economics, Law

Joined Chartered Surveyors, De Groot Collis, and retired as a partner in 1971 to become property director of a public company, from which I retired in 1978 to run my own companies and practice. Married, three children.

In the 1950's the Jewish Society was a friendly Shabbat dining club for the once a weekers like myself and a little more for those who enjoyed Kosher lunches daily.

Bennun, Naomi (Dr. Nevo)
L.S.E. 1942-45
Sociology

Left in January 1946 for erstwhile Palestine, ostensibly on fieldwork for M.A.; returned to London November 1946 to burn my bridges; returned to Palestine December 1946; married Yosef Nevo 1948 (see *O Jerusalem*); worked continuously as sociologist; 1979 Ph.D. Soc. Anthropology. Active feminist.

The Jewish Society when I first joined was not actively Zionist. Hermie Pearlman and a few others, including myself, founded Habonim in Cambridge and this influenced the Jewish Society. A 'Palestinian' (Yes! That's what they were in those halcyon (?!) days) called Levine, an amputee, became chairman of the Jewish Society. The very warm friendly network of Jewish students was due to the Jewish Society and its intellectual activities were particularly rewarding. I hope the centrality of Israel still exists there.

Bergbaum, Edwin M.
Peterhouse, 1977-80
Engineering

Worked as a Consulting Civil Engineer in High Wycombe for one year and in Leeds for eighteen months. Qualified in 1983, and married. Joined firm of Structural Engineers in 1984.

I was the second chairman of the reconstituted CUJS Building Committee which prepared a set of plans for extending and modernizing the synagogue. Due to legal difficulties dating back to the setting up of the CUJS, these plans were never activated although 50% of the money was available. The problem of ownership of the building was finally resolved in 1981, by my successor Mr. A. Burnside.

Berkman, Lydia (Mrs. Callender)
Homerton College, 1945-46
Youth Leadership & Social Welfare

1946 joined Jewish National Fund forming youth groups; 1948 transferred to Joint Palestine Appeal; 1950 Magen David Adom, organizing secretary; since 1952, on executive Council of M.D.A. and founder and Chairman of their Functions Committee; since 1978, founded and run Casting Information Service in England, liaising with Producers and Directors in Film, Television and Theatre. Three children.

The Jewish Students Society in 1945 was a vibrant and active group, providing Friday night services and Kosher meals and the opportunity of socializing with other Jewish students.

Berkoff, B.
Trinity Hall, 1926-29
Natural Sciences, Economics

After qualifying as a Solicitor and working in London I joined a firm of

Solicitors in Calcutta in 1934. During the War I joined the Royal Artillery, fought in Burma and ended as Captain I.G. Returning to England in 1946 I joined the Metal Box Co. Ltd. and later the Commonwealth Development Finance Co.. Ltd. in a legal capacity, finally becoming Managing Director of the latter. Since retirement I have been lecturing on development topics. Married, three children, five grandchildren.

My memories of the Society are rather dim now. We used to meet for Sabbath services in a room in Sydney Street, and held about four meetings a term to discuss matters of interest (such as the numerus clausus in some European Universities) or to hear a visiting speaker. As there were no other practising Jews in my college I tended to remain rather on the outskirts.

Berkoff, Nelson A.
Trinity Hall 1935-38
History

British Army and Jewish Brigade 1939-46. Taught in England till 1948. Emigrated to Israel in 1949 and taught in Haifa till 1958. PhD in Linguistics, Cornell University. Commander of Artillery Regiment in Israel Army Reserve from 1950-1967. Senior lecturer in English Language and Linguistics at the Hebrew University of Jerusalem from 1958 till retirement in 1985. Lives in Jerusalem. Married with two children and two grandchildren.

Sometime in 1936 it was decided to launch an appeal for the building of a permanent synagogue at Cambridge. Bernard Waley-Cohen was up then, and so his father Sir Robert, took an active part in fund raising. I remember attending — as a representative of the Cambridge Hebrew Congregation and Schechter Society — an appeal meeting in October 1936, and on 25 April 1937 Sir Robert Waley-Cohen laid the foundation stone of the new synagogue. In June 1937 the three undergraduate Jewish societies — the Schechter Society, the Zionist Society and the local branch of the Anglo-Jewish Association — united to form the Cambridge University Jewish Society. I was the first president of CUJS and so had the honour of conducting part of the Service when the new Synagogue was opened by Mr. Lionel de Rothschild on 21 October 1937, and I led the procession of those carrying the Scrolls with the Chief Rabbi, Dr Hertz, following behind me.

Another thing I remember is that we did not start using the kitchen immediately for our Friday night suppers because we knew that in the following year, 1938, Pesach would be in term time, so we kept the new dishes and cutlery for then.

Berkowitz, Sidney (Rabbi Dr.)
St. John's College, 1937-39

Dr. Berkovitz, who died in 1983, was ordained at Hebrew Union College, Cincinatti in 1936, and did graduate work at Cambridge, Oxford and the Sorbonne. He received his doctorate at Cambridge in 1939. He was a chaplain during World War II, serving 42 months in the Pacific. In 1946 he became the spiritual leader of the Rodef Sholom Temple in Youngstown, Ohio and retired from that position shortly before his death. He was active in Jewish and Civic affairs, particularly in civil liberties and inter-faith relations. As a result of his Cambridge days he remained 'a staunch admirer of the British and their way of life'.

Berkowitz, Ivan (Dr.)
Trinity, 1973-75
Law

Rejoined New York bankers Rosenthal & Rosenthal. Moved to Los Angeles in 1978 to form investment banking partnership dedicated to financing company buy-outs and real estate. Returned to New York in 1986 to establish an eastern office for the firm. Have given lectures and seminars at colleges and law schools and contributed to legal and financial journals. Am also a board member of various companies and charities.

The simple act of attending the Minyan on a regular basis and the friendships that developed there are sufficient testimony to the immense value of the role played by the Society. A most memorable occasion was the annual breaking of the fast after Yom Kippur services, at the home of Lady Rachel Lauterpacht, a true Zionist matriarch.

Berlyne, Anita R. (Mrs. Abrams)
Newnham, 1947-50
Modern Languages, Psychology

Postgraduate diploma in Abnormal psychology at Maudsley Hospital. Assistant lecture at Leeds University, then to Child Guidance in Sheffield, later in Enfield. Since 1973 in private practice. Currently involved in developing a professional association for Clinical Psychologists. Five daughters, two (so far) Newnham graduates *q.v.*

J.Soc. contained brilliant people. They could do Ximenes crosswords, and seem to have met each other through Study groups in London. I.U.J.S. was strong. The J.Soc. produced romance for several members.

Berman, Marcelo S.
Queens', 1983
Physics

Returned to Brazil in 1984 and soon became financial director of Construtora Gustavo Berman. Published two books on Physics, in Portuguese. Married.

Bernstein, Ian A. (Dr.)
Emmanuel, 1982-84
Medicine

Left Cambridge in 1984 to cox for the University of London and then the National Lightweight Squad (1986). Expect to finish medical degree in 1987.
J.Soc. was rather cliquey, but good fun!

Bernstein, Paul
Jesus, 1985-
Engineering

Berry, Elliot M.
Christ's 1964-67
Medicine

Aliyah 1973; General Physician in internal medicine at Hadassah University Hospital, Jerusalem; special interest — eating disorders. Married, four children.

The Society was an oasis for meeting fellow students without fear of religious polarization or brain washing.

Bier, Hannah (Mrs. Manne)
Newnham, 1973-76
Natural Sciences

Moved to Israel. Graduated from Bar Ilan University with MA in Clinical Psychology. Now work as clinical psychiatrist in public mental health clinic with kibbutzim and a private clinic. Moved to border town, Kiryat Shmona in 1983, and enjoy life in Galilee. Married, one daughter.

215

CUJS was a meeting place for Jewish students, including synagogue and meals. Also a place to meet some of the Jewish residents in town with whom relationships developed outside the J.Soc proper.

Biermann, David
St. John's, 1964-67
Music

PGCE at Leeds University 1968. Since then teacher and lecturer on music education. At present, Director of Music, Woughton Campus, Milton Keynes. *Attended Shabbat and festival services, and occasionally lectures. I particularly remember the way in which Cambridge residents and students collaborated so magnificently together.*

Blackburn, David Michael
St John's 1956-59
Mathematics, Law

Qualified as Solicitor in 1962; partner to Courts and Company 1962-78; left professional practice to join the Board of Rosehaugh P.L.C.; Director Rosehaugh P.L.C. 1979-85; currently Property Project Consultant and Director of Rosehaugh Stanhope Developments P.L.C. Married (twice), four children.

I have fond memories of Friday evening dinners that were well attended by members having a multiplicity of views, religious and otherwise. The Synagogue services were conducted with enthusiasm and a high degree of competence in many varying styles. Senior members of the University then active in the Society included Albert Cherns. Raphael Loewe was also in evidence from time to time maintaining the association of his late father (Herbert Loewe) with the C.U.J.S.

Blain, Martin Alfred
King's, 1985-
Engineering, Law

Blaukopf, Ruth Beatrice
Newnham, 1969-72
English

Emigrated to Israel 1972; studied at Hebrew University, Jerusalem leading to Assistant Lectureship in Faculty of English 1973; joined Israel Radio as trainee 1974; Editor, English News department 1976; Reporter 1979-82; seconded to Israel mission to UN as researcher till 1984; Producer, Israel Radio 1984-86; Joined WTN (Worldwide Television News), Bureau chief, Israel as producer 1986. Am currently Bureau chief, WTN Israel, responsible for Israel news coverage and transmission by satellite to Europe, USA, Australasia and the Soviet Union.

Together with my Jewish contemporaries at Cambridge, I was unremittingly critical of CUJS, but, looking back, it gave a focal point of Jewish identification at Cambridge, and brought us into contact with one another and with Jewish residents of Cambridge whose hospitality provided a home away from home. Occasionally it gave us not only kosher meals but food for thought. I would have wished then that CUJS had brought about greater interaction with the larger student world of Cambridge, involving itself more in the issues of our time. I hope this synthesis and dialogue may be realized by future generations at CUJS.

Bohm, Peter
Queens' 1970-73
Law

Spent nearly six years in legal department of Ladbroke Group; now a partner with Courts & Co., Solicitors. Married, two children.

Have very happy memories of Friday nights in particular at Thompson's Lane, where I made enduring friendships. The Society provides a marvellous opportunity to meet Jews from different places and backgrounds.

Bornstein, Israel I. 'Sonny' (Bar-On)
Emmanuel, 1943-46
Natural Sciences, Psychology

IUJF Summer School Convenor 1945; IUJF Zionist Convenor 1946; qualified M.B., B.Chir. 1949; served in R.A.F. until 1953 (for two years in Egypt, Canal zone); immigrated to Israel 1953; served in Israeli Air Force until 1968 (as Chief Psychiatrist to the Air Force and Chief Medical Officer of the Air Force 1963- 66). Presently Consultant Psychogynecologist at Serlin Maternity and Gynecological Centre, Tel Aviv University. Married, two children, two grandchildren.

My late brother, the Rev. Harry Bornstein was a graduate of Emmanuel where he read History. He was later domiciled in Cambridge when he was Army Chaplain in Newmarket, 1942-43, but died in North Africa in 1943. Together with Rabbi B.D.Klein, I founded the Luncheon Meals Service at Thompson's Lane in 1944. In 1950, when the then Rabbi of Cambridge died suddenly before Yom Kippur, I stood in as Ba'al Mussaf on Yom Kippur! (I was then a Medical Officer at R.A.F. Wutton, Hants.)

Bower, Marcus
Trinity, 1936-40,45-46
Classics, Law

Joined National Coal Board in 1946, becoming Deputy Legal Adviser. Left in 1947 to become director of major power engineering group, first in Midlands, later in North East. Retired in 1983 and returned to London. Was Chairman of Northern Institute of Directors, member of Newcastle University Council and director of Port Authority. Currently Health Authority member; Vice-chairman, Reform Synagogues of Great Britain. 1949 married Anne Rubinstein *q.v.*, have two sons *q.v.* and four grandchildren.

...We were a very catholic group in those days, mainstream orthodox (with a fair sprinkling of Rabbinic students) mixing happily in Synagogue and socially with Reform and Liberal, secular and Zionist. The Cambridge 'minhag' was somewhat to the left of Hampstead United Synagogue, and innovations (such as Adon Olam to the tune of Chu Chin Chow) were accepted... This tolerant relationship had begun to change by the time I returned in 1945 and the trend has apparently continued so that it is now only the conformist Orthodox who can find a home in Thompson's Lane. I should like to see a return to the 'open' tradition of CUJS which to me is of the essence of Cambridge.

Boxer, Eric I. (Dr.)
Bart's, 1941-42
Medicine

Qualified in 1947. G.P. in Greenford, Middlesex since 1953. Married in 1953 and have four children and four grandchildren.

A happy time in spite of the War and Home Guard. I acquired many friends and two brothers-in-law.

Braun, Lavinia
Gonville & Caius, 1980-83
History

> After graduation I wandered around a little and attempted a doctorate on 'Alliance Israelite Universalle', which failed through lack of funds. In 1984 Rotary International awarded me a scholarship at the Hebrew University, Jerusalem for a study on 'Anglo-Israel relations'. In 1985-86 I was librarian and history teacher at Carmel College, and since then have begun reading for an M.Phil. in Modern Jewish Studies at Oxford.
>
> *A memory of warmth and a longing for Israel in young hearts. Good food on Friday evenings! I hope it continues to thrive.*

Brecher, David John
Trinity 1948-50
Law

> Commenced legal career as a Solicitor in May 1950. Now a senior partner of substantial firm of Solicitors in the West End of London. Married with two children and two grandchildren.

Briscoe, Sheila M. (Dr. Kaplow)
Girton, 1948-52
Zoology

> Obtained D.Phil after working at the Department of Pharmacology, Oxford. I came to USA on a Fulbright to teach Pharmacology for a year at the University of Vermont, where I met my husband, so one year has stretched to thirty three. Am currently an Associate Professor of Biology teaching Physiology at Quinnipiac College in Connecticut. Have two children and two grandchildren.

Brittan, Leon (The Rt. Hon.)
Trinity, 1957-61
English, Law

> Yale 1961-62; Barrister, Q.C. 1978; Bencher of the Inner Temple 1983; M.P. Cleveland & Whitby 1974-83; M.P. for Richmond since 1983; Minister of State at Home Office; Chief Secretary to Treasury; Home Secretary; Secretary of State for Trade & Industry. *See Who's Who.*
>
> *CUJS was a very active social, religious and cultural centre in my day. I hope it will continue to be so.*

Bronstein, Michael Simon
Christ's, 1976-79
Law

> Spent one year as Tutorial Assistant, Kings College, London, Law faculty. Qualified as a solicitor in 1983, and now practice in London.

Brooks, Suzette
Kings, 1981-83
Economics

> Having graduated from Harvard Law School, am now a corporate lawyer in New York City specializing in health care law and trying to get involved in NYC politics and community work.
>
> *Cambridge was like stepping backwards in time. It is the antithesis of the New York ethnic melting pot where I grew up. Probably the two most intellectually stimulating and socially active years of my life.*

Brown, Brendan David (Dr.)
Trinity, 1969-72
Economics
> Joint M.D. of family company 1971; M.B.A. University of Chicago 1975. Ph.D. London 1979; Bank of England, Economic research 1976; Consultant, International Finance, Philips & Drew 1976; Director, County Nat. West Capital Markets Ltd. and Nat. West Investment Banking Ltd. 1986. Editor, *Currency and Bond Outlook*. Author of seven books on financial topics.

Brown, Morris Jonathan (Professor)
Trinity, 1968-71
Medicine, Classics
> Clinical course at University College Hospital, London; elective at Hadassa Hospital, Jerusalem; Senior Lecturer and Consultant Physician, Royal Postgraduate Medical School, Hammersmith; Professor of Physical Pharmacology, Cambridge 1985. Married, three children.

Brownstein, Martin Ian
Fitzwilliam, 1967-70
Mathematics
> 1970 Joined National Mutual Life. 1974 Qualified as Fellow of the Institute of Actuaries. Currently Deputy Secretary and Corporate Planner for NML. Married 1971, two sons. Warden, Chigwell & Hainault Synagogue.
>
> *The Kosher canteen was full every lunchtime. The centre of Shabbat, with interesting speakers and a friendly atmosphere. I particularly remember the May Ball when we provided a meal for about 50.*

Burston, Neville
St. Catharine's, 1948-51
Economics, Law
> 1951-55 Executive trainee at Houndsditch Warehouse. 1955-76; Founder and chairman of Burston & Texas Commerce Bank; 1976- Corporate finance activities in both North America and U.K. 1961 -76 Councilman and Alderman, City of London; 1965 appointed J.P. for Inner London. Since 1955 London Vice-President J.N.F.; currently Vice-Chairman, British Technion; committee member, British Friends of the Israel Museums; member, International Council, Israel Museum.

Burton, Raymond Montague
> *See* Jewish Yearbook

Caller, Alan
Emmanuel, 1945-48
Mechanical Sciences
> After National Service spent time with various engineering companies, moving into export marketing operations. Now run small export consultancy specializing in Eastern Europe.
>
> *I was a fairly regular attendant at Friday night suppers; still remember most of the Zmirot. Pleasant memories.*

Caller, Martin (Dr.)
Emmanuel, 1942-44
Natural Sciences
> Clinical Studies at Guy's Hospital. R.A.M.C. 1950-52; GP in Battersea, London since 1952.
>
> *Those happy Friday nights are really all I remember well.*

Cantor, Raphael
Trinity Hall, 1958-61
Natural Sciences

Qualified in Medicine at University College Hospital, London in 1964; entered General Practice in Cardiff in 1966. Married with three children.

Two happy memories — 1) Eleanor Bron singing a song about making love to the devil from the ladies' gallery at a Jewish Society party: 2) A special long vacation luncheon catered by John Cappin who produced a gourmet's delight that was by far the best meal that we ever had in Thompson's Lane.

Casper, Bernard Moses (Rabbi)
Trinity 1936-39
English, Anthropology

Left Cambridge 1939. Rabbi, Higher Broughton Hebrew Congregation. 1941 joined Royal Army Chaplain's Department; service in England and then in Egypt, Italy and across to Belgium and Holland. Senior Chaplain Jewish Infantry Brigade Group from its foundation until my demob in 1946. Returned to Manchester. Moved to Western Synagogue, London in 1954. In 1956 first Dean of Students at Hebrew University, Jerusalem. Since 1963 Chief Rabbi, South Africa. Have two children and eight grandchildren.

Charkham, Jonathan Philip
Jesus, 1949-52
Law

Chief advisor, Bank of England, since 1985. *See Who's Who.*

Charles, Julian A.
Queens', 1971-74
History

Qualified as Solicitor, 1978. Married 1984. Live and practice in London.

Chayen, Joseph (Dr)
Christ's 1948-49

Ph.D (London): Biophysics (1951); D.Sc (Biophysical and Biochemical Cytology), London, 1961. Lilian May Coleman research fellow, Royal College of Surgeons of England (1960-1966); Head of division of Cellular Biology, Kennedy Institute of Rheumatology from 1966 until present. Gold Medal of the Biochemical Society for advances in Analytical Biochemistry, 1984. Member of the World Health Organization Committee on Biological Standardization 1975 to present.

Cherns, Albert Bernard (Professor Emeritus)
Trinity, 1940-41,46-48,54-59
Mathematics, Moral Sciences, Psychology

After research at the Nuffield Unit, Cambridge Psychological Laboratory, I spent seventeen varied years in the Scientific Civil Service, before being appointed Professor of Social Sciences at Loughborough University in 1966 from which I retired in 1984. Now Professor Emeritus, I am a visiting fellow at the Science Policy Research Unit, University of Sussex. My publications include 7 books as author or editor and numerous articles on organizational topics and utilization of the social sciences. (Albert Cherns died in May 1987, shortly after sending this information).

The Society was not only more hierarchical and formal but also more tolerant in 1940 than in later years. I think I was the last to hold the office of secretary to the AJA in 1941. Friday night suppers and lectures were the highlights of the week and Shabbat morning services decorous and expedi-

tious, marked regularly by the arrival of Charles Fox, former head of the Department of Education, in gown and bicycle clips. The Society's tenth anniversary in the Easter term of 1947, at which I took the chair, was marked by the attendance of a formidable array of distinguished alumni. For the future, I hope the Society finds a way continuously to accommodate to a changing world — but not too quickly!

Chigier, Norman (Professor)
Queens', 1956-60
Engineering

> International Flame Research Foundation, Holland 1960-63; Department of Aeronautical Engineering, Technion, Israel 1964-66; Department of Fuel Technology, University of Sheffield 1966-1981; William J. Brown Distinguished Professor of Mechanical Engineering, Carnegie Mellon University, Pittsburgh, PA, USA 1981 to present. Married with three sons. Author of several books, 140 papers, and editor of international review journal on Combustion. Research at NASA Ames Center, California on aircraft wake turbulence (Scientific American, March 1974).
>
> *I greatly cherished the opportunity to Daven and eat at the Thompson's Lane Synagogue. The Friday night services and the Festivals allowed us to have some spiritual experience. During vacation times we missed the service and meals. I hope that the CUJS will continue to flourish and benefit from the renewed interest in religion that is being found on campuses.*

Chinn, Trevor
King's 1953-54
Economics

Citron, David B.
Gonville & Caius, 1964-67
Economics

> Qualified as Chartered Accountant in 1970. Lived in Israel till 1975, where I married, and then in Montreal till 1979. Returned to England and became a lecturer in Accounting, first at North London Polytechnic and now at City University. Have four children.

Citron, Neil
Trinity, 1969-72
Medical Sciences, Physiology

> Senior Registrar, Orthopedic Surgery at the Royal National Orthopedic Hospital. Specialist in hand surgery. Married, three children.

Cohen, Bruce J.R.
Jesus, 1958-61
Economics, Law

> 1962 LL.M. at Cambridge. 1964 qualified as Chartered Accountant. 1965 joined Courts Furnishers plc where am now chief executive. 1966 married, now have 5 children, the eldest having just started at Jesus. Father, brother, son, 2 uncles and 5 cousins all at same college (all under name Cohen).
>
> *I still have several friends whom I met at the CUJS. I hope that Jewish students will continue to benefit from its homely atmosphere and chicken soup on Friday nights.*

Cohen, Charles (Dr.)
Pembroke, 1945-48
Natural Sciences (Medicine)
> Qualified in Newcastle, served for two years in R.A.M.C. in Kenya and four years in as a Medical Registrar. Since 1959 have been in General Practice in Sunderland. Married with four children and two grandchildren.
> *My most happy memories of Jewish life in Cambridge were the Erev Shabbat meetings and meals at Thompson's Lane, and also having evening meals in 45/46 at Rabbi Ehrentreu's home in company with Sam Stamler, Cyril Rashbass, Ken Alberman, Henry Lachs and others.*

Cohen, Donald David
Jesus 1938-41
Law
> 1941-46 in Army. Wounded in action in Burma campaign. Since 1947 Director of family furniture business in Newcastle-upon-Tyne. Formerly President and Treasurer, now Trustee of synagogue. J.P. and Chairman of Northumbria Probation Committee. Married, two daughters, one grand-daughter.
> *Used to enjoy the Friday evening Services followed by supper at Thompson's Lane. Clear memories of good food and fellowship. I especially recall a visit of Chief Rabbi Dr. Hertz and his address to a large audience there. During the early years of the war the numbers were increased by students from L.S.E., Bedford College and other colleges.*

Cohen, Edmund G.
Jesus, 1948-50
Economics
> Chairman, Courts Furnishers Plc. 1976-86. Married, two children, two grandchildren.

Cohen, Murray Howard
Downing, 1950-54
Law
> Practice as a Solicitor. Married, three children.

Cohen, Solomon Ben-Tov
Trinity, 1979-83
Mathematics
> Obtained scholarship to study violin with Yfrah Neaman at Guildhall School of Music and Drama. Also developed business interests in securities and currently work for James Capel & Co.

Cohn, Paul M. (Professor)
Trinity, 1944-45,46-51
Mathematics
> Spent 1951-52 at Nancy University, France as CRNS Fellow in Mathematics, then lecturer at Manchester University until 1962. Came to London, first Queen Mary College, then Bedford College (until its merger with Royal Holloway College in 1984), then at University College, since 1986 as Astor Professor of Mathematics. Married, two daughters.

Colb, Sanford (and Paula)
St John's 1970-72
Law

> Harvard Law School June 1972; Aliyah 1974. Has own Law firm for the practice of patents, trademarks and copyrights in Tel-Aviv and Rehovot. Four children.
>
> *We were the closest Jews to the Shul and were often called on to make a minyan. One winter we scraped the peeling paint behind the Aron Kodesh and repainted that whole wall. We return every few years for visits and this year were pleased to see the big crowd on Shabbat, many children (more than in 1970-72) and the Landys — ever present.*

Cole, Louise Sylvia (Mrs. Mestel)
Newnham, 1943-46
Economics, Psychology

> Stayed in Cambridge until my marriage in 1951 to Leon Mestel q.v. Then mainly concerned with bringing up our four children. 1962-64 took Postgraduate Certificate in Social Anthropology at Cambridge. When my children were older had various research and administrative jobs relating to social deviance (drug addiction, psychiatrically disturbed offenders, care of disturbed adolescents). Now retired and working as a consultant in family history.
>
> *CUJS was a magnificent shadchan — I met my husband there! Some of my best friends date from that time too. It was also the best Jewish community I have ever belonged to. I shall always remember the warmth of its Services and the breadth and tolerance of the outlook. My hope for its future is that it will still remain a home for all Jewish students and never succumb to the fatal polarization of contemporary Jewry.*

Coleman, Clive I. (Dr.)
Gonville & Caius, 1966-69
Natural Sciences

> Ph.D. at Imperial College, London 1974. Research assistant, then Lecturer in Department of Physics and Astronomy, University College, London. Joined Marconi in 1981; now Manager, Electro- Optics. Married, four children.

Collins, Stephen Paul,
Trinity, 1969-72
Economics

> Joined Bank of England and worked in various departments. Assistant Private Secretary to the Governor of the Bank 1980-83. Seconded to International Monetary Fund, Washington D.C. 1983-85. Married, two surviving children.
>
> *The Society provided a welcome change on Friday evenings, where one could enjoy good company, a fine religious service and — let's face it — indifferent food, in a 'heimische' atmosphere. Long may it continue, hopefully in improved premises.*

Conway, Anthony Malcolm
Trinity Hall, 1957-58
International Law (Postgrad. diploma)

> Qualified as Solicitor in 1960 and joined the family firm, and am today the Principal. During my first two years of practice was also on staff of Law department of Leeds University. Formerly President of Leeds Jewish Representative Council. Currently Vice- president of Leeds Council of Christians and Jews. Married, two sons.

The Society was extremely active. Lunch was provided daily and Mincha was davened immediately afterwards. Friday evening Service and meal was followed by a talk, and generally attracted 60 or more people. Services were conducted by students themselves...I hope the Society will always be a focal point for Jews in Cambridge.

Cowan, Jonathan M.
Magdalene, 1985-
Law

Invaluable for its Kosher meals. Hope that in the coming years the Society will prove more attractive to all the levels of student religiosity, rather than its present predominantly very orthodox appeal.

Crystal, J. D.
Corpus Christi 1936-40
Modern Languages and PGCE

War service 1940-46; Mentioned in Dispatches; Commissioned in Royal Artillery; demobilized as lieutenant-colonel. Worked in education in England as departmental head, headmaster and examinations officer. Widowed in 1979.

Darcy, Ken
Gonville & Caius, 1983-86
Medical Sciences, Zoology

At present studying in Yeshiva in Jerusalem; plan to continue medical career after one or two years of study here.

Davidson, Jeffrey E.C.
Robinson, 1981-84
Classics, Law

Training as chartered accountant. Getting married in September 1987.
The most notable benefit that I derived from CUJS is that I met my wife there.

Davidson, Jonathan
Pembroke 1960-63
History

Joined Foreign Office: served in India, Thailand, Senegal and Washington. Left Foreign Service to settle in Washington. Represented since then University of South Carolina as Washington representative, Director of International Programmes and special assistant to President. Married with two children.

Davis, Robert Jonathan
Gonville & Caius, 1976-79; Wolfson, 1979-80
Economics, Social & Political Science, Law

Qualified as Solicitor in 1983, and in practice since then. 1977- 81 Active in Tory Party. Since 1982, Westminster City Councillor. Active in many aspects of Local Government, and author of papers on related topics.

de Rothschild, Edmund L.
Trinity, 1934-37
Science, Military History

See *Who's Who*. In 1952 I was junior partner of N M Rothschild & Sons who were signatories to the Principal Agreement with the Province of Labrador and Newfoundland to explore 50,000 square miles in Labrador and 10,000 square miles in Newfoundland for minerals, a timber forest of 1500 square miles and the unalienated water rights. The latter included the Hamilton Falls, later renamed the Churchill Falls, and was the largest development in Canada this century up to 1970. I have re-established the Exbury Gardens of some 250 acres, which are open to the public from March to July and to which over 100,000 visitors come annually.

Diamond, Judy
Pembroke, 1986-
Economics

Doll-Steinberg, Alfred
Gonville & Caius, 1952-56
Natural Sciences, Chemical Engineering
> Worked in Oil and Construction Industries until 1972; now in Finance. Married, three children.
> *The Society was a significant component of my four extremely enjoyable years at Cambridge.*

Domb, Ann (Mrs. Ebner)
Newnham, 1958-61
History
> Bridge in Britain award to Israel; taught in U.S.A. and travelled, lecturing in Far East; career in teaching and adult literacy (Churchill Fellowship 1981); currently lecturer in College of Technology. Member , Supplementary Benefits Appeal Tribunal and a J.P. Married, three children, Jo q.v. at Homerton.
> *Amazingly busy centre of Jewish life. Canteen and Friday night speakers the most important aspect for most students. A comfortable base for Jewish students who were, like myself, active in other aspects of C. University life.*

Domb, Cyril (Professor)
Pembroke, 1938-41, 46-49, 52-54
Mathematics
> 1941-46 Radar Research, Admiralty; 1949-52 ICI Fellow, Oxford; 1954-81 Clerk Maxwell Professor of Theoretical Physics, Kings College, London; F.R.S. 1977; Professor of Physics, Bar Ilan University 1981; Academic President, Jerusalem College of Technology (secondary appointment) 1986. Married, six children, four grandchildren.
> *My undergraduate period during the War years was characterized by the presence of a large evacuee Jewish community in Cambridge. Among the evacuees were a former Chief Rabbi, Dr. Hertz, and a large number of refugee Rabbis from Germany and Austria. The students had to fight hard to avoid becoming submerged, but, in fact, they managed to retain their independence and to take the lead in all Jewish affairs.*

Doran, Alan
Clare 1968-1971
Engineering, History and Philosophy of Science.
> Left Chartered Accountancy for Postgraduate Economics, then worked succesively for Schumacher, Economists Advisory Group and now freelances in economic research and consultancy. Has published several books and reports mainly on small firms sector. Also runs small market statistics firm from home. Increasingly active in Masorti movement: co-founder of local Shul. Married, two children.
> *In my day the Jewish Society fought externally to gather in the exiles, and*

internally over the purpose of the harvest. The food tasted better than it looked. Our year was a great one for Aliyah.

Drake, Stephen Keith (Kedar, Shmuel)
Fitzwilliam, 1976-79
Hebrew, Arabic, Law

Married Deborah Baum *q.v.* and made Aliya in September 1979. Served in Israeli Army, Judge Advocate General Corps as Prosecutor and Defence Counsel for 'wayward' soldiers. Demobbed 1983 with rank of Lieutenant. Since 1982 reside in Kibbutz Kfar Etzion, work in Gas equipment producing factory. Three children.

The food was greasy — but the Society had a heart of gold!

Drukker, Cyril Mark
Sidney Sussex, 1938-41
History

1941-46 Royal Air Force; 1946-80 Civil Service (Assistant Secretary, Department of Trade and Industry and Office of Fair Trading). Honorary Secretary, Jewish Historical Society of England. Three children, eight grandchildren.

The CUJS provided in our day a unique example of complete undergraduate control of the Synagogue and its various activities which now seems to have been compromised.

Eban, Raphael (Dr.)
Pembroke, 1943-46
Medicine

Qualified at University College Hospital, London 1950; National Service as doctor 1951-53; since then NHS Consultant Radiologist; 1960-87 at Ealing and as Hon. Senior Lecturer at the Royal Postgraduate Medical School; retired 1987 to become a hospital manager. Divorced and remarried, two children.

To be honest, material considerations rather than spiritual ones drew me to Thompson's Lane; the canteen in the hungry years of the War had food, not only Kosher, but good and satisfying! It is a pleasure to acknowledge this, forty years on.

Ebner, Jo
Homerton, 1985-
B.Ed — Education & Religious studies

Edgar, Leslie I. (Rabbi Dr.)
Christ's 1924-1928
History, Oriental Languages

Post-graduate King's College, London, 1928. Associate Minister Liberal Jewish Synagogue, London 1931-48, Senior Minister 1948-61, Minister Emeritus 1961-1984. R.A. Chaplain's Department Jewish Chaplain to H.M. Forces 1940-45. Honorary Rabbi Hebrew Union College Jewish Institute of Religion, Cincinnati. U.S.A., 1951. Co-chairman London Society of Christians and Jews 1954-78, Co- president, 1981-84. President of the London Society for the Study of Religion, 1949 and 1966. Honorary Life President, Union of Liberal and Progressive Synagogues. Honorary Life Vice-President, World Union for Progressive Judaism. Deceased, 1984.

Honorary Secretary of Cambridge Hebrew Congregation and the Schech-

ter Society, 1927, and subsequently President of the Hebrew Congregation. Took part in the Consecration Service of the Cambridge Synagogue, 1937.

Ehrenstein, Janine
Jesus 1981-84
Medical Sciences, Natural Sciences
> Royal Free School of Medicine 1984-87; M.B. B.S., 1987.

Eilon, Daniel (Dr)
Gonville and Caius 1977-85
English
> Stayed in Cambridge to write Ph.D on Jonathan Swift. Secretary of Cambridge Traditional Jewish Congregation. Lectureship in Department of English and Comparative Literary Studies, University of Warwick, 1984; currently lecturing there. Married.
> *I have very pleasant memories of davening at the kabbalat shabbat services, eating appalling overcooked food, listening to some very tedious and pompous speakers, and dozing at the crazy Tickun Leil Shavuoth. Like everyone else, I loved the Simchat Torah riot, where one year Ann Gainsford (yes, a woman) got an aliyah, to the highly comic chagrin of a couple of residents (guess!). I also have fond memories of friends of mine as Presidents of the Society. The Jewish Society Building Committee was an old joke in my brother Amir's day (up at Caius ten years before me). Are there any plans for rebuilding this century?*

Elata, Chaim (Professor)
Trinity
> Visiting Professor, now President of Ben Gurion University.

Ellenbogen, Gershon
King's
Classics, Psychology, Law
> R.A.F. 1940-46; Bar exams 1939; Called to the Bar 1948. Deputy Circuit Judge 1977-81; elected to the Bar Council 1952 and 1955; committee member Bar Musical Society and formerly of Bar Theatrical Society; has acted as interpreter and translator at international legal conferences; Fellow of the Chartered Institute of Arbitrators; Supervisor at several Cambridge colleges 1952-60; Part-time lecturer in Law at Sussex University, 1970-72 and at Reading University 1973-78. Has published widely on various legal topics. Vice President of the Maccabeans; Member of the Council of Friends of The Hebrew University. Married (Eileen Alexander *q.v.*); one child, two grandchildren.

Ellis, David Leon
Trinity Hall, 1976-79
> Read for the Bar. After a brief stint as pupil barrister and a student of Brussels University, changed to a career in the City. Spent five years in the international division of Warburgs and am now recovering from the traumas of the 'big bang'. Married to a divine young lady introduced to me by Cambridge friends.
> *CUJS will be remembered by me for its excellent cameraderie, and the constant striving for a cuisine that matched. It brought me together with a fabulous group of people who, I hope, will remain my friends for life.*

227

Ellison, Mark
Clare, 1970-73
Mathematics, Economics
> After three years articles in Manchester, my home town, two years in London, two in New York and two in Paris with an international accounting firm, I took an MBA at INSEAD (Fontainebleau). Am now financial director of Reynolds European, a French metals trading company. I live in Paris with my French wife and two very young children.
>
> *I hope that the CUJS has made some gastronomic progress since I was senior canteen officer!*

Epstein, E.N. 'Teddy'
Trinity 1933-36
Engineering
> Went into family firm then Army (R.E.M.E.); returned to family firm, later as M.D.; on its take-over joined partnership in Merchant Bank; retired in 1981. Married, three children, six grandchildren.
>
> *I recall Herbert Loewe leaving a Shabbat service in disgust at the speed of my reading the Prayer for the Royal Family after accelerating because we were running late.*

Epstein, Jonathan A.
St. Catharine's 1963-66
Geography
> Did a P.G.C.E. in Bristol and then began teaching at Tiffin School, Kingston-upon-Thames; am still there as Head of Upper School; recently contributed to *Anglo-Jewry in Evidence* and am involved in education within the Reform movement. Married, two children.

Fairmont, Moss
L.S.E. 1939-41
Economics, Statistics
> Directed to essential government work at the Ministry of Supply, Ministry of Aircraft Production; after end of war worked in National Coal Board, Road Haulage Executive; Aliya in 1951; worked in various Government departments, currently with Ministry of Communications, Head of International Relations Department. Married, three children.
>
> *CUJS and Thompson's Lane was where we 'evacuees' met our fellow students and the locals, and was a pleasant refuge in those days of war. It played a vital role in enabling Jewish students, away from home, to keep in touch with Jewish life, and provided an intellectual forum for learning about Jewish and non-Jewish affairs.*

Falk, A.
Downing, 1972-75
History
> Qualified as teacher. Education Director, Association for Jewish Youth 1976-77; Housemaster, Carmel College, 1977-82; Jerusalem Fellowship, 1982-85; currently Headmaster, Independent Jewish Day School. Married (Stanton, q.v.), three children.

Fenner, Trevor I. (Dr.)
Selwyn, 1962-66
Mathematics, Computer Science
> After leaving Cambridge took lecturing post in Computer Science at Birkbeck College, University of London. Married in 1969. Spent 1971-72 as

Visiting Assistant Professor at Queen's University, Kingston, Ontario where my elder daughter was born. Have now returned to Birkbeck. Have two daughters and a son.

I recall washing-up the Cholent pot after Shabbat — is there still a duty rota for this? CUJS showed that Jews of all inclinations can get on together with a little tolerance and goodwill. I hope it is successful in helping to reverse the current trend of polarization.

Filer, David Samuel (Dr.)
Fitzwilliam, 1951-54
Natural Sciences (Medicine)

Qualified at London Hospital, and have been in General Practice in London since 1958. Appointed Police Surgeon in 1965. Active in medical journalism for past 15 years. Currently researching into medico-legal incidents in the Tanach. Married, four children.

One of the our CUJS problems was that of keeping the meat fresh. It used to come from the Hassidic 'settlement' at Letchworth weekly. There was an uproar when I bought, for five pounds, a small 'frig' from the son of our non-Jewish cook. How do you Kosher a 'frig' — the orthodox wanted to know, whilst other members were not so worried.

Filer, Paul Andrew
King's 1976-79
Economics

Joined Price Waterhouse in 1979; qualified as an accountant in 1982; 1987 joined Guinness plc..

I was a passive member of the Society. It was always a vibrant religious and social centre — and provider of chicken soup.

Fineberg, Naomi A. (Dr.; Mrs. Bergbaum)
Girton, 1978-81
Medicine

Clinical Medicine at Guy's Hospital. At present training in Psychiatry at St. Mary's Hospital, London. 1984 married Edwin Bergbaum *q.v.*

I was President of CUJS in the Lent term 1981, at a time when there were major rifts in the Cambridge Jewish community, revolving round synagogue matters.

Finlay, Ronald Adrian
St John's 1976-79
Economics

Joined British Market Research Bureau in September, 1979 as Research Executive; joined Merrill Lynch in 1982, working as a broker in London and New York; moved to Valin Pollen in 1983 to combine marketing with financial experience; appointed to the board in 1986.

Fireman, Bruce A.
Jesus, 1963-66
Law

Qualified as a solicitor 1970; law practice until 1974 when I joined a merchant bank; became a director in 1976, originally specializing in corporate finance, then head of technology department; 1986 founded my own business specializing in financing technology and communications.

I have fond memories of the Society, especially as I met my wife (Barbara Mollett q.v.) there.

Fliegelmann, Margalit (Margaret)
Newnham, 1977-80
Anthropology, Archaeology

Born in Rumania; grew up in Venezuela. Harvard 1976-77. After Cambridge went to USSR for two weeks and have lived in Israel ever since. Have been free-lance editor and translator; currently Assistant to the Curator of Tribal Art, Israel Museum. Divorced, one child.

The CUJS was especially important for me as I was 30 when everyone else was 18-21. I was foreign and so had no family to go to for a Friday evening or holydays. I remember with special fondness evenings around the bonfire on Lag BaOmer or Israel Independance Day.

Florentin, Clive
Churchill 1983-86
Engineering

Started working for Austin-Rover in Birmingham.

Fluss, Sev S.
Trinity Hall, 1956-57
Agriculture (Postgrad. Diploma)

After a marvellous year at Trinity Hall went to University of Wisconsin in Madison where I did research in agricultural science. Returned to Cambridge in 1960 to work for Commonwealth Agricultural Bureaux as scientific abstractor. Joined World Health Organization in 1965 as editor in Health Legislation Unit. Have been Chief of that Unit since 1984. Member of international Council on Environmental Law and International Editorial Board of *American Journal of Law and Medicine*.

Memorable lectures by George Steiner, George Mikes and many others. Disappointed, though, not to have heard some of the eminent Jewish academics at Cambridge, who often seemed indifferent to the remarkable example of Jewish self-governance displayed by CUJS. Quite a contrast to the paternalistic approach to Jewish student activities that I witnessed soon afterwards at the Hillel Foundation at the University of Wisconsin.

Fox, Howard
Trinity, 1956-59
Economics

Chairman of Inter-University Jewish Federation 1960; qualified as chartered accountant 1960; married 1965; Honorary Treasurer B'nai Brith Hillel Foundation, 1971-77. Financial Representative, Muswell Hill Synagogue, 1980-86.

Fox, Kevin Francis
Jesus, 1984-
Natural Sciences, Medicine

Fox, Stephen Michael
Gonville & Caius, 1968-71
Natural Sciences

Spent two months doing research at the Technion, Haifa. Then worked for seven years at the National Institute for Medical Research in London. I joined Merck, Sharp & Dohme Ltd in 1978, eventually reaching the position of Manager, Sales Research and Information Services. After six and a half years at MSD I left to work in the international business development group of IMS (Intercontinental Medical Statistics). I am currently assigned to the creation of a new range of products and services for IMS in America.

Frankel, William
L.S.E. 1940-3
Law

> Practiced at the Bar in London 1944-55; General manager of the Jewish Chronicle 1955-58; Editor 1958-77. Represented CUJS on Board of Deputies 1941-3. C.B.E. 1970.

Frankenberg, Ronald J.
Gonville and Caius 1947-50
Natural Sciences, Archaeology and Anthropology

> Postgraduate work in Anthropology with Max Gluckman at Manchester; research in Wales; was Education Officer to South Wales Area National Union of Mineworkers; returned to teach at Universities of Manchester, Zambia and Keele; retired early to develop Medical Social Anthropology still at Keele. Married three times, five children.
>
> *I was Treasurer of the Society — probably the worst ever; I was also Secretary of Jewish Society. It was central to my life at Cambridge.*

Freedman, B. Clive
Pembroke, 1974-77
Law

> Called to the Bar 1978; practiced at the Bar in Manchester since 1980. Married.
>
> *Memories: Police arrest of ex-Yeshiva Bocher at Jesus for drunkenness on Purim; falling off ladder in synagogue while trying to repair clock. The J-soc was a second family — it's all about the warmth and friendship of the members.*

Freedman, Laurence S.
Trinity Hall, 1966-69
Mathematics

> Spent one year in Yeshiva in Israel; returned to London to study Statistics; career in medical statistics with Medical Research Council, the last ten years in Cambridge; due to move to Washington D.C. in 1988. Married, four children.

Freeman, Alan
Trinity, 1947-50
Modern Languages, History

> Joined Inland Revenue Department 1951; District Inspector of Taxes at various offices in London and provinces; currently at Head Office. Activities include voluntary work for Jewish and non-Jewish organizations, solo singing, scrabble, walking. Married, three children.
>
> *It attracted (and still does) too few of the total Jewish student population. It probably has less appeal to non-practising Jews and Reform and Liberal Jews, than to Orthodox Jews, and should try to widen its appeal.*

Freeman, Harvey
Trinity 1984-87
Classics

> Interest in word games has produced a second and third place in National Scrabble Championships (1980, 1985) and victory in Channel 4's 'Countdown' Series, 1986, and its 'Champion of Champions' tournament, 1987.
>
> *Active in Jewish Society, serving as Senior Canteen Manager and Secretary. The Society caters extremely well for the minority who most need it, but at the expense of the irreligious majority. It is difficult to see this long-established polarity being conquered, but a new and better equipped building would increase the society's appeal.*

Friedman, Joan Enid
Girton, 1937-40
Classics

Wartime experience: as translator in the Foreign Office, at Bletchley Park. Postwar career in librarianship: posts held successively in Birmingham University Library; as Assistant Librarian at University College of North Staffordshire (now University of Keele); as Librarian and secretary, Cambridge Institute of Criminology; as Senior Lecturer, Sheffield University Postgraduate School of Librarianship and Information Science. Retired in 1980.

Membership of CUJS played an important part in my student life. I hope the Society will continue to flourish.

Fromson, Bernard (Dr.)
Emmanuel, 1977-80
Medical Sciences, Computer Science

Qualified as a doctor from Charing Cross Medical School in 1983. Spent three years in hospital medicine. Now undertaking a Ph.D. in the use of computer-aided imaging techniques as a diagnostic tool. Married 1978, Sarah Hubert *q.v.*

Furst, Lilian R. (Professor)
Girton, 1952-55
German

Taught German at Queen's University of Belfast 1955-66; Headed Comparative Literary Studies, University of Manchester 1967-71; emigrated to U.S.A. 1971. Have taught at Harvard, Stanford, Dartmouth, Texas, William & Mary. Published seven scholarly books and many articles. Hold Bataillon Chair of Comparative Literature at University of N. Carolina.

I was a member of CUJS and looked forward to Friday night dinners as an oasis of warmth and conviviality.

Gaba, Phyllis (Dr. Hackett)
Newnham, 1967-70
English

Went to Israel on graduating and taught at Hebrew University for some years. Now work as Hebrew-to-English translator. Married with two children.

Games, Stephen
Magdalene, 1974-77
Architecture

Reviewed for the *New Statesman* while at Cambridge; 1977-78 free- lance writing, followed by eight months on the design department at BBC TV; 1979-81 Deputy Editor, Journal of the Royal Institute of British Architects; 1979-84 Architecture correspondent, *The Guardian*; 1981-86 wrote and presented documentaries for BBC Radio 3; 1984-86 presenter, *New Premises* a new weekly Arts magazine on Radio 3; Summer 1986 joined *The Independent*.

I look forward to seeing a new building on the site of the old one.

Gamse, Ian
Christ's, 1979-83
Mathematics

1984-87 Hebrew Studies; research in Hebrew at St. John's College.

Garcia, Philip Marc
Trinity, 1981-84
Mathematics

> I am working for a firm of International Management Consultants and studying to be an actuary.

Gergel, Simon
Trinity, 1984-
Mathematics

Gibson, Stephen L.
Sidney Sussex, 1984-87
Economics, Management Studies

> Went on a round-the-world tour; am about to embark on a postgraduate computer science course at Cambridge.

Gillis, J. (Professor)
Trinity, 1929-35

> 1937-39 and 1945-47 lectured in mathematics at Queens University, Belfast; 1939-45 War Service; 1947-76 Professor of Mathematics at Weizmann Institute, Rehovot; since 1976 Professor Emeritus.
>
> *Have held in turn all the offices of the late Schechter Society and C.H.C., in the days when the synagogue was a shed behind a sports shop in Sidney St. and the Schechter Society used to have its communal Friday night dinner and subsequent meetings at Thurston's cafe in Emmanuel St. I suppress a whole collection of reminiscences, to save wear on the editor's scissors.*

Gilroy, Keith Stuart (Dr.)
Churchill, 1977-80
Physics

> 1981 Joined Central Electricity Generating Board at Leatherhead, Surrey. Moved to CEGB Wilmslow in 1984, to develop NDT techniques for power station inspection. Married.

Glass, Antony Julian
Gonville & Caius, 1959-62
Law

> Qualified as a Solicitor and set up my own practice. I was President of Wembley Chamber of Commerce in the 70's and am presently Chairman of the Jewish Youth Orchestra. Also a confirmed Zionist and heavily involved in the J.I.A.
>
> *Was President of CUJS Michaelmas 1981 when we celebrated 25 years of the Society by holding a Ball in London. Abba Eban, the first President of CUJS wrote the introduction to the Ball brochure.*

Glass, Jennifer (Mrs. Hillman)
Newnham, 1962-66
Music

> Taught for three years at Frances Holland School NW1 while writing music reviews for *The Times* and giving occasional piano recitals. 1969-70 Lectureship at Homerton College, Cambridge. 1970 married and taught at Trinity College of Music and Guildhall School of Music and Drama, London. Took several years 'maternity leave'. 1979 returned as Professor of Musicianship and Piano to Guildhall School of Music and have remained. Still composing; various performances and publications. About to embark on a concert tour

to Canada with piano duo.

Occupied much of my time during my first year. Many pleasant meals, lectures, encounters. Thereafter music took up most of my time. Still in contact with many good friends from J.Soc.

Glynn, Sarah Rosalind (Mrs. Tillotson)
Trinity, 1978-81
Architecture

1982-84 Completed the Diploma in Architecture at Oxford Polytechnic. 1984 Married. 1985 Qualified as an architect.

Goehr, Alexander (Professor)

One of the leading figures in British musical life today. After study at the Royal Manchester College of Music (where fellow students included Harrison Birtwistle, Peter Maxwell Davies, John Ogden and Elgar Howarth) and a year in Messiaen's master class in Paris, he worked as a copyist, translator and BBC producer. He became Professor of Music at Leeds and since 1976 has held the Chair at Cambridge. Goehr's catalogue of works includes the opera *Arden Must Die*, a triptych of music-theatre pieces and two large-scale choral and orchestral works. A book of articles and interviews, *The Music of Alexander Goehr*, edited by Bayan Northcott, is published by Schott. A second opera, *Behold the Sun*, received its world premiere in 1986 in Düsseldorf.

Goldberg, Jonathan
Christ's, 1978-82
Natural Sciences, Chemical Engineering

D.Phil. at Balliol College, Oxford since 1982. Submitted thesis summer 1986 and awaiting viva. Since 1985 am computer programmer for CEGB. Married, one daughter.

I was active in the Society during my stay, and found it and its members a wonderful experience. In my day the Society found the right balance between catering for the needs of its more observant members while at the same time welcoming all Jews to its activities. I hope it manages to continue like this in the future.

Goldenfeld, Nigel David (Professor)
Pembroke, 1976-82
Natural Sciences

After obtaining my Ph.D. I spent three years at the Institute for Theoretical Physics, Santa Barbara, California. Currently on faculty at the University of Illinois at Urbana-Champaign, doing research in condensed matter physics, teaching and participating in a physicists' boycott of Star Wars. I was co-author of a booklet *Your Career and Nuclear Weapons: A Guide for Young Scientists and Engineers*. I publish widely and have given many talks about my work, Star Wars, and the involvement of the United States in supporting fascist regimes throughout the world.

My main participation in the Jewish Society was in trying to respond to anti-Semitism at Cambridge.

Goldhill, Simon David (Dr.)
Kings, 1975-78, 79-
Classics

Cambridge, England to Cambridge, USA (Harvard) and back to Cambridge. Teaching Classics at King's since 1982. Married Shoshana Rosenfeld q.v., one son. Published two books on Greek tragedy.

Goldinstein, Edgar (Dr. Bendor)
Christ's, 1946-49

Spent four years at Imperial College and four in the aircraft industry. Migrated to Canada in 1957, married and moved to USA three years later. Settled in the same Long Island community for twenty seven years. Following twelve years in two Universities and the aerospace industry, opened my own business in 1972. Married, two children.

Remember with affection the many friends made at Thompson's Lane and regret that I have now lost contact with almost all.

Goldrein, Neville Clive
Pembroke, 1942-43
Law

Joined Army, commissioned, served in Italian East Africa. On demobilization qualified as a solicitor and established my own practice. Now Consultant with Deacon Goldrein Green. Public life consisted of 29 years in Local Government including Mayor of Crosby, Vice-Chairman and then Leader of Merseyside County Council and numerous other appointments. *See Who's Who* etc.

The most interesting recollection was a Seder. There were numerous American Air Force servicemen stationed at the Bull Hotel (which we called Bull College) who joined us. It was the first time I had heard the four questions *with a strong American accent. The role of the Society was vital then and I am sure it is just as vital now.*

Goldstein, Gabriel
King's, 1960-63
Mathematics

Took post-graduate training for teaching mathematics. Taught, and researched into teaching maths and computing. Joined Unilever Ltd. as analyst in 1969 and became manager and later director of product development with the CRC Group. Have been a member of Her Majesty's Inspectorate of Schools since 1976. Married, three children.

The Society's strength was that it succeeded in catering for such a broad spectrum of religious commitment and belief. Although it was never easy to find individuals willing to serve as officers in most capacities, there was undoubted commitment by a large minority, a variety of study groups and much humour. It was a DIY community and enhanced the meaning of Judaism for me.

Goldstein, Michael Robert
Trinity 1979-81
History

Returned to United States; worked as a political Scientist in Washington D.C.; currently completing Law School and a Ph.D. at the University of California at Berkeley.

Goldstein, Robert B.
Magdalene, 1962-65
Mathematics I, Economics II

Career in Management Consultancy, involving considerable overseas travel.

The Society played a key role in introducing me back into Judaism. I especially remember the Friday night dinners, and the opportunity to meet other Jews.

Goldstone, Andrew F.
Emmanuel, 1984-
Law

Goldwhite, Harold (Professor)
Queens', 1950-56
Natural Sciences, Chemistry
> Post-doctoral, Cornell University 1956-58; Lecturer at UMIST 1958-62; since 1962 Professor of Chemistry at Cal. State, Los Angeles. Married, four children.
> *I was treasurer of CUJS for a year or two; money was always tight because of the difficulty of collecting for Friday night dinners! I recall lively Friday night services and some impressive Purim plays.*

Golker, Ivor
Queen Mary College, London, 1943-44
> RAFVR — demobbed in 1947. Afterwards 'Hachshara' training farm at Bosham and Habonim leader in Manchester until going to Israel in 1950. Married in Kibbutz HaEmek where we live.

Goodhardt, Gerald J. (Professor)
Downing 1950-54
Mathematics, Statistics
> After twenty years in industry and commerce, returned to academic life in 1975. Currently Sir John E. Cohen Professor of Consumer Studies at The City University Business School. Married, two children.
> *My most vivid memories of Thompson's Lane (apart from the food) are of the triannual general meetings. How often did we try to repeal the laws of thermodynamics in order to save on fuel costs?*

Goodman, Elliot R.
Queens', 1983-86
Medical Sciences, Natural Sciences
> *President, CUJS 1985; Chairman, CUJS Building Committee 1984-; Secretary, CUJS 50th Anniversary Appeal 1986-. CUJS is a social, cultural, religious and educational focus for Jewish students. A breeding ground for communal leaders. A happy place -long may it prosper!*

Goodman, Peter A.
Gonville & Caius, 1974-77
Law
> Spent one year in Israel after Cambridge; returned 1978 to London to Qualify as a Chartered Accountant; 1987 admitted to partnership, specializing in taxation. Married, one daughter.

Goodwin, Stephen Paul
Emmanuel, 1977-80
Economics
> Joined DVA Yerushalayim Yeshiva in Jerusalem; returned to England 1981 to train as a chartered accountant; qualified in 1984; now work part-time as an accountant and pursue Rabbinical studies at the London Academy of Jewish Studies in Golders Green. Married, two children.
> *Friendship with other Jewish students within an Orthodox, yet tolerant, environment as a result of which I increased my interest in Judaism and eventually went to Yeshivah. The Society should increase its commitment to Jewish education.*

Goorney, Norman Jacob (Dr.)
Clare, 1937-40
Anatomy, Physiology, Biochemistry, Pathology

> Completed Medical studies at London Hospital E.1.; 1942-45 various appointments at London hospitals; 1945-48 medical practice at Haverhill, Suffolk; 1949 medical practice in Tottenham with appointment as police surgeon; 1970 onwards lived in Israel, working for Kupat Cholim; now retired. Married, two children, four grandchildren.

Gottlieb, Aviva (Dr. Zornberg)
Girton, 1962-65, 66-70
English

> Taught English Literature at Hebrew University 1969-76. Published translation of Biblical commentary. Teach Bible and Midrash at Michlelet Beruria and at the Jerusalem College for Adults. Married with three children.
>
> *The Society provided a lively focus for Jewish student life. Organizing cultural activities, running the canteen, a term as President, all were an important part of my total Cambridge experience. I wish the Society growing success in engaging Jewish hearts and minds.*

Gottlieb, Paul
St. Johns', 1964-67
Economics

> Morrison Research Fellow, University of Nottingham and Hebrew University for M.Phil. thesis on 'Jewish Social Mobility'. Joined Post Office 1970, becoming Investment Manager Girobank in 1975, Director in 1982, with Board post as Director Corporate Banking in 1986. Subsequently joined Greyhound Corporation as Managing Director, Greyhound Guaranty Ltd. Lived in Ealing on return from Israel. Active in local politics. Councillor 1974-78; Chairman of Planning; Chairman of Labour Group; Chairman of Brent Community Health Council 1976-78. Active in early days of British Friends of 'Peace Now'.
>
> *Remember being J.Soc. President and Israel Society Chairman in the days before extreme religious polarization. It would be good to feel that tolerance and mutual respect between the variety of approaches to Jewishness could be properly established by the Cambridge Jewish student body.*

Grant, Warren Lewis
St. Catharine's 1973-76
Law

> Called to the Bar in 1977; went to Jerusalem in 1979; worked at the Bar for six years in London; now practice as a solicitor. Still play jazz. Married with two children.
>
> *I was Synagogue Secretary and Canteen Manager. I went back to the Jewish Society in 1984 and the food tasted much better than in my day.*

Green, Anthony L. (Dr.)
Downing, 1975-78
Medicine

> Since 1985 in General Medical practice in Leeds. Married, one child.

Green, Jeremy B.A.
Peterhouse, 1980-83
Natural Sciences

> Worked on virology at the Weizmann Institute, Rehovot before starting Ph.D. research at Centre for Biotechnology, Imperial Institute, London.

Green, Stuart H. (Dr.)
Trinity, 1957-60
Natural Sciences

Completed clinical training at Middlesex Hospital; worked in various hospitals in and around London for about five years; specialized in pediatrics and spent two years in Lexington, Kentucky, USA; returned to Birmingham in 1970; Senior Lecturer at University of Birmingham, Pediatrics and specialist in Child Neurology from 1976 to date.

For me the JS was a home from home; lunch very often, Friday evening meal almost without fail. A very eclectic group incorporating a wide range of religious and political beliefs. Excellent discussions and very good visiting speakers. One year Pesach fell in term and we had an excellent Seder. Soon after coming down I helped arrange a 25th anniversary celebration in London. I will be sad to see the Society split into too many factions.

Greenberg, Daniel
Trinity, 1982-86
Law

Reading for the Bar.

Greenberg, Michael (Dr. Green)
Trinity, 1933-39, 47-49
History, Economics

After academia (Fellow of Trinity, Visiting Fellow, Harvard) mostly involved in international economic affairs: Board of Economic Warfare (Washington), IMF, GATT, Central Bank of Ceylon (Director of Economic Research); also editorial staff of *Petroleum Economist, The Banker* (Editor); currently in the City as an economic advisor. Married, three sons, one journalist, two scientists (J.B.A.Green *q.v.*).

One vivid memory is of a Spring day in May 1948, when a number of us spontaneously gathered in somebody's rooms at Trinity to drink to the just declared State of Israel and sing a rather solemn Hatikvah.

Greenburgh, Edna Patricia (Mrs. Chayen)
Resident

Bar practice 1954-61. Settled in Israel 1964; Called to Israel Bar 1972; Teacher in Tel Aviv University Law Faculty 1972- 75. Married, two children.

My father was appointed Public Analyst for Cambridge at about the time I was born. Among my earliest memories I recall going to the old 'Schule' in Sidney Street. I was among the children under Emil Marmorstein's Tallit on Simchat Torah. I remember the excitement of the opening of the new synagogue and the stress laid on the fact that this was the students' synagogue to which we, the residents, were invited to attend.

Greenwood, Jeffrey Michael
Downing, 1954-57
Law

Admitted as a solicitor 1960. Joined firm of Nabarro Nathanson, where I am presently Senior Partner. Have lectured and published articles on Property Law. Chairman, Jewish Welfare Board, Member, Executive Council of the Anglo-Israel Association and Trustee of the English Friends of the Jerusalem College of Technology.

My enduring memory of CUJS is of a very tolerant community where Jews of diverse views and differing religious practice met happily together. It was the embodiment of K'lal Yisrael.

Gross, Frances L.
Queen Mary College, 1944-45
Mathematics
> Taught in secondary schools in London until the chance of early retirement allowed me to settle in Israel in 1980. Here I am enjoying life with a series of voluntary jobs including guiding at the Israel Museum.
> *The Society was the centre of much social activity, a great deal based on the synagogue and the Services there. Friday night suppers waited on by the men students. At that time, there was a kosher meal each weekday.*

Gruder, Jeffrey Nigel
Trinity Hall, 1973-76
Law
> Bar practice since 1977, mainly commercial cases. Married, two children.
> *The Society was warm and friendly. The food, however, was appalling. Unfortunately the Society was not attractive to the broad mass of Jews in Cambridge. It had an over-orthodox reputation. My hopes are that it could become a Society which attracts all Jews in Cambridge.*

Guttman, Egon (Professor)
Pembroke, 1945-48
English
> Studied at L.S.E. for Ll.B and Ll.M. Middle Temple Practice 1952-53; Sudan Political Service and Khartoum University 1953-58; Founder editor Sudan Law Journal and Reports. Lectured at Heidelberg University 1958; Professor North Western University 1958-59; Rutgers University 1959-60; University of Alberta 1960-62; Howard University since 1962; American University since 1964. Advisor to various U.S. Government Agencies. Several books and articles on Legal subjects.
> *A warm place where one was accepted whatever one's strength or weakness.*

Haberman, Philip
Trinity, 1974-77
Mathematics
> Qualified as chartered accountant 1980; spent 1984-85 in New York; now a Senior manager at Peat, Marwick McLintock. Married.

Haberman, Steven (Professor)
Trinity, 1969-72
Mathematics
> Joined Prudential as actuarial trainee in 1972. Left to join City University as Lecturer in 1974. Qualified as Actuary in 1975. Promoted via Senior lecturer (1979), Reader (1983) to Professor of Actuarial Science in 1985. Married, three children.
> *CUJS was an important focus of student life, both at lunch times during the week, and more importantly, on Friday night and Shabbat morning. It enabled me to meet people from wide range of social and religious backgrounds. Many of the friendships established there have continued over the past 15 years.*

Halford, Miles Benjamin David
Trinity Hall
Economics
> Chartered Accountant 1961 specializing in corporate finance and securities industry regulation. Member of The British Mycological Society, London

Natural History Society and Itchenor Sailing Club. Member of Islington Council 1968-71. Married, four children.

The three years that I spent at Cambridge were a very happy period of my life: not that I have had many miserable periods. The Jewish Society made a large contribution to my enjoyment of Cambridge. The generally tolerant attitude of the members to each others' views, even though they came from a wide spectrum of observance, is something which I hope will remain a permanent feature of the society and enable all members to associate and worship together amicably.

Halpern, Adina
New Hall, 1978-81
Law

Studied in Brussels for a year; joined Slaughter & May as an articled clerk where I still work as a commercial solicitor.

Halpern, Vivian (Professor)
Jesus, 1957-61
Mathematics, Physics

Postgraduate at Mathematical Institute, Oxford 1961-64. Post-doctoral research at Department of Electrical Engineering, Imperial College, London 1964-66. Since 1966 at Bar Ilan University, Physics Department, Associate Professor since 1974. Married, four children.

Harris, Ansel Zev
St. Catharine's, 1943-44, 47-50
History, Political Economy

1950-54 Israel, Prime Minister's Office. 1954-84 Executive, Marks and Spencer. Since 1984, Partner, MBA Consultancy. Community activities have included Member, Board of Deputies; Chairman, Jewish Council for Social Responsibility; National Treasurer, OXFAM. Two children, *q.v.* Katerina.

Was President CUJS Michaelmas 1948. Most vivid relevant memory was the Service to mark the establishment of the State of Israel in May 1948.

Harris, Katerina
St. Catharine's, 1983-86
Law

Management trainee, Lloyds Merchant Bank.

In my first year a Jewish Women's group was established. Despite the feminist connotations the meetings proved to be a stimulating mix of companionship, support and intelligent discussion.

Hartstone, Jeffrey
Queens', 1975-78
Economics

Worked for Boston Consulting Group and then qualified as a chartered accountant. Now a partner in a London practice. Married, two children.

CUJS filled an important role for me in providing Kosher meals and Jewish company. I remember Friday nights in Cambridge with much affection.

Hayman, Zvi
St. John's 1936-39
Natural Sciences

Immigrated to Palestine, December 1939; Research student, Department of Physical Chemistry, the Hebrew University of Jerusalem, 1940-46; Ph.D.

1947; served in I.D.F. during the War of Independence; since then, continued working in above department of the Hebrew University; now working on Stereoscopy as a teaching aid in science and medicine. Married.

During my time at Cambridge, the Thompson's Lane Synagogue was built and the C.U.J.S. formed by the amalgamation of a number of constituent societies, thus encouraging constructive contact between Jews from widely different backgrounds and holding a multitude of opinions. I hope that such a broad-minded attitude still persists since it seems to me to be more necessary today than ever before.

Heller, Charles
Trinity Hall 1965-68
Natural Sciences

Held posts as Science and Music teacher at Hasmonean Boys School, London, and was a Science teacher at the Jewish Free School. Currently Music Director, Beth Emeth Bais Yehudah Synagogue, Downsview Toronto, Ontario. Has published several articles on Jewish Musicology and Hazzanut. Major contributions include setting of the Prayer for the Welfare of the Queen and Government of Canada, which was performed in the presence of Her Majesty in 1984.

Heller, Michael A.
St. Catharine's, 1955-58
Economics, Law

Qualified as Chartered Accountant in 1961. Chairman of following public companies: London & Associated Investment Trust plc; Bisichi Tin Company plc; Electronic Data Processing plc.

... Main memory was of Friday evenings and spontaneous warmth of the experience. Hope it will continue to be a medium by which those who wish to identify can.

Herwald, Basil M.J.
Queens', 1972-75
Law

After completing Articles in London and Brussels returned to North West England, eventually to be a partner in own firm of Solicitors. City Councillor, special interests: education and housing. Chairman of Manchester Jewish Bicentennial Commission.

Herzog, Chaim
University College, London 1939-41
Law

See Who's Who, Jewish Year Book. President of State of Israel.

Heymann, Michael (Dr.)
King's, 1953-57
History

Joined staff of Central Zionist Archives in Jerusalem, of which I became director in 1971. Have published some scholarly articles and edited collections of historical documents.

I joined the Society mainly to disprove the notion that Israelis kept apart from diaspora Jews. Attended services on Holydays and occasionally Shabbatot. Also came to lectures which I thought interesting. Made several Jewish friends at Cambridge, but none through the Society. To me, an Israeli Yekke, the kind of Jewishness represented by the Society was not only foreign but also not very attractive.

Hill, Oscar William
Gonville & Caius, 1950-53
Natural Sciences
> Consultant Psychiatrist at the Middlesex Hospital. Married, three children.

Hoffmann, Ian Michael
Magdalene, 1981-84
Computer Science, Natural Science
> Joined a computer consultancy in Manchester in October 1984. Moved to Stockholm, Sweden in May 1985 to work on an assignment with Shell.

Hubert, Sarah (Mrs. Fromson)
Girton, 1977-80
Natural Sciences
> Married in 1978 to a fellow student *q.v.* Spent four years with various commodity broking houses. Completed MBA course at the London Business School. Since August 1986 portfolio manager with American Express Asset Management.
>
> *...It was brilliant being married in Cambridge — like playing house whilst having the opportunity to study with the best people in my field and to socialize and make friends with a wide variety of people. The experience changed my life after growing up in a small provincial community with few Jews.*

Hulbert, David Ian
Pembroke 1972-1975
Natural Science
> Joined Civil Service and worked for five years at the Ministry of Defence; left Defence for Postgraduate Medical School gained an MSc in toxicology; subsequently worked as an analyst in the City; currently training for the rabbinate at Leo Baeck College.
>
> *I have the warmest memories of CUJS as a real chavurah that did much to help me and others survive feelings of isolation in the initial period at University, when we felt lost amidst the enormous sea of anonymous students. To belong one did not have to pretend to be clever or talented or ideologically committed — all that was required was that one should be oneself. I always looked forward to the Erev Shabbat communal supper, despite the food and the premises. It seemed an oasis far from the frenetic pressures of University life.*
>
> *Just as CUJS answered social needs, so the small group of progressives under the wing of Rabbi Nicholas de Lange (Reader of Rabbinics) met spiritual needs. Four members of that group in the early 70s went on to become rabbis. Soon I hope to become the fifth. Although I was a keen member of Dr Simon Schama's History group and attended several of Dr Stefan Reif's occasional shiurim, I regret that in my time there was no opportunity for regular formal study of the classic Jewish texts properly taught in classes, such as are available at any American university with a sizeable proportion of Jewish students.*

Huttner, Bruno
Kings, 1983-84
Mathematics
> French military service in Antarctica 1984-86; started studies towards a Ph.D. in Physics at the Technion, Haifa in 1986.

Isaacs, Gillian D. (Dr Yudkin)
Newnham 1961-64
Natural Sciences

Clinical studies at University College Hospital, London and qualified as a doctor in 1967; worked in Mwanza, Tanzania on the V.S.O.; returned to London to train as a General Practitioner; went back to Tanzania in 1975 and worked for two years in Child Spacing Clinics; returned to London in 1977 as a part-time G.P.; in 1980 became a Principal in my training practice in Kentish Town; currently still working there. Married to John Yudkin (St John's, 1961-64) with two children.

I have never been particularly religious, but joined the Jewish Society more for social reasons. I enjoyed teaching the young children in the Sunday morning Hebrew classes.

Isaacs, Jonathan Michael
Queens', 1982-83
Law

Worked for a firm of Solicitors in London for a year, then joined a stockbroking firm and was sent to Hong Kong, where I now work as a stockbroker. Married.

Very much enjoyed hearing interesting speakers at Friday night dinners, like Leon Brittan before he became Home Secretary. My father, Alan Isaacs, an old Queensman, remembers much the same Friday nights at Thompson's Lane and we both wish CUJS every success for the next 50 years.

Israel, Norman C.
Perse School, 1944-48

Left Perse July 1948 on closure of Hillel House, and completed schooling at City of London School. After National Service became a solicitor and subsequently Deputy County Court Registrar. Married, three children.

During my four years at the Perse School, and particularly during vacations, I acted as substitute Ba'al Koreh at the University Synagogue. I have vivid memories of Dr. Fox, at one time Senior Treasurer of the Society, regularly standing at his lectern during the reading of the Torah and being most annoyed if someone had taken it before he arrived.

A particularly memorable incident occurred on Simchat Torah 1945 when Rabbi Kahana was in residence reading for his Ll.M. He led the dancing in the Synagogue holding a Torah Scroll in one hand and a bottle of whisky in the other. Among the other congregants was Mrs. Loewe, the widow of Herbert Loewe, sometime Reader in Rabbinics, and mother of Raphael Loewe, subsequently a Professor at University College, London. From an Anglo-Jewish patrician family, she was horrified and aghast at the Rabbi's antics and vowed loudly never again to enter the Synagogue. Tragically, she kept her vow, for she died before the end of the year.

The Perse had a long standing connection with the synagogue. Harry Dagut, who was Housemaster at Hillel House from 1928 until his untimely death in 1944, was a founder member of the I.U.J.F.

It was compulsory for all boys to attend the Synagogue on Saturday and on the first days of those festivals which occurred in term time. A small number of boys, of whom I was one, who came from orthodox homes, attended also on the second day. During vacation particularly there would barely have been a Minyan had the boys not attended.

The most long-lasting impression, however, on my adolescent mind was the ecumenical manner in which the Synagogue was conducted. The Synagogue was open to all Jews, of whatever persuasion.

Jackson, Paul Leslie
Magdalene, 1984-
Classics

Jacobs, Laurence
Queens', 1979-82
History
> Returned to Cambridge, a year after graduating, to undertake postgraduate research at King's College into modern political thought.

Jacobs, Lesley (Mrs. Robinson)
Churchill, 1976-78, 79-80
Modern & Medieval Languages
> Began Masters course in phonetics in London, but gave it up due to lack of funds. Married in 1981 and left for United States where I worked for 2 years for the Head Start program. I am now a full time mother looking after my daughter and loving every minute of it.

Jacobs, Sam
Selwyn, 1978-81
English
> Worked for Union of Jewish Students as National Chairman and then as General Secretary of Poale Zion; married in 1985 and travelled to Far East and South America with my wife; currently working in software industry having spent 1986 working in High Technology industry in Israel.
> *I hope that the J.Soc. food has improved.*

Jaffe, Victor
Emmanuel 1972-75 1979-80
Medicine
> Clinical Studies at Westminster Hospital, London; returned as Honorary fellow, Anatomy Demonstrator and Pathology Tutor at Emmanuel College, 1979-80; F.R.C.S., 1983; Burghard Research Fellow, Royal College of Surgeons 1985-87.

Janner, Daniel Joseph Mitchell
Trinity Hall
Law
> Barrister; editor *Litigation Law Journal*; Parliamentary candidate (Labour) 1983; joined Conservative party 1986. Member, Board of Deputies Law and Parliamentary Committee. Married, one daughter.
> *As President of the Union, the J.Soc was a fabulous base for political votes and excellent nearby meals! The J.Soc's London social evening a week before I went up for my first term, was the first and most influential of all Cambridge meetings I ever went to: I met many who later became my best friends — no less than two were ushers at my wedding. I hope that J.Soc will never move out of Thompson's Lane, which being next door to Trinity Hall's annexe makes life highly convenient for orthodox Hall men.*

Janner, Greville (Hon.- Q.C.,M.P.)
Trinity Hall, 1949-52
Economics, Law
> Harvard Law School, 1952-53; called to Bar 1955; M.P. for Leicester North West/West 1970; President, Board of Deputies 1979-84; President, Commonwealth Jewish Council, Jewish Museum etc.; Member, Select Committee on Employment; Vice Chairman, Parliamentary British Israel and Soviet Jewry Group; Secretary, War Crimes Group; author, journalist, lecturer.
> *Regular Friday night dinner, source of lifelong friendships, and fond memories of Jewish arguments which stretch on...*

Jay, Barrie (Professor)
Gonville & Caius, 1946-49
Medicine

Left Cambridge for University College Hospital, London. Studied ophthalmology at Moorfields Eye Hospital. Consultant Ophthalmic Surgeon The London Hospital, 1965-79. Consultant Surgeon Moorfields Eye Hospital since 1969. Dean, Institute of Ophthalmology, University of London, 1980-85. Consultant Advisor in Ophthalmology, DHSS, since 1982. Professor of Clinical Ophthalmology, University of London, since 1985. President, Faculty of Ophthalmologists, 1986. Married with two sons.

Jayson, Raymond Victor
St. John's, 1957-60
Mathematics, Business Management

Qualified as Chartered accountant 1963. Joined Swiss Israel Trade Bank 1965 as member of London Directorate. Joined First National Finance Company 1968, became a Director of the Bank and Managing Director of its Industrial Leasing Company. Formed own small merchant Bank in 1974. I was senior warden of Elstree Synagogue for seven years and represented the synagogue on the United Synagogue Council and at the Board of Deputies where I was on the Foreign Affairs Committee. Emigrated to Israel in 1983. Married, two children.

I greatly appreciated the friendship and support of the Society, where I met my wife. I hope the Society will assist Jewish students to retain and strengthen their Judaism in their University years and believe it has a vital role to play in this respect.

Jedwab, Michael R.
King's, 1979-82, 1983-
Engineering, Aerodynamics

Spent a year from July 1982 at Hebrew University, Jerusalem. Currently completing Ph.D. thesis.

In the six years that I have been a member the Society has grown in strength, and now caters for religious, political and cultural activity.

Joseph, Anthony Peter (Dr.)
Trinity, 1955-58
Medicine

While training at St. Bartholomew's Hospital, London married Jane Mindelsohn, grand-daughter of Rev.Dr.A.Cohen. Worked at Bart's until 1963, then one year in Sydney, Australia. Currently in General Practice in Smethwick (since 1964). Actively interested in Genealogy and Heraldry. First wife died in 1984 leaving three children. Married Judith Levy in 1986, thereby becoming brother- in-law to Rabbi Vivian Berman, a Cambridge contemporary.

CUJS was very much a focal point, and was impressive as being able to house all wings of opinion from very orthodox to very liberal.

Joseph, Neil (Dr)
Gonville and Caius 1968-71
Medical Sciences

Represented The United Kingdom in Maccabiah games, Israel 1969; Clinical Studies at Westminster Hospital; full medical qualification 1974; moved to Manchester from London 1975; currently General Practitioner in Bury, Lancs.; Governor of Broughton Jewish Cassel Fox Primary School, Salford. Married, three children.

The Jewish Society helped to buffer the break from home to independence. It was instrumental in consolidating my commitment to Judaism, and allowed unlimited culinary experiment. The society was directly responsible for enabling me to meet my future wife in the term after I went down from Cambridge.

Kahn, Richard (Professor Lord)
Trinity
> See *Who's Who.*

Katz, Jordan I.
Darwin, 1981-82
History, English
> Playwright, Screenwriter working in New York and Los Angeles.

Kay, Sarra
Queens', 1984/5
Law
> Presently completing the rigorous training of an Articled clerk in City solicitors firm specializing in shipping law.
>
> *Although J.Soc was principally for undergraduates, I was a regular participant and I got a great deal out of attending; friends, education and spirit. I never ceased to be impressed by the standard of religious enthusiasm of the members and by the fact that it was so positively active. I was very fortunate, but I would like to have seen a greater participation of postgraduate students, who were somewhat abashed at turning up to Friday night sessions.*

Kaye, Alan
Christ's 1969-72
Mathematics
> Fellow of Institute of Actuaries.
>
> *C.U.J.S. filled a very useful role as a meeting point for all those committed to or wanting to find out more about Judaism.*

Kaye, Andrew
Clare, 1985-
Natural Sciences

Keidan, Joshua Marcus
St. John's, 1930-34
Classics, Law
> 1934-36 at London School of Economics. Called to the Bar 1936. Joined Ministry of Health in 1938. 1942-46 in Army. Retired from DHSS 1927. Married, two sons.

Keller, Alex (Dr.)
Peterhouse, 1950-53, 61-63
History
> Research at Oxford on Late Byzantine Empire 53-56. Hebrew University 1956-57; I.D.F. 1957-60. Worked at Whipple Science Museum, Cambridge 1960-63; teach History of Science, and History (including Jewish history) at Leicester University since 1963.
>
> *The Friday night suppers at J.Soc. are among my most vivid and most enjoyable memories of Cambridge, where friendships were made more firmly*

*and more warmly than in College. Even if I changed ideas on many subjects,
the atmosphere of the Jewish society somehow remains. I remember Charlie
Kuper (now a Professor of Physics) abolishing the laws of thermodynamics
in an attempt to keep the place warm.*

Kelly, Vivian H.

St. John's, 1953-56
Mathematics

> Worked on computer software and applications since 1956. Married, two
> children.

Kessler, David F.

Clare, 1924-27
Economics, Law

> Entered commercial life in London and Paris. 1930 in Aden for A.Besse as
> Shell Co. agent. 1934-35 in Palestine with Palestine Potash Co. 1936 joined
> Jewish Chronicle as Managing Director. 1940-46 war service, from Gunner
> to Major in R.A. and Iraq Levies and PWE. 1946 returned to Jewish
> Chronicle, later becoming Chairman. Married, four children, seven grand-
> children.
>
> *In my time the Schechter Society, as it was then called, was a happy ship
> and truly ecumenical; services were held in Sidney Street and were conducted
> by undergraduates of all sections of the community.*

King-Cline, Anthony L.

Trinity,1954-57
Natural Sciences

> Qualified as a Chartered Surveyor. Married to a Sculptor, three children. I
> work for a large property company and am Master of a pack of Basset
> Hounds.
>
> *Happy Friday nights — my hope is that the tolerance to all Jews returns.*

Kleinman, Philip

Jesus, 1951-54
History, English

> Spent two and a half years in Kibbutzim; returned to England in 1957;
> journalist since 1959 including three years with AFP News agency in
> France, *Jewish Chronicle* columnist, freelance editor of *Marketing Break-
> through* newsletter, and *World Advertising Review*. Three children.

Klug, Aaron (Sir)

Trinity, 1949-52
Natural Sciences

> Research student at Cavendish Laboratory Ph.D. 1953; Research on virus
> structure, London 1953-61; returned Cambridge 1962, as Fellow of Peter-
> house and Director of Studies in Natural Sciences and as member of staff
> of MRC Laboratory of Molecular Biology, of which am now Director. Various
> honours, including F.R.S. 1969 and Nobel Prize for Chemistry 1982.
>
> *Used to come to Kosher lunches which were attended by non-orthodox as
> well. In my day there was an absence of the deep division between the
> orthodox students and the rest which is prominent today, and which I
> deplore. John Rayner, and others like him, used to come to Shabbat morning
> services. I hope the extended synagogue and centre will serve as a focus for
> gathering in non-orthodox students who seem to be regarded as marginal by
> the activists in the Society.*

Knapp, Alexander V.
Selwyn, 1963-70; Wolfson, 1983-86
Music

Churchill Fellow 1976; travelled to North America to study Ethnomusicology with special reference to Jewish music; lecturer, Goldsmiths College 1976-77; Assistant Director of Studies at Royal College of Music 1977-83; Visiting Scholar, Wolfson College, Cambridge 1983-86; at present freelancing as musician and musicologist. Married, two children.

Irregular attendance at Thompson's Lane and also 'Progressive' group, but glad to keep in touch with friends made there at the time.

Knopf, Chanoch — Henry (Dr.)
Queens', 1965-72

Assistant under-librarian at the University Library with responsibility for Taylor- Schechter Genizah Collection. Aliya 1972 to Bar-Ilan University Jewish Sciences Library. Married, three children.

Enjoyed seven 'fat' years of Jewish contentment on the whole with the Sassoon and Fachler families providing homely environment at Letchworth especially for invigilation periods.

Kochan, Anna Nadya
Kings, 1974-76
Engineering

Completed Engineering degree at Sussex University, and then trained as a technical journalist. I am the editor of four publications on automated manufacturing technology, and published my first book — on computer integrated manufacturing in 1986.

I shall never forget Saturday nights at J.Soc when the 'cholent' pot had to be washed out.

Kohorn, Ernest I. (Professor)
Downing, 1946-49
Medicine

Qualified at University College Hospital, London. Came to United States in 1968, to Yale University, where I am currently Professor of Gynecology.

Kopelowitz, Lionel (Dr.)
Trinity, 1944-47
Natural Sciences

University College Hospital 1948-51. General practice in Newcastle upon Tyne since 1953. Married 1980. Have been active in Jewish communal life since undergraduate days. Currently President, Board of Deputies; World Vice-president, World Jewish Congress; President, European Jewish Congress; President, National Council for Soviet Jewry. Active in Medical affairs: Member, Council of British Medical Association; Member, General Medical Council; Member, General Optical Council, appointed by Privy Council.

Korn, Peter J.
Emmanuel, 1986-86
Law

Am presently at Law School in London, and hope to qualify as a solicitor.

In my days the Society was strong, religious and male-dominated. I would like to see it reach out more to the less committed, but not by religious coercion. I also hope that more women will become involved.

Kornberg, Justin Anthony
Trinity, 1947-50
Natural Sciences

> Bradford Technical College 1950-53. London School of Economics Diploma in Business Management 1956. Joined family business which became Listers & Co. PLC of which am now chairman. Warden, New London Synagogue 1982-85; First Chairman and President, Anti- Boycott Campaign of British Israel Ch. of C.; Member of Council, British Israel Ch. of C.; First Chairman, Industrial Property Group, Bradford and founder of the Trans-Pennine Club.

> *CUJS is a good institution. Made many friends and contacts there which have withstood the test of time. The contribution to my development was more social than cultural. Lunches and Friday night dinners in those days of rationing played an important part — Floreat CUJS!*

Kornbluth, Jonathan S.H. (Professor)
Queens', 1963-66
Mathematics

> Took Doctorate at Imperial College, London; in 1972 came to live in Israel, teaching Operations Research at the Hebrew University. Two children.

> *The chickens at the Jewish Society seemed to have more than two legs each! I hope that the Kosher food continues to improve.*

Kuper, Charles G. (Professor)
Fitzwilliam, 1946-52
Maths, Physics

> Liverpool University ICI Fellow 1952-56; St. Andrew's University 1956-67; Professor at Technion since 1967. Widower, two children.

> *CUJS served as a social centre for all Jews — apikorsim (like myself), Reform, Traditional and Ultra-orthodox, with a degree of mutual tolerance sadly lacking in present-day Israel. I understand from friends that CUJS has lost this balance, and I hope that it will regain it.*

Lachs, Henry L. (Judge)
Pembroke, 1945-49
Modern languages, Law

> Called to Bar, Middle Temple and practiced on the Northern circuit 1951-79; Chairman, Merseyside Mental Health Review Tribunal 1969-79; Circuit Judge since 1979. Got much involved in Jewish education as Chairman of Governors of Liverpool King David Primary School 1965-70, and High School 1970-8. President and teacher at Liverpool Yeshiva for many years. Married, four daughters.

Landes, Susanne (Mrs. Ottenstein)
Newnham, 1951-54
History

> Awarded Smith-Mundt fellowship for postgraduate study at Harvard, but did not take it up because of marriage to George Ottenstein (Pembroke 1952-54). Worked for I.C.I. in New York 1955-60. Have done a variety of volunteer jobs, notably the recording of numerous books for the Jewish Braille Institute. Two children.

Landy, Aron (Dr.)
Jesus, 1980-86
Mathematics, Engineering

> Completed Ph.D. in 1986. Deserted academia for a job in a bank in the City.

Landy, Barry
Jesus, 1956-63
Mathematics

Stayed on at Cambridge, doing Maths III followed by research in Nuclear Physics. In 1963 I switched to the Cambridge University Mathematical Laboratory and have been engaged in 'computing' ever since. Married in 1961 and have three sons.

Since 1963 I have been Senior Treasurer of CUJS and have seen a steady growth in the size and vigour of the Society, paralleled by a similar growth in the local community, and in the contacts between the two groups. In my student days the CUJS was responsible for the maintenance of the premises, and for the conduct of most services, other than the High Holydays. Now three-quarters of the running costs are paid by the residents, who make good use of the premises when not required by the students, and contribute in many other ways to improve Jewish student life. I hope that this will continue and flourish in modernized and enlarged premises.

Landy, Francis (Dr)
Jesus 1966-69
English

Wrote Ph.D at Sussex University on *The Song of Songs*, published as *Paradoxes of Paradise: Identity and Difference in the Song of Songs* (Almond, 1983); became Assistant Professor of Jewish Studies at University of Alberta, July, 1984.

The Society was entering one of its more dynamic, if pietistic phases, with an unusual conglomeration of bright people. Somewhat elitist. Definitely not a sixties phenomenon, except in so far as an interest in kabbalah and Hassidut was developing.

Landy, Joshua
Churchill, 1984-
French, German

CUJS is a focal point for social life in Cambridge; sure to continue producing its own idiosyncratic mixture of Cambridge 'types'.

Landy, Rosalind (Mrs.)
Clare, 1980-82
Medieval & Modern Languages (French)

After graduation stayed in Cambridge doing research into 19th century French literature. Now am teacher of Latin. Married in 1961, three children.

I recall 'generations' of undergraduates playing with our children, Michael Brandeis, Eliot Berry and many others.

Lang, Charles A. (Dr.)
Emmanuel, 1957-60
Mechanical Sciences

After working at Mullard Laboratories and Massachusetts Institute of Technology I returned to Cambridge in 1965 to lead a Computer- Aided Design research group at the Computer Laboratory. Founded Shape Data Ltd. in 1974 and Three-Space Ltd. in 1986, both in Cambridge. Married, three children.

I hope the Jewish Society will always be equally welcoming to all Jewish students in Cambridge.

Lass, Jonathan D.
Downing 1965-68
Law

> Qualified as a solicitor in 1972; in private practice until 1977, specializing in Corporate Law; joined Citibank as European legal Counsel until 1986; returned to private practice as partner in Lovell, White and King, London in 1986.

Lassman, Jack
Fitzwilliam, 1951-54
Natural Sciences

> Belgian Government scholarship at University of Brussels 1954-55. Research chemist at Glaxo 1955-60; later worked with Fisons, Smith Kline and French, and Beecham Pharmaceutical until I set up my own chemical company in 1973. Am on committee of Fitzwilliam Society and on the Technical Committee of the British Israel Chamber of Commerce. Married, three children.
>
> *At Cambridge I was college representative and an officer of the Society.*

Lasson, Kenneth (Professor)
Wolfson, 1985
Visiting Scholar, Faculty of Law

> At Cambridge I did research concerning British law on incitement to racial hatred, and taught in the area of American civil liberties. Resumed duties at University of Baltimore School of Law, conducted seminars on Dispute Resolution, Law and Social Reform, Civil Liberties. Published book (Mousetraps and Muffling Cups). Married, three children.
>
> *Have pleasant memories of the Cambridge community which welcomed us with warm and open arms. We still feel very much a part of the community and miss it, particularly the walk to Thompson's Lane every week through the park. We hope that Thompson's Lane will continue to flourish, its physical facilities improved and expanded, but its spirit and character(s) forever intact.*

Latchman, David S.(Dr.)
Queens', 1975-81
Natural Sciences

> Research for Ph.D. at Cambridge then at Imperial College, London; currently Lecturer in Molecular Genetics at University College, London.
>
> *Revived the Schechter Society in 1980 and chaired it for a year.*

Lawson, David N. (Dr.)
Emmanuel, 1960-63
Natural Sciences

> Took Ph.D. at Imperial College, London; worked for Shell, I.C.I., and now am Managing Director of Lauter (UK) Ltd., a subsidiary of Tootal. Married (Judith Rich, met at J.Soc.), two children.

Lee, Alix (Mrs. Pirani)
Newnham, 1948-52
Modern languages, English

> Taught English in schools and colleges 1952-74 while bringing up four children; became psychotherapist and group facilitator, taking degree in humanistic psychology 1980, with special emphasis on creative process; now dividing time between therapeutic educational work, and writing poetry, plays, fiction and non-fiction. Particularly concerned with exploring and

encouraging women's spirituality and creativity.

It was important as a social educational centre, and since I was very orthodox for most of my years at Cambridge, a religious centre. I hope it will survive with variety and flexibility in its Jewishness.

Leighton, Jeremy D.

St. Catharine's, 1977-80

Economics, Management studies

Joined London On-Line Local Authorities in 1980 as a trainee programmer, and am currently a Principal programmer. Unmarried.

Lesser, Henry

Queens', 1965-68

Law

Married Jane Michaels *q.v.* in 1969. Called to the Bar 1969; taught at Fitzwilliam and at Lincoln College, Oxford 1969-71; Harkness Fellowship, Harvard Law School 1971-73; emigrated to USA 1976; practiced corporate law in New York until 1983; currently a partner in the Los Angeles office of a national law firm, specializing in corporate takeovers and mergers; widely published on that topic; for relaxation run marathons.

The synagogue played an important role in my adjustment from school to university but, most importantly, it brought me and my wife-to-be together.

Levi, Michael

Robinson, 1984-

Political Economy

Levin, Naomi Sara

New Hall 1984-87

Mathematics

The Society acted as a social group with relaxed and informal Friday night meals and speakers, as well as protecting Jewish interests within the University. I hope it continues to provide such a nice atmosphere.

Levine, Edward (Dr.)

Pembroke, 1980-83

Medicine

Graduated as Doctor of Medicine at Westminster Medical School in 1986.

Was canteen manager for two terms, and largely achieved ambition to improve service and meals and thereby attract more students especially to the Friday night meals.

Levy, Dennis Martyn

Gonville and Caius 1956-60

Law

Called to the Bar 1960; Granada Group Limited 1963; Time Products Limited 1963-66; 1967 to present in practice at the Bar; called to Hong Kong Bar 1985. Married, two children.

Levy, Ismay Caer (Mrs. Emanuel)

Newnham 1936-39

Mathematics

Practiced as a school teacher and private tutor; served on the Jewish Guide Advisory Council as Treasurer and Chairman. Married (divorced in 1952), two children, two grandchildren.

I was a member of C.U.J.S. and attended services regularly. I also served on the committee in various capacities.

Lewis, Jonathan Malcolm
Downing, 1965-68
Law
> Qualified as Solicitor 1968; now joint head of commercial department of D.J.Freeman & Co. Writer and lecturer on various aspects of commercial law. Married, two children.
> *The Jewish Society embodied a traditional yet tolerant form of orthodox Judaism from which the Anglo-Jewish community can learn much. Through its members, may it remain a light to the Anglo-Jewish community!*

Lieberman-Leigh, Sara (Dr. Levene)
King's, 1972-79
Natural Sciences, Medical Science
> Worked in hospital medicine, obtained MRCP in pediatrics. After two years in medical research married and broke off work to raise son. Currently part-time medical advisor to Child Accident Prevention Trust.

Lightstone, Liz (Dr. Goodman)
Newnham, 1977-80
Medical Sciences
> Qualified at Kings College Medical School, London in 1983 and married Ian Goodman q.v. Currently on low — middle rung of career in hospital medicine and managing to bump into my GP husband on occasion.
> *J. Soc. played a very prominent part in my student days, not the least as source of gossip and intrigue! I was involved in the running of the society and designed the programmes. Its legacy is a cohort of friends that I still see and my husband. I hope it continues to provide a similar comfortable 'heimische' setting for students for years to come.*

Linger, Angela M. (Mrs. Benson)
Newnham 1951-54
Modern and Medieval Languages
> Worked in export department of Horrochses Crewsdon, Preston; moved to Manchester 1955; began teaching French at the primary school in 1966 and is currently holding the same post. Married, three children.
> *I have pleasure in reading of the success of some notable contemporaries. I wonder at the degree of tolerance then evinced by members of such varying shades of orthodoxy within the society — so patently lacking in the wider Jewish community of today. The society gave me a feeling of warmth and 'coming home' on Friday evenings; it was my first exposure to serious intellectual orthodoxy.*

Lipson, Eric
> Was President of the Cambridge Hebrew Congregation and Schechter Society from 1927. '... was a contemporary of Judge Gillis (Kyanstiy), Brodetsky junior, Leo Genn, Lord Kahn and many others who have left a mark. In my day we began our Friday evening Supper Meetings, obtaining fried fish from Polly Nathan...'.

Lipson, Henry (Professor)
Cavendish Laboratory, 1938-45
Physics — Crystallography
> See *Who's Who*.
> *The sudden influx of European refugees and evacuees from London led to the formation of a Resident's Committee, of which I was Treasurer, and for a short period Senior Treasurer of CUJS.*

Lipton, Jane A.
Newnham, 1980-84
Modern Languages
> Worked on a minor feature film. Joined a marketing communication agency.
> Currently Public Relation Officer with Chinacraft Group.

Littman, Jeffrey
St. Catharine's, 1961-65
Natural Sciences, Social Anthropology
> Barrister, married, two children.

Loewe, Herbert M.J. (d.1940)
Queens'
Oriental and Theological Triposes
> Brother of Lionel Loewe. Jewish Scholar. University Reader in Rabbinics
> 1931-40. Commemorated by library in the CUJS Synagogue.
> *See* Encyclopedia Judaica, Who was Who 1930-40.

Loewe, Lionel Louis (Major)
Jesus, 1911-14
> Brother of Herbert Loewe.
> Served through First World War remaining in Army until end of Second
> World War. Then practiced as a barrister.

Loewe, Raphael James (Professor)
St. John's, 1938-40, 45-48
Classics
> Served in Second World War in North Africa and Italy, where wounded.
> Thereafter devoted himself to Hebrew and Jewish Studies. Occupied various
> academic positions including Cook Bye-Fellowship at Caius, 1954-7, Finally
> Goldsmid Professor of Hebrew, University College, London until retirement
> in 1984. Two daughters: Elizabeth (Girton), Camilla (Newnham).

Lopian, Jonathan B. (Dr.)
Gonville & Caius, 1978-86
History
> Graduated in June 1981 and remained in Cambridge to complete a doctorate
> on crime and law-enforcement in the early twentieth century. Joined the
> merchant banking group, Morgan Grenfell, as Corporate Finance Executive
> in May 1986.
> *How can one rationalize the appeal of a Society whose meals were often*
> *uneatable and whose guest speakers were often unspeakable? I was simply*
> *very fortunate in being in Cambridge at a time when the Jewish Society was*
> *led by a core of students whose aim almost was to prove that religion and*
> *intellect were complementary. I wish the Society, and future generations who*
> *use it, well.*

Lovitch, Lionel (Professor)
Christ's, 1957-60
Postgraduate studies for Ph.D.
> Assistant Lecturer, Department of Mathematics, Queen Mary College,
> University of London, from September 1960. Resigned a year later to assume
> a research post under the Pisa section of the Italian national institute of
> nuclear physics. A leave of absence during the academic year 1965/66 was
> spent as Research Associate at the Physics Department of Columbia

University, New York with a couple of months stay at the Argonne National Laboratory. Married in New York in September 1965. Associate Professor of Physics at Pisa University from 1967 through 1977; Chair at University of Calabria from 1977 until 1979; Chair of Nuclear Physics at the University of Ferrara since November 1979 and Director of the Physics Department of that university since 1981.

The CUJS was an excellent reference point for Jewish students coming from abroad. I made several lifelong friends although I see them nowadays quite infrequently. I hope that the Friday evening dinner meeting, the canteen and the synagogue continue to attract the student and local Jewish population, and express felicitations and best wishes to the present generation of frequenters on the occasion of the anniversary of the consecration of the Thompson's Lane Synagogue.

Lyons, Louis (Dr.)
Gonville & Caius, 1955-58
Natural Sciences

Went to Oxford D.Phil. in Nuclear Physics, and have been there ever since apart from periods as Visiting scientist at Weizmann Institute, Berkeley and CERN (Geneva). Currently Senior Physics Tutor at Jesus College, Oxford and researching in elementary particles at Nuclear Physics Laboratory, Oxford. Married, two children.

Very happy memories of the Jewish Society. I hope it maintains the spirit it then possessed.

Magrill, Henry
Christ's, 1965-68
Natural Sciences

1968-69 Took M.Sc. in Administrative Science at City University Business School; 1969-82 Beechams Pharmaceuticals, various UK and International marketing positions; 1982-85 with Teva Pharmaceuticals, Israel; currently Senior analyst, Pharmaceutical sector, CIBC Securities Europe Ltd.

Malachi, Zvi (Dr)
1970
Hebrew

Worked on the Genizah for a year; currently senior lecturer at Tel-Aviv University; founded research institute for Literary Research in Lod, 1983.

Enjoyed participating in the activities of the Society: kosher meals, Sabbath and Festival hospitality. I greatly value the work of the Society, as it enabled me to live in Cambridge in a Jewish environment.

Marcuson, Roger W.
Christ's, 1955-58
Natural Sciences

Completed medical training at Middlesex Hospital, London. I am now a Consultant Surgeon at Hope Hospital, Salford, which is part of Manchester University Medical School. I have a special interest in Vascular Surgery.

I cannot claim to have been the most regular attender at the CUJS although I did frequently come to the Friday night services and supper meetings. I have to admit that my most vivid memory was of the appalling table manners at the meals.

Margulies, Alice (Professor Shalvi)
Newnham, 1944-47
English Literature

Studied Social Work at L.S.E. (1947-49) prior to going on Aliyah. Since 1950 I have been teaching at the Hebrew University, specializing in Shakespeare and drama. Since 1975 I have been head of Pelech, a unique experimental high school for religious girls. Since 1984 I have been chairperson of the Israel Women's Network, a non-party group that has been making its mark on our society. Married, six children, nine grandchildren.

Main events recalled: our involvement with DP adolescents in 1946-47 (which brought me to social work); my being the first woman to sing 'zmirot' at Friday night supper (one of my first feminist acts); the ardour of the Shabbat prayers and the delight of our annual 'Purimspiel' — i.e. the 'Yiddishkeit' of the CUJS in my time — coupled with the Zionist fervour that found expression in the Zionist Study Circle; Martin Buber lecturing at Trinity. Our sense of Jewish identity, that is what I hope the Society will continue to foster.

Margulies, William
L.S.E. 1940-43
Economics

1942-45 War work; 1945-83 business career; 1983 retired.

Markham, Maurice Ian
Queens', 1982-85
History

Visited USA, returning late '85 to work for parents. Since May 86, manager of fabric department of small wholesale company.

CUJS served as a useful venue for meeting other Jewish students, and establishing contact with the local community. I would hope this could be extended in the future.

Marks, Fiona Kate (Mrs. Hulbert)
Homerton 1975-76
Postgraduate Certificate in Education

Taught at two Jewish primary schools in London; moved to the Akiva School at the Sternberg Centre for Judaism in Finchley; spent 1986-87 studying sculpture, pottery and graphic design at the Israel Museum. Married to David Hulbert *q.v.*, one child.

Marks, Leon
Sidney Sussex 1958-61
Law

Solicitor, Local Authority Councillor for 10 years. Board of Deputies, initially for CUJS, subsequently for local community. Married, three children. Workaholic longing for retirement. Wistful appreciation of the academic life lingers. Commitment to matters of Jewish interest remains total.

Remember visits to the Society of Lord Waley-Cohen, Rabbi Louis Jacobs, Dr. Israel Brodie; the impressive 'leyning' and fluent Ivrit of two (subsequent) Tory Ministers. The Society then had a United Synagogue orthodox orientation, but was broadly based, with no significant attempt by Reform or other groups to 'split off'. As such, was comparatively strong and healthy. On a Friday evening 70 plus attended (a large number in relation to the total number of Jewish undergraduates). CUJS fulfilled a vital, and to some an indispensable role. Number of Jews in my college — 3.

Maroudas, Celine E.
Clare, 1983-86
Natural Sciences, Experimental Psychology
>Travelled and worked with Missionaries of Charity in India before making Aliyah in December 1986. Hope to study clinical psychology in Israel in the future.
>
>*The Society was important both socially and as a place where one could be openly Jewish. It could sometimes be exclusive, even to Jews, but hopefully this will change as the Presidents become more aware. A new and better building would also be a great help.*

Marsden, Julian
Jesus, 1984-
Engineering, Electrical and Information Sciences

Maurice, Jack
Sidney Sussex 1953-56
Law
>Bar exams 1956; called to the Bar 1957; family business until 1977; six years in Bar practice; joined Institute of Chartered Accountants as Under-secretary in 1983. Married (twice), three children and two stepchildren.
>
>*Though I was college representative for the Society for a year, I wasn't very active, alas, saw more of Thompson's Lane during undergraduacy of my daughter Nicole — same college, course and Director of Studies; better degree.*

Mendoza, Eric (Professor)
Trinity, 1937-40, 45-48
Natural Sciences
>Spent WW2 working with radio in the Admiralty and Navy. Rest of working life entirely academic, at Bristol University, then Manchester and as head of Physics Department in the University of Wales at Bangor, North Wales. Made Aliyah to Jerusalem in 1973 as Professor of Science Teaching at Hebrew University. Published many articles and some books on physics, science teaching and history of physics. President of the Spanish and Portuguese Congregation in Israel. Married, four children, six grandchildren.
>
>*Was the first Suppers Secretary after the Synagogue opened. Previously Friday night suppers had been held in Thurston's Cafe and had become an important part of Jewish student life; an Erev Shabbat and a pleasant alternative to compulsory meals in Hall. In the synagogue it was possible to serve meat. The first menus were not popular and heavier menus were soon substituted. The cooking was done by a lady, Mrs. Gair, who lived in the road opposite and in those carefree days Chief Rabbis ate her meals.*

Merzer, A. M. (Dr)
Churchill 1964-71
Theoretical Physics, Geophysics
>Lecturer in Geophysics in Tel-Aviv University, 1971-76; 1976 moved to the Technion to lecture in Mechanical Engineering; since 1973 has worked on electromagnetic waves at A.D.A., Haifa. Married, eight children.
>
>*Cambridge changed my life. I entered Cambridge non-religious and came out orthodox. The memories — from the pleasant times to the moments of crisis are unforgettable.*

Mestel, Leon (Professor)
Trinity, 1945-51
Mathematics

Research Fellow, Leeds 1951-54; Princeton 1954-55; University Lecturer, Cambridge 1955-66; Fellow of St. John's 1957-66; Visiting Fellow, Weizmann Institute 1966-67; Professor of Applied Maths, Manchester 1967-73; Professor of Astronomy, Sussex 1973-; Elected Fellow of the Royal Society 1977. Married Louise Cole *q.v.*, four children.

CUJS was most important for me. I met my wife there, as well as lifelong friends, Cherns, Stamler, Sciama, Alberman, Loewe, Korner, Squires.

Meyerhoff, Henry J. (Dr.)
Pembroke, 1959-62
Control Engineering (Ph.D.)

Went to Toronto, Canada to work on geophysical instruments and some part-time lecturing. Moved to San Francisco in 1965 and later to Houston, Texas to look for oil. 1968 moved to Washington D.C., into Satellite communications and in 1976 to Geneva to regulate frequencies for the I.T.U. Married, one daughter, one horse and two dogs.

CUJS was a friendly meeting place, especially Friday evenings, for normal and nutty people. Hope it continues in the same way.

Michaels, Jane M. (Mrs. Lesser)
Homerton, 1965-68
Maths and Pottery

Married Henry Lesser *q.v.*, 1969; taught maths in London and at Ely High School, 1969-71; took a degree in computer science from a college in Boston, 1971-73; emigrated to USA, 1976; occupied various data processing positions in New York until 1983; currently a senior systems engineer and project leader with Los Angeles based life insurance company; drive around in a convertible, soaking up the sun.

The Society was a great help to me in adjusting to living away from home for the first time and in making good friends, as well as in enabling me to discover my own Jewish identity. It must remain a permanent part of the Cambridge environment.

Michaels, Leonard
Jesus, 1938-40, 45-46
Architecture

Joined Royal Navy 1940; active sea duty, Mediterranean 1941; operational intelligence at Admiralty 1942-45. Returned to Cambridge 1945-46; Regent Street Polytechnic 1946-48; Registered Architect A.R.I.B.A. 1948. Designed large public housing projects and post-war reconstruction in London. Wrote *Contemporary Structure in Architecture*, New York 1950. Faculty member, University of California, Berkeley 1952-54. Since 1953 in Architectural practice. Designed several synagogues, many public, commercial and housing projects. Married, three children, two grandchildren.

I came from an orthodox home and the Society provided a spiritual and psychological umbrella in an unfamiliar environment. The common culture and interests shared with new friends; the stimulating lectures by distinguished guests; the joyful Friday evening community suppers, complete with singing of Shabbat Zmirot; and the well-conducted services on Shabbat morning (I met my wife at one of these) and other festivals. All these and much more provided a memory never to be forgotten. With Hitler on the doorstep, these were ominous years and the Society provided a strong Jewish identity and political activism against the forces of anti-Semitism which were building up under the leadership of the Nazis.

I have read that these are difficult times for Jewish students at British Universities. I hope that the C.U.J.S. is maintaining today the vigour which it displayed in my time, and is able to provide Jewish students with the support, confidence and pride in their heritage which is so necessary when anti-Semitism rears its ugly head. My prayer for the Society members is 'Be strong and of good courage'.

Michaelson, Harold Montague (Dr.)
St. Catharine's, 1943-46
Natural Sciences, Anatomy, Physiology

> Clinical training at Middlesex Hospital, London; took finals at Cambridge 1950. First Doctor appointment at St. Luke's Hospital, Bradford 1950-51; R.A.M.C. Military Service 1951-53 ending as Major in charge of forty bed Military Hospital, Hadrian's Camp, Carlisle; Senior House Officer, St. Luke's Hospital, Bradford 1953-54 prior to emigration to Canada; Family circumstances compelled me to abandon emigration plans and to assume responsibility for family business; am now Managing Director of the several companies comprising the now much enlarged family business. Nevertheless I remain a Registered Medical Practitioner and retain a close affinity with the profession and regularly attend Medical Refresher courses. Married, two children.
>
> *CUJS was a welcome oasis in the midst of a predominantly non-Jewish community. I recall with warm nostalgia those Friday evening gatherings for Sabbath eve service and supper. Though the meat was sometimes tough, and the meals hardly 'haute cuisine', one readily accepted these shortcomings in return for the happy sing-song (zmirot) after supper, the often interesting talks by a learned member of the Society or by a visiting Speaker, and the warmth of a weekly social occasion shared with others having the same religious, spiritual and educational interests. Oh! happy days! May they long continue for succeeding generations of Jewish undergraduates.*

Miller, Barrie
Trinity, 1941-44
Civil Engineering

> Joined Babcock & Willcox; after the War went to America and joined a store group for English imports; returned to England and entered the Fashion Industry, first as a wholesaler, then a manufacturer and now as a retailer. Have four children (Richard, Daniel *q.v.*), 5 grandchildren. Died 1988.

Miller, Daniel (Dr.)
St. John's, 1978-81
Archaeology & Anthropology

> Lecturer in Anthropology, University College, London.
>
> *Went to J.Soc for Friday night suppers, and married the then President of the Israel Society (Rickie Burman).*

Miller, Harvey I.
St. Catharine's 1943-45, 47-48
Natural Sciences

> 1945-47 Radar Officer, R.N.V.R.; 1947 returned to Cambridge; May 1948 joined Hagana and went on underground route to Israel; established Radar in Israeli Navy; returned to England in 1950 and married; succeeded my Father-in-law in 1955 as publisher of Phaidon Press until 1968; since then have published under my own name. Have three children (Malcolm *q.v.*) and five grandchildren.
>
> *CUJS was a place to maintain contact with Jewish life, religious and*

secular. It was a jumping off point for those exservicemen, like myself, who were not prepared to see the Holocaust followed by the destruction of the Yishuv. I hope it will continue to be a place where each generation of students can develop and express their own relationship to their roots.

Miller, Malcolm B.B.
St. Catharine's, 1976-78
Music

Transferred to Sussex University where I obtained First Class Honours in 1981; continued academic research in London, obtaining M.Mus at King's, London in 1984, where currently engaged in doctoral work; as performer, have concertized extensively as pianist, singer,and conductor; I also write reviews and articles.

The Jewish Society formed a dynamic and central component in the exciting flux of my undergraduate life, adding an essential stability and sense of purpose to the fragmentary and transitory student existence. As well as meeting intelligent Jews in a warm ambience, I was attracted by the creative tension generated by diverse attitudes to Judaism. I hope that diversity will continue to flourish, and to express both the richness and beauty of our tradition, as well as the infinite potential of individual creativity.

Miller, Richard Joel (Dr.)
St. John's, 1972-75
Biochemistry

Joined M.C.R. for a short time, then Burroughs Wellcome at their Research Triangle in Raleigh, South Carolina; currently Professor at University of Chicago heading a team researching into Neuropharmacology.

Moleman, Jason Martin
Trinity, 1985-
Mathematics

Mollett, Barbara R. (Mrs. Fireman)
Newnham, 1962-65
English

Subeditor, Cambridge University Press 1966-67; Educational consultant 1967-81. Married (Bruce Fireman *q.v.*).

It was at the Jewish Society that I made proper contact with fellow Jews, despite not being brought up as one, experiencing an affinity with them which has remained with me.

Mond, Daniel R.
Kings, 1985
Philosophy (Postgraduate)

I came to Cambridge from Australia in 1985, having completed a B.A.(Hons) at Monash University and taught for a number of years at Bialik College in Melbourne.

Having come from overseas, I found the Society very supportive.

Montagu, Joyce Mary (Mrs. Tyrer)
Girton, 1952-55
Modern Languages

1956-61 Worked in Information Research Department of the Foreign Office. 1961 married John Tyrer, (Information Dept., F.C.O.). Three children.

Morris, Geoffrey
Downing, 1953-56
History

After spending fifteen years working for multinational companies, including eleven years with IBM, I founded with a colleague in 1973 Intermatrix Ltd., a management consultancy, now with offices in USA, Italy, France, Indonesia, Switzerland, Thailand. Married, three children.

CUJS in the early fifties was the sole Jewish Society comprising both traditional and progressive elements harmoniously. The programmes were full and varied. It saddens me to learn from my children of the divisions that exist in the Cambridge Jewish community.

Morris, Michael S.
St. Catharine's, 1942-43, 46-48
Mathematics

See *Who's Who*.

I deplore the divisive behaviour of the CUJS since my time and wish to have nothing to do with it so long as this attitude continues. I am therefore not very interested in your proposals.

Moschi, Gabriel
Magdalene, 1945-48
Economics and Politics

Occupation, Managing Director of companies dealing in residential and commercial properties, crude oil and product slops.

The Society formed a valuable nexus for undergraduates to meet and exchange viewpoints. It is to be hoped that this tradition will continue and be extended due to the improvement of the Thompson's Lane facilities.

Mushin, Bernard
London Hospital 1939-41

Retired. Married, three children.

Great friendship and much happiness emanated from C.U.J.S. then. May it go from strength to strength and bring commitment from more Jewish students of all religious shades.

Myers, Braham Jacob
Magdalene, 1939-41, 46-47
Classics, History

Served in Royal Artillery 1941-46; wounded in N.W.Europe 1945; returned to Cambridge 1946-47; Managing Director and Chairman, J.W.Myers Ltd. (Leeds Headwear Manufacturers) and Director, A. & J.Gelfer Plc.; retired 1985. Served on various Health Authorities 1961-86. Awarded MBE in 1985 for services to British Limbless Ex- Servicemen's Association.

Myerson, Arthur Levey (Judge)
Queens', 1948-51
Law

Practice at the Provincial Bar since 1953. Recorder 1972; Q.C. 1974; Circuit Judge 1978; B.A. (Open University) 1985. Married, two sons.

A welcome to all who considered themselves as Jews. One community, one congregation. One would like to see a return to this basic concept, for if we don't hang together we will hang separately!

Nabarro, Rosemary (Mrs. Ross)
Newnham 1957-60
Mathematics
> Computer Programmer – Ferranti, I.C.L.; Mathematician – Weizmann Institute; Systems Analyst – Sheffield University, I.C.L. Stevenage; Mathematics teacher Stevenage College; Deputy Head of Mathematics, St Paul's Girls School; returned to computer world as Senior Project Manager F. International. Married, two children.
> *Fond memories of Friday evenings at the Jewish Society. Grateful for large circle of acquaintances which C.U.J.S. provided.*

Naftalin, Adrian Paul (Dr.)
Trinity 1956-59
Natural Sciences
> Qualified at The Middlesex Hospital in 1962; F.R.C.S. 1967; specialized in Plastic Surgery; entered General Practice 1974. Past secretary, Chairman British Fellowship Israel Medical Association; currently World Executive member I.M.A.; Past Vice President, London Jewish Medical Society. Married, three children.
> *Happy memories of Friday night suppers with lots of singing and laughter. Disappointed that so many Jewish undergraduates did not participate. Strong belief that students should be encourage to identify — the Society should make itself attractive culturally, religiously and Zionistically.*

Nagel, William
Fitzwilliam, 1950-53
International Law
> Am now a Diamond Broker, representing De Beers, in London. Married, four children.

Nagler, Neville A.
Jesus, 1964-67
History
> Joined H.M. Treasury as Assistant Principal in 1967. Various posts in Treasury included Private Secretary to Chancellor of the Exchequer (1970-71). Transferred to Home Office in 1975. Currently Assistant Secretary responsible for policy on drugs and extradition. UK representative at UN Commission on narcotic drugs. Married in 1979, two children. Financial representative of Pinner Synagogue
> *I used to come to the Society on Friday nights. I have many happy memories of stimulating speeches. I remember a delightful communal Seder in 1967, and visits from London groups to whom we showed the sights. An important role for the Society is keeping Jewish life alive for those away from home, despite competition of other social activities.*

Nathan, Lawrence David (O.B.E.)
Emmanuel, 1928-31
History
> After coming down I worked in London as an accountant. About 1935 I worked for a year with the Central British Fund trying to secure permits for German refugees to emigrate to Australia. In 1936 I joined the family firm in Auckland and, except for war service with the New Zealand forces in the 8th Army in Africa, remained with the company until 1977. Married 1947, four children. President, Auckland Hebrew Congregation. Published autobiography As old as Auckland.
> *In 1931 I was for one term President of the Cambridge Hebrew Congre-*

gation and associated Schechter Society. Our synagogue was an unused lecture hall rented from Sidney Sussex College, behind a bicycle shop. In about 1932, while living in London, I was Joint Secretary with Richard D. Barnett, of committee set up to obtain a site, approve plans and organize an appeal for the Synagogue ultimately built in Thompson's Lane. The Chairman was Sir Robert Waley-Cohen, the joint treasurers were Bernard Waley-Cohen and E. de Rothschild.

Nemeth, Cyril (Dr.)
Downing, 1946-49
Medicine

Westminster Hospital; General Practictioner, Northwood and Harley Street. Justice of Peace, Hillingdon; formerly, Hertfordshire County Councillor; now Westminster City Councillor, Vice-chairman Social Services; Member, Bloomsbury Health Authority; Vice-chairman, Hillingdon Family Practitioners Committee.

Neville, Alexa Esther
Sidney Sussex, 1986-
Classics

Newman, Aryeh 'Laibel'
Emmanuel, 1941-44
English

After short experience in England in Rabbinic and English teaching field, emigrated with wife and family to Israel in 1949. Worked with World Zionist Organization in Jerusalem for 25 years in information and Jewish educational fields editing and compiling numerous English publications; With Hebrew University English as Foreign Language Dept. since 1958. Author of *Mapping Translation Equivalence* and translator of Nehama Leibowitz's *Studies in the Weekly Sidra* (six vols.); mission to Australia and New Zealand Jewish community as cultural officer for World Zionist Organization 1962-64. Married, four children, four grandchildren.

Nissimoff, Nico (Professor Nissim Bar-Yaacov)
Fitzwilliam, 1953-54

On returning to Israel joined academic staff of the Hebrew University, Jerusalem and have been there ever since. Married Claire Stonehill *q.v.*, three children.
Pleasant memories of the meetings of the Society.

Niven, Mark Jonathan (Dr.)
Sidney Sussex, 1975-78, 78-80

Junior Hospital posts in Southend, Cambridge, Luton, Bow and Newham; currently Lecturer in Medicine at the London Hospital Medical College. Married (Ruth A. Rose q.v.), one child.
Was an active member of the Society and met my wife there. I have maintained informal contact with the Cambridge community.

Nyman, Regina (Mrs. Allen)
L.S.E. 1943-45
Sociology

Trained as a social worker; worked for I.B.G. and then for the Institute of Marital Studies; now in child and adolescent psychiatry and works as a private counsellor. Married, one child.

I recollect the Society with great affection. Through it I met my husband (S. Allen q.v.) and many dear friends.

Oppenheimer, Andrew
Trinity, 1970-73
Law

Studied EEC Law in Brussels 1974-75; called to Bar 1978; studied at Gateshead Yeshiva 1978-84; now work in legal publishing and as freelance legal translator. Staff member, Research Institute for International Law, University of Cambridge; Fellow, Institute for Advanced Talmudical Studies, Gateshead; Lecturer for Seed/Arachim 'Challenge' seminars for Jewish awareness. Married, two children.

The Society was a meeting place for religious and non-religious Jews. I started off as one of the latter and ended as one of the former. So did several others of my contemporaries, many of whom, like me, came from very assimilated backgrounds! My hope is that the Society can act as a focal point for those who want more than just superficial social life, and, through its educational program can challenge Jewish students to search for a meaning of Jewish existence and come to a truer and deeper understanding of Judaism.

Pearlman, Adrienne
Christ's, 1982-85
Mathematics

Training as a Cost and Management accountant with Mobil Oil Company.

Pearlman, Chaim Zundel (Rabbi)
St.John's 1967-70
Economics

Qualified as Chartered Accountant, practising as sole practitioner from home address. 1986 appointed as Rabbi to Machzike Hadath Synagogue, London NW11. Married, seven children.

CUJS brought together Jewish students from widely differing backgrounds. Many students from less committed and less observant backgrounds became more committed as a result of friendships formed within the Society.

Pearlman, Herman (Chaim)
Queen Mary College, 1942-44
Aeronautical Engineering

Made Aliyah in 1950, initially on a Kibbutz then the Israeli Air Force. On completion of service joined El Al where I became Chief Engineer during the period of absorption of the Bristol Britannia and the Boeing 707. 1964-66 obtained Masters at M.I.T. 1966-68 worked at Boeing-Vertol. On returning to Israel joined Israel Aircraft Industries to undertake sales of the Arava aircraft, the first to be designed and built in Israel. Married, two children.

Pearlman, Joseph
St. John's, 1965-68
Law

Solicitor in London. Chairman, Menora Grammar School; Editor, HaMeir, a weekly commentary on the Sidra; active in North West London Orthodox Community. Married, nine children.

CUJS played a valuable and central part in the formation of the character of the emergent Jewish youth. It is to be hoped that it will continue to inculcate responsibility, a caring attitude, tolerance without compromise of religious principle, and a harmonious co-existence in respect of all its membership.

Pearlman, Robert H.
Churchill, 1985-
Engineering

Perlman, Robert
St. Catharine's, 1962-66
Economics
> On editorial staff of the Economist Newspaper until 1969; then set up a business consultancy in the UK and the USA advising companies in commodity industries; am now primarily involved in property investment and development.
>
> *Friday evenings were often pleasant occasions, but my most immediate memories are of the canteen facilities. They left much to be desired; nevertheless CUJS meals were a welcome relief from the almost unending series of omelettes that were served up at college for anyone who explained that they were vegetarian or on a kosher diet.*

Philipp, Elliot (Mr., FRCS, FRCOG)
St. John's, 1933-36
Medicine — Nat. Sci. Tripos
> Qualified as a doctor from Middlesex Hospital 1939. RAF to 1946 — Squadron Leader, mentioned in dispatches. Married 1939. After training became consultant obstetrician gynecologist at the Royal Northern Hospital and Whittington Hospital and in Harley Street. Two children and four grandchildren.
>
> *I was President of the Jewish Society and was succeeded by Aubrey (Abba) Eban. It was my aim to link the Zionist Society and the Jewish Society, which was successfully accomplished by Eban. It was also my desire to have a permanent synagogue and I was responsible together with Bernard Waley-Cohen and the Sebag- Montefiore brothers and cousins, as well as other undergraduates such as Teddy Epstein, in buying the site in Thompson's Lane. I was not so keen on having the architect chosen by Sir Robert Waley-Cohen nor on his design for the synagogue and argued a*
> gainst this unsuccessfully, preferring a much more imaginative design.

Podhoretz, Norman
Clare, 1950-53
English
> Have been editor of *Commentary* magazine since 1960, and have published six books and many articles. Married, four children, eight grandchildren.

Podro, Michael (Professor)
Jesus, 1951-54
English
> In 1955 went to the Slade School and then to the Philosophy Department, University College, London. After teaching at Camberwell School of Art and the Warburg Institute I went to the University of Essex where I have taught ever since. Married, two children.
>
> *At CUJS I remet old friends and made most of the others with whom I have remained in contact.*

Polack, Bennie H.
King's, 1942-43, 46-48
Classics, History
>   1948-49 Bristol University, Education Department; 1949-86 Sixth form
>   Classical Master (from 1970 Senior Classical Master) Wolverhampton
>   Grammar School. Retired 1986. Married, three children.

Poyser, C.A.
Emmanuel, 1928-31
Maths (Wrangler- 1st class)
>   Joined Yorkshire Insurance Company in London and qualified as Fellow,
>   Institute of Actuaries 1936; joined R.Watson & Sons, Consulting Actuaries
>   1935; became Senior Partner 1971; retired 1974; with Admiralty during the
>   War years. Joint Author of book on Pension Funds.
>
>   *Jewish students met each Friday evening during terms for a meal and*
>   *discussion, during my years of residence before the Thompson's Lane Syna-*
>   *gogue.*

Prawer, S.S. (Professor)
1944-48
English and Modern languages
>   See *Who's Who.*
>
>   *I met my dear wife at a meeting of the Jewish Society; gave several Friday*
>   *night talks to my fellow members; and served as 'Shames' during Synagogue*
>   *services.*

Prevezer, Sidney (Professor)
St. Catharine's, 1948-51
Modern Languages, Law
>   Taught Law at University College, London (Assistant Lecturer, Lecturer,
>   Reader) 1951-63; Qualified as Solicitor 1956; practiced in London 1956-79;
>   spent post-graduate year at Harvard Law School 1956-57; Professor of Law
>   at Sussex University 1979-. Married, four children.
>
>   *I have only dim but happy memories of the Society during my years at*
>   *Cambridge.*

Priestley, Maurice (Professor)
Jesus, 1951-55
Mathematics, Mathematical Statistics
>   Appointed Lecturer at University of Manchester 1957, Professor of Mathe-
>   matical Statistics 1970. Married, two children.
>
>   *The Society was extremely active during the early 1950's, with sub-groups*
>   *organizing meetings on Zionist activities and Hebrew studies. The Society*
>   *also conducted regular Services on Shabbat, and, where appropriate, on*
>   *Festivals. There were also very enjoyable inter-functions with the Oxford*
>   *Jewish Society, the venues alternating between Oxford and Cambridge. A*
>   *joint Dinner and Dance was held annually.*

Rabinowicz, Ernest (Professor)
Emmanuel, 1944-50
Physics, Physical chemistry
>   Went to MIT for post-doctoral year in 1960, and have been there since then,

researching and teaching Mechanical Engineering. Married, three children, four grandchildren.

The Society was my home more than my College ever was. Most of the friends I keep in contact with are people I interacted with in the Society.

Raines, Mrs. Sylvia
Resident

Married at Thompson's Lane, 13th May 1945.

Raphael, Dov Laurence
Gonville and Caius 1972-75
Mathematics

Studied for Actuarial profession; Aliyah 1978; Actuary for Klal Insurance Company, 1980-86; from 1986, planning and control manager of Confectionery Division at Elite Ltd. Married, three children.

Yom Kippur War 1973. Term started in October 1973 immediately after Yom Kippur. Israeli students at Cambridge left their studies in order to fight in their units. Members of the Jewish Society were mobilized to explain Israel's point of view at the Union, and to arrange donations of blood. A large group travelled to a protest rally in Trafalgar Square. The regional television news reported these events and showed Jewish students in the Succah at Thompson's Lane.

Rappaport, Charles David
St. John's 1931-34
Oriental Languages

After Army service in the Intelligence Corps succeeded the late Professor I. Talmon as Secretary of the Palestine Committee of the Board of Deputies for the last two years of the Mandate; later rejoined the Board as Secretary of the Israel and Foreign Affairs Committees and their representative and that of the International Council of B'nai Brith at the U.N. Commission for Human Rights etc., for ten years; later three years as Educational lecturer etc. for the Council of Christians and Jews; finally, thirteen years as Assistant Director and then Director of the Jewish Colonization Association (I.C.A.); now am a voluntary assistant at the Institute of Jewish Affairs. Married, two children.

About two years prior to amalgamation had been President of Schechter Society and Congregation, and also of C.U. Zionist Society. Preliminary proposals for acquiring permanent site for Synagogue were made during my Presidency with invaluable support of Lord Kahn, our Senior Treasurer. My philosophy and career were largely influenced by tolerance and interchange of thoughts between all shades of Jewish views, whether ultra-orthodox, moderate (like myself), Reform or Liberal, Zionist or anti- Zionist, members of old Anglo-Jewish families or of recent immigration or refugee families. 'Kol Yisrael Chaverim'.

Rappaport, Rosa (Mrs. Druiff)
L.S.E. 1943-46
Sociology and Economics

Did Research in Sociology under Professor Morris Ginsberg; later was inter alia;- curator of the William Morris Museum, London; a psychiatric social worker; a J.P.; a Governor of schools in Shipley, Yorkshire. Married, four children. Died 1986.

Rashba, Jeffrey David
Clare, 1982-83
History

> After my year at Cambridge I returned to U.S.A. and completed my B.A. at Columbia University, New York. Received a Masters degree in Middle Eastern studies from University of Chicago in 1985 and am currently studying Law.
>
> *My only wish is that I should have spent more time with the Society. As a foreigner, nothing made me feel more at home than the Society.*

Rayner, John D. (Rabbi Dr.)
Emmanuel, 1947-53
Modern Languages, Moral Science, Oriental Languages

> Ordained 'Reverend', served South London Liberal Synagogue 1953-57; joined Ministry of the Liberal Jewish Synagogue, St. John's Wood, where I have been Senior Minister since 1961. Also studied at Hebrew Union College, Cincinatti where I received my Rabbinic Ordination and hon D.D. Since 1966 I have also taught (mainly Liturgy and Codes) at Leo Baeck College London. Married, three children.
>
> *In my time the tensions between Orthodox, Progressives and Secular-Zionists were strong, but good sense and good manners* usually *prevailed. My hope is for even greater tolerance as well as greater interest in what is going on in the world of Jewish (especially critical-historical-scientific) scholarship.*

Reitman, T.H.
Queens', 1940-42, 45-46
Mechanical Sciences

> 1946 went to Palestine and Israel. Returned to UK in 1949 and joined family business; 1955 Director of Perseverance Banking Trust Co. Ltd.; 1957 joined in the creation of man-made fibre industry in Israel.

Reynold, Nick
St. Catharine's, 1956-59
Economics, Law

> Came down with only one clear idea, to have no contact whatsoever with family catering business. 1962 entered family catering business and remained for 22 years. 1984 made Aliyah with one clear idea, never to go near a catering business ever again. Am considering my next move.
>
> *CUJS was a very important part of my three years, where I made many good friends. It was the only Jewish institution unbesmirched by petty politics and machers; a lesson for all to be learned here.*

Reynold, Tony
St. Catharine's. 1952-55
Law

> Did not complete Solicitor's Articles but have had various businesses. Am now an Antiquarian Print and Map dealer.
>
> *Attended orthodox section at University, but was married in the Liberal Jewish Synagogue by Rev.Rayner, who was a contemporary.*

Richardson, Montague (Monty)
Emmanuel, 1938-41
Economics, Hebrew

> Welfare and Youth of the United Synagogue, London directing the Jewish Institute in East London. Actively involved in welfare and youth work, primar-

ily for the Jewish Community. Was Chairman of the Brady Boy's Club and Association for Jewish Youth (now Vice- President). Now, activities include the following: Chairman of the Zekenim Club in East London (first of the Jewish Old People's clubs); Vice-Chairman of the Governors of Tower Hamlets Adult Education Institute; Chairman, Social Security Appeal Tribunal; Chaplain to Jewish prisoners in H.M. Prisons.

Throughout my years at Cambridge the Jewish Society was the active centre for every aspect of Jewish life and attracted the support of the majority of Jewish undergraduates from all sections of the community — Orthodox, Reform, Liberal, Zionist without distinction. From 1940 it welcomed evacuated students from many London colleges, evacuees and distinguished Jewish refugees. We were responsible for every aspect of Jewish communal life, arranging weddings, funerals, services etc. Distinguished evacuees included Chief Rabbi Dr.J.H.Hertz, the former Chief Rabbi of Vienna Taglicht, Professor Samuel Krauss and Ted (Kid) Lewis the famous boxer. I hope that in the future CUJS will welcome Jews of all denominations as it did in the past.

Rickaysen, Gerald (Professor)
Christ's, 1951-54
Theoretical Physics (research)
Main appointments since leaving Cambridge: Research Fellow in the Admiralty; Research Associate at the University of Illinois; Lecturer at Liverpool University; Reader, the Professor and now Deputy Vice-Chancellor, University of Kent. Fields of research have been Solid State and Liquid Physics. Married, four children.

Although I attended the synagogue occasionally, I was not a staunch member and have no useful memoir to offer.

Rogowsky, Zvi (Professor Rigbi)
Queen Mary College, 1939-42
Engineering
Joined I.C.I. and managed to get transferred to Israel before the end of the War. Served in Israeli Air Force, worked in industry, mostly rubber and plastics. Joined the Technion in 1967. Married in Thompson's Lane, one of the first marriages there recorded by the Registrar. Have three children, twelve grandchildren, three adopted.

Recollect with pleasure my part in organizing the Palestine evening (when Palestinians were Jews!!) at Trinity (or Jesus?) attended by everybody who was anybody.

Rose, Diana
Kings, 1974-77
History and S.P.S.
Took Postgrad Cert. of Education at Oxford in 1978; have taught History and Politics ever since; am presently Head of Department at a mixed Grammar School in Aylesbury. Married, one child.

Met interesting people. Good social centre, homely and friendly.

Rose, Ruth Alison, (Dr. Niven)
Clare, 1977-80
Natural Sciences
Qualified in 1985 at the London Hospital Medical School; junior hospital posts in Harlow and the London Hospital; am due to return to work after

birth of child, as Vocational Trainee for General Practice. Married (Mark Niven *q.v.*), one child.

Active member of Society, met my husband there. Maintain informal contact with the Cambridge community.

Rosen, Jonathan A.
Clare 1975-78
Law

Called to the Bar, 1979; went to Jerusalem 1983 and since has studied at Harry Fischel Institute on Advanced Rabbinics Course.

Rosen, Stuart D. (Dr)
Pembroke 1979-82
Medicine

Clinical studies at Charing Cross Hospital; Qualified in 1985; subsequent posts in Hull and Charing Cross; currently Research Senior House Officer (Cardiology) at Charing Cross Hospital. Married (Ann Vecht, *q.v.*, originally met at C.U.J.S.).

Rosenberg, Danny
Gonville & Caius, 1981-84
Law

Law school in London until July 1985. Currently working with Slaughter & May, Solicitors. Married Helena Rudie *q.v.*
Apple crumble.

Rosenfeld, Shoshana Shira (Mrs. Goldhill)
Newnham, 1980-83
Classics, Law

Qualified as a Solicitor. Married, one child.

Rosenfelder, Walter Jacob (Dr.)
Trinity, 1943-46
Natural Sciences

Ph.D. at Imperial College, London, then post doctoral fellow at Harvard, followed by the Weizmann Institute; I have been a director of a number of RTZ Borax and RTZ Chemicals companies for over thirty years. Married, three children.

A pleasant informal group of colleagues both from the Cambridge Colleges and from LSE and UC evacuated from London during the War.

Rosenhek, Steven F.
St. John's, 1984-85
Law

Returned to Toronto, Canada, where am presently engaged in practice of Law.

Rosenne, Shabtai (Professor)
Magdalene, 1985-86
Arthur Goodhart Visiting Professor in Legal Science

See Zionist Organization *Who's Who.*

Rosenstock, Michael
St. John's, 1956-59
Medieval and Modern Languages

> Qualified as a librarian. Worked in University libraries in California and Ghana, before becoming head of the Department of Book Selection, University of Toronto Library, in 1966.
>
> *I was CUJS librarian for a year or more, before I has decided on a career. Of the many factors which made me choose librarianship as a profession, my year as the Society's librarian was undoubtedly one.*

Rosenstock, Werner (Dr.)

> *...The Thompson's Lane Synagogue evokes happy memories also for myself. I was Director of the Association of Jewish Refugees from its inception in 1941 to my retirement in 1982. During the War and early post-war years we had a lively close-knit group in Cambridge, composed mainly of elderly retired refugees with a professional background. I spoke at several meetings which were held in the Synagogue, and whenever I visited Cambridge on later occasions I did not fail to pass Thompson's Lane, which is also a landmark in the history of our community.*

Rosenthal, Colin
Clare, 1982-
Physics, Mathematics

Rosenthal, Erwin I. J.
Pembroke
Oriental Studies

> Emeritus Fellow, Pembroke College (fellow 1962-71); Lecturer in Hebrew 1948-59; Reader in Oriental Studies 1959-71; Supervisor of Islamic Studies. Vice R.A.S.C. 1944-45 P.I.D., F.O. Mission to M.E. Cairo 1945-46; PoW Division London 1946-48. Visiting Professor Advanced Arabic Studies Columbia University, New York, 1967-68

Ross, Jacob Joshua (Professor)
Trinity, 1952-54
Moral Sciences

> Completed doctorate after leaving Cambridge and while residing in London 1955-56; returned to Ponevez Yeshiva in Israel 1956-60; Taught at Bar-Ilan University until 1963; Deputy-Principal and Tutor, Jew's College, London 1963-68; since then teach at Tel Aviv University. Served as General Supervisor of Religious Secondary Schools, Israeli Ministry of Education (1968-72); Director of Studies, Midrasha, Harry Fischel Institute, Jerusalem (1973-74); Senior Lecturer in Jewish Thought, Michlalah — Jerusalem College for Women (since 1973). Married, seven children.
>
> *I came to Trinity College (and to digs in Jesus Lane) straight from Ponevez Yeshiva and Bnei Brak, where the Chazon Ish (Rabbi A.I.Karelitz), of Blessed Memory, had told my friends he would give me personally a halachic ruling forbidding me to leave the Yeshiva to take up my post-graduate scholarship to Cambridge. I avoided taking personal leave of the sage, but came to Cambridge with a bad conscience which never completely left me for the whole of my stay. The Thompson's Lane Synagogue was for me, during those first few months, an oasis in which I could feel my Jewish identity. Not only the kosher meals (after the first few months I preferred to cook for myself), but the daily Mincha-prayers (we never managed to organize regular prayers for Shacharit) at the Synagogue came to serve as the Jewish anchor of my existence.*

271

The regular Shabbat services which we all took some part in running, certainly contributed towards making our lives in Cambridge more pleasant. It was through the Synagogue that I came to be acquainted with Cyril Domb and Sigmund Price, both of them already dons. It was there too that I met a group of fresh young students such as Norman Solomon, Stuart Simons, John Rau, Phil Chody and many others whose names I no longer easily recall. I was, at the time, the only former yeshiva-bocher at Cambridge, and the thought that my presence may have had some influence on a few of them was my small consolation. After the first few weeks Norman Solomon and I began to have regular sessions in which we learnt together, and this too assuaged my guilty conscience.

I am not sure that I, personally, got much, at the time, out of the meetings and lectures of the Jewish Society. When, in the second year of my stay, I took digs at the home of Mrs. Margulis, I remember meeting many of the invited lecturers at the regular Shabbat meals at her home. But I confess to a certain feeling of fulfilment when I was invited by the Jewish Society to deliver the Annual Solomon Schechter Lecture in the Synagogue Hall in 1966 or 1967.

My recollection of my period at Cambridge (and I have heard similar reports of the situation at other periods) is that for most of the Jewish students this was a period of crisis in which one's Jewish identity was tested. Many, I think, were lost to the Jewish community as a result. But a small group (not necessarily those with the better Jewish background) came out better for the experience, with a heightened Jewish awareness. The Thompson's Lane Synagogue centre certainly had a part to play in this. Thanks are, therefore, certainly due to those who, fifty years ago, had the foresight to realize that the setting up of the Synagogue could be a genuine contribution to the Jewish community.

Ross, Pamela Esther (Mrs. Foa)
L.S.E., 1943-45
Geography

Studied soil surveying at Oxford. Aliyah 1949. Soil surveying land use for new settlements while member of Kibbutz Lavi. 1953 — soil surveying and drainage work in Western Emek Yizreel. 1956 — married and moved to Jerusalem. At Water Commissioner's office worked on problems of underground water: prevention of over- pumping and contamination. From 1975, at Physical Planning branch of Ministry of Interior, siting quarries, solid waste sites, electric plants etc. In 1985 retired and now work part-time, voluntarily, for Yad Sarah, which loans out Medical equipment for home use. Three children, seven grandchildren.

The synagogue was full of activity with Kosher canteen six days a week. Over seventy people attended a Friday evening supper in my term of office! Many of us came on Aliyah; perhaps the Zionist sessions helped! Hopefully the Society may thrive as it did in the last years of the Second World War.

Rossiter, Mary Anne (Dr.)
Girton, 1956-59
Natural Sciences

From Cambridge to Guy's Hospital Medical School, qualifying as a doctor in 1962. Since 1974 am a Consultant Pediatrician in North London.

I remember the Jewish Society as a happy place to meet one's friends and set time apart from other aspects of Cambridge life.

Roth, Carol Susan (Mrs. Eini)
1967-69
Secretarial Course

Came to Israel in 1969; attended Ulpan on Be'erot Yitzhak; moved to Haifa in 1970. Has worked at Dov Chemicals Ltd for nine years; started as typist and is now head of the office of the company. Married, two children.

The Society helped to bring Jewish students together; it also brought us into contact with the local community and with other universities.

Roth, Gabriel
Christ's, 1950-52
Economics

Research Officer, Department of Applied Economics 1960-63. Left D.A.E. to pursue my interest in the economics of transport, and in 1967 moved to America to work on this subject for the World Bank, until 1986. Age and experience resulted in increasing disillusion with the capabilities of the public sector, especially in 'developing countries', and I am now atoning by heading a consultancy that specializes in market-oriented approaches to economic development. Married, three children, one grandchild.

I was impressed by the way the CUJS provided a centre in which Jewish groups, both 'Orthodox' and 'Reform' co-existed in harmony. I hope it will long continue to do so.

Rothschild, Walter Louis (Rabbi)
Fitzwilliam, 1973-77
Theology

Whilst at Cambridge ran Progsoc (Progressive Jewish Society); developed from this to run P.J.S.C. nationally. Taught in Hemel Hempstead one year, then went to Leo Baeck College. Ordained 1984, now Rabbi at Sinai Synagogue, Leeds. Lived in Holland for a year, and in Israel for a year. Have researched and published articles on Palestine Railways, and Israel Railways.

Rubinstein, Anne (Mrs. Bower)
Girton, 1944-47
Modern Languages, Psychology

Practiced social work before marriage in 1949 to Marcus Bower *q.v.* Two sons, four grandchildren.

Rubinstein, Eric (M.B.E.)
Corpus Christi, 1929-32
Law

Practiced under the name of H.E.Aston and Co. and finally with Janners. Served with Royal Tank Regiment during the War. Retired 1985. Married, two children, seven grandchildren.

Rudie, Helena (Mrs. Rosenberg)
C.C.A.T., Hughes Hall, 1980-84
Economics, Sociology, P.G.C.E. in Secondary R.E.

Teacher training then teaching post at Ilford Jewish Primary School, Essex. Married Danny Rosenberg *q.v.*

Rudoe, Wulf
Peterhouse 1935-39
Mathematics, Statistics

Operational research R.A.F. 1939-45, and Ministry of Works 1946- 48; Statistician and Chief Statistician, Board of Trade 1948-66; Director of Statistics and Research, Ministry of Health 1966-76. Assistant Secretary, Price Commission 1976-79; Advisor to Government of Ghana 1980-81; Honorary Secretary Royal Statistical Society, 1964-74. Married (E. Trilling, Newnham,1938-41), two children, two grandchildren.

Rudolf, Anthony
Trinity, 1961-64
Modern Languages and Social Anthropology

> From 1964 till the present: Various jobs of no interest to me or anyone else, endured in order to subsidize my literary work. Have written/translated/edited 12 books and edited/guest-edited several magazines. I run a one-man-band publishing company, the Menard Press, which specializes in poetry (esp. translations) and politics (esp. nuclear). Married (and divorced) with two children.

> *I was involved enough in Jewish life and the Jewish Society to be an officer one term. I enjoyed listening to the speakers on Friday evenings.*

Rydz, Simeon L.
Jesus 1955-58
Modern and Medieval Languages

> Assistant Cashier to a firm of cloth merchants 1958-61; a director of Incorporated Trade Protection Agents 1961-70; Secretary and subsequently administrator of South Manchester Synagogue. Married.

> *I was fortunate to be drawn in the right direction, and my active participation in the C.U.J.S. nurtured an interest in conducting Synagogue Services. At the same time my post as canteen manager developed an interest in accounts. Conducting services and working with accounts have both been constant and absorbing features of my life ever since.*

Sachs, Leo (Professor)
Trinity, 1948-51
Biology (Ph.D. student)

> Joined Weizmann Institute, Rehovot 1952; currently Otto Meyerhoff Professor of Biology; Head, Department of Genetics.

Sacks, Brian Zachary
Gonville and Caius 1970-74
Mathematics, Statistics

> Management Science in the Civil Service 1974-80; taught Mathematics and Computing at a Sixth Form College, 1982-83; took an MSc in Computing, and have since worked in the Computer Industry. Married, two children.

> *The Society provided an environment to develop one's personality and attitudes to Judaism, freed from family influences. It brought us into contact with people from a wide range of backgrounds. The experience was surprising and stimulating.*

Sacks, Eliot Edward
Gonville & Caius, 1979-84
Philosophy

> Spent Academic year 1982-83 at the Hebrew University of Jerusalem as Lady Davis Visiting Fellow. Transferred to L.S.E. in 1984. At present completing Ph.D. in philosophy of Jewish Law and Ethics, and lecturing in Jewish Law and Ethics at Jews' College, London.

> *Drunken punt parties. Drunken Purim parties. The extraordinarily hospitable resident community. Distinguished Friday evening guest speakers questioned aggressively by pretentiously intellectual students. Friday nights in students' rooms, drinking, singing, learning, talking until the early hours.*

An oasis of warmth and communal spirit in what is otherwise an often competitive and elitist University. An opportunity for students from a wide variety of Jewish backgrounds to meet, talk and share a common community. My hope for the future is that the Society continues to be a force in fostering unity, communal responsibility and intellectual integrity among its members, many of whom are the Jewish leaders of the future.

Saffman, Philip Henry (Professor)
Trinity, 1950-60
Mathematics

Resigned Assistant Lectureship in Mathematics at Cambridge in 1960 to go to King's College, London until 1964, when I brain drained to become Professor of Applied Mathematics at the California Institute of Technology, where I have been ever since. Married, two children, two grandchildren.

Saltman, Avrom (Professor)
Gonville & Caius, 1943-45
History

Continued studies at London University, Ph.D. 1951 (Life and Times of Archbishop Theobald). Lecturer, Birkbeck College, London University 1948-57. Married Ilse, sister of Ernst Rabinowicz (Emmanuel *q.v.*) 1953. Associate Professor, Dept. of General History, Bar-Ilan University, Israel 1957-61, Professor of History, Bar Ilan University since 1961. F.R.Hist.Soc. since 1956. Awarded Israel Prize for History 1983. Publications in Medieval and Biblical Studies.

The Society played a decisive role in the maintenance of Jewish national identity and pride, as well as religious tradition, in the years of the Holocaust and destruction. Such thoughts may assuage, if only partially, the enduring feeling of guilt, that we were having a good time while millions of our fellow-Jews were being done to death.

Samet, Paul Alexander (Professor)
Christ's 1950-53
Mathematics

Civil Service 1953-57, working at Royal Radar Establishment; Lecturer, Durham University 1957-60; Director of Computation, Southampton University 1961-66; Director of Computer Centre, University College, London, 1967 to present; Professor of Computer Science since 1970. Married.

Sampson, Eve (Mrs. Bolchover)
Newnham, 1954-55 Law

Called to the Bar; University lecturing 1956-60 (Dublin and Manchester); since then have lived in Manchester; now work in local government. Married, four children.

Samuel, Andrew Phillip
Corpus Christi, 1952-55,62
Economics. Law

In 1955 went into business and in 1962 admitted as a solicitor. Married in 1965 and have four sons. Since 1967 in private practice in Sydney.

The Society at its best involved and interested a lot of folk in Jewish affairs who perhaps might not otherwise have been touched. Who could resist that weekly call to the Talmud Shiur in number 4 Chapel Court, Jesus! May it go from strength to strength.

Samuels, Diane
Sidney Sussex, 1979-82
History

Teaching drama in one school and three youth clubs around London. Involved in the work of a blossoming Jewish Women's Theatre Group.

Very grateful for the financial assistance given by J.Soc towards setting up the tour of 'Hannah' in July 1983. Hope the Society will expand the range of its activities and provide a base for Jews of all interests and opinions in Cambridge.

Samuels, Pamela J. (Dr. Talalay)
Girton, 1947-52
Natural Sciences

In 1953, while pursuing postgraduate studies in Cambridge, I met and married Paul Talaley. Moved to Chicago where Paul was on the Faculty of University of Chicago. Completed Ph.D. in 1954 and since then have worked on and off as a biochemist and scientific editor. Left Chicago in 1963 to come to Johns Hopkins University, Baltimore where Paul is now Distinguished Service Professor and I am on the faculty. Have four children.

CUJS was an integral part of my University experience, not merely as a means of meeting other Jews, but also because it stood for a strong social and moral commitment for all members. Arguments and discussions were particularly intense and made a lasting impression. Many of the members were not only highly intelligent and broadly knowledgeable, but their eccentricities were particularly memorable. I hope this tradition will continue for at least another 50 years.

Sandelson, Brian H.
Magdalene, 1945-49
History, Law

Solicitor. Married, two children.

Sanders, Valerie (Dr.)
Girton, 1975-78
English

Spent four years in Oxford writing a D.Phil. thesis. Since 1983 Lecturer in English Literature at the University of Buckingham.

Found CUJS disappointing. Its ultra-orthodox, North London, male-dominated atmosphere was offputting, and I soon drifted away. I would like to see this and all University Jewish societies doing more to attract the moderates — women as well as men — who don't want to spend all their free time talking about Israel or the Talmud. Would like to have seen more theatre and concert trips, walks, picnics, punting, and informal, relaxed parties where people could talk and get to know each other. Unless Jewish Societies move in this direction, most moderate students will just disappear, leaving an extremist minority in control.

Sands, Joan (Dr. Kimelman)
Newnham 1944-47
English

Moved to U.S.A. in 1955; did doctorate on Clinical Psychology; now work as a Psychotherapist. Married, three children.

The Society was tremendously important to me and introduced me to what became my substitute family. It gave me a feeling of community and belonging and anchored me to a stronger Jewish identity. I hope it will continue to do so for subsequent generations.

Sasieni, Peter
Gonville and Caius 1981-84
Mathematics
> Graduate Student at University of Washington 1984 to present.

Sassoon, Robert M.E.
Trinity Hall, 1985-
Engineering

Sattin, Gerald
Christ's, 1945-48
Natural Sciences
> 1949 Commissioned and joined 5th Regiment, Royal Horse Artillery. 1953 Director, Mitchel Maer Ltd.; 1955 M.D. Onalite Ltd. (manufacturing costume jewellery); 1964 M.D. International Division, Eothen Films; since 1969 Gerald Sattin Ltd., Antique Dealers in Burlington Arcade. Married, three children, two grandchildren.
> *When I was at Cambridge the Jewish Society was not very active except on High Holydays. I hope the Society will provide and maintain Jewish traditions for the undergraduates as this appears to be on the decline with the present generation.*

Savitz, Alan Melville
Clare, 1949-53
Classics
> Taught Classics in South Wales, Wigan, Chesterfield, Liverpool (Deputy Head, King David High School 1960-82), Chester (The King's School) and Manchester (Girls' High School).
> *As President of CUJS for one term I found that it catered for students of every shade of opinion. It was warm and friendly... I came back some years later and found it appealed mainly to orthodox students. I hope it will broaden is appeal...*

Schonfield, A. E. David (Professor)
Emmanuel, 1941-43, 48-50
Psychology, Moral Sciences
> Following research on ageing at Cambridge and a year's training in abnormal psychology at the Maudsley, educational psychologist at Bolton for 4 years; then back to Cambridge as clinical psychologist and unsuccessful applicant for university positions anywhere; to Calgary in 1975, retired in 1986 but still part-time teaching. Widowed, one child, one grandchild.
> *(Apocryphal or true memoir?) Chief Rabbi (Hertz) having started his sermon to crowded Cambridge congregation one Shabbat was interrupted by a very late student in full regalia, looking for a seat. Chief Rabbi stopped talking, hushed silent audience watches aghast, and Chief Rabbi says, as student goes up and down the aisles, 'Beadle, take the wandering Jew outside!'.*

Schwab, Harry C.
Trinity, 1935-38
> Joined Marks and Spencer plc as a management trainee, with whom I remained until retirement in 1977. Served in R.A.S.C. from Feb 1940 to May 1946, having served in Iceland, Middle East (8th Army), Italy (mentioned in dispatches) and in France, Belgium, Germany and Denmark. Commissioned in 1942, Captain from 1943. Executive Secretary of British Israel Chamber of Commerce; joint administrator of the B'nai Brith Housing Society. Under the guidance of Herbert Loewe, I was largely responsible for the preparation and publication of the Cambridge 'Roll of Honour' and

Memorial booklet, and together with Geoffrey Block prepared a survey of Jewish students at the universities which was published in the Jewish Year Book 1938. Married, two children, seven grandchildren.

During my undergraduate days I was much involved in the merger of the Hebrew Congregation, the Schechter Society, the CU Zionist Society and AJA branch into the C.U.J.S. and in the opening of the Thompson's Lane Synagogue. The resident community was at that time very small. Undergraduates enjoyed the warm hospitality in particular, of Herbert Loewe, the Reader in Rabbinics, and his family, of Mr. Harry Dagut, master of the Jewish house at Perse school, and of Dr. and Mrs. Sidney Greenburgh.

Schwab, W.M.
Trinity, 1931-34
Medicine

Taught and active in Refugee committee; member of kibbutz 1936-38; returned to England as *shaliach* 1938; war service 1939-45 (Dunkirk, North Africa, Italy); civil servant (Dept. of Environment) 1946-83. Have published and edited books on Jewish history. Vice-President, Jewish Historical Society; Chairman, Ben Uri Art Society. Married, one daughter (Julia *q.v.*), two grandchildren.

Society was very orthodox in attitude. Friday evening dinners were held at Thurston's Cafe. George Yates nailed a manifesto to the door of the Synagogue complaining of the rigidity of its attitude.

Schwartz, Jonathan Stephen (Dr.)
St. John's 1975-78
Medicine

Qualified in 1981 at London Hospital Medical College; currently medical registrar in London.

Sciama, Dennis William (Professor)
Trinity, 1944-70
Mathematics and Physics

1949-52 Research student; 1952-56 Research Fellow, Trinity; 1961-70 Lecturer in Mathematics and Fellow of Peterhouse; 1970-85 Senior Research Fellow, All Souls, Oxford. Since 1983 Professor of Astrophysics, International School of Advanced Studies, Trieste, Italy; since 1986 Extraordinary Fellow, Churchill College. 1982 Foreign Member, American Philosophical Society; 1983 Fellow of the Royal Society; 1984 Foreign Member, Accademia dei Lincei; 1984 Fellow of the American Academy of Arts and Sciences.

...I have not put anything under 'memories' because CUJS meant so much to me that I cannot express it adequately...

Seaton, A. Trevor (Dr.)
Trinity, 1954-57
Natural Sciences

Clinical Medicine at St. Bartholomew's Hospital. Now Senior Partner in General Practice. Married, two children.

Sebag-Montefiore, Nathaniel
King's, 1959-62
Archaeology & Anthropology

Led Cambridge expedition to Northern Peru 1962; Export Director, Alginate Industries 1963-77, exports of chemicals made of seaweed; Grindlays Bank 1977-86; Stockbroker since 1986. Married, two children.

I much appreciated the comradeship and breadth of contact the Society provided. I much regret that this breadth appears to have been lost and that the Jewish undergraduates I know find the Society unwelcoming and less able to tolerate the non-orthodox non-Zionist Jew. I hope that the atmosphere of an earlier era will one day return.

Segal, J.B. (Professor)
St. Catharine's, 1932-36
Oriental Languages
> *I hope that the Synagogue and the Society will be a centre to which all shades of Jewish opinion will be welcome.*

Selby, Philip M. (Dr.)
Jesus, 1957-60
Natural Sciences
> Completed medical studies at Middlesex Hospital, London and spent four years in hospital practice. 1968-70 Hadassah Medical School, Jerusalem. Since 1970 in Geneva, first with W.H.O., then Geneva University. In 1974 co-founder of Sandoz Institute for Health & Socio-Economic Studies, and in 1982 of Health Management Institute. Since 1984 Executive Director of International Union against Cancer, with 260 member organizations in 85 countries. Author or editor of 5 books.

Selig, D. Adam
St. Catharine's, 1980-83
Natural Sciences
> Joined Marconi, and then the computer department of a well known retail partnership, which I left when they objected to my leaving early on Fridays; did an M.Sc. in Computer Science at Imperial College, London; joined a software house; now work for an Oil company. Married, one child.

Selig, H. Michael
St. Catharine's, 1977-80
Mathematics
> Qualified as an accountant; emigrated to Israel in 1983; now work on Operational Research.

Senior, Bryan
Christ's, 1954-57
Modern Languages
> Professional Artist. One-man shows in London, Edinburgh, Leeds, Exeter, Dublin, Florence, Milan, Boston (USA). Portraits, figure groups, streets, landscapes and still-lifes in oils and acrylic. Cambridge painting prize 1957; GLC 'Spirit of London' prize 1981; Hampstead Millenium prize 1986.

Shaerf, Paul Simon
Gonville and Caius 1968-71
Moral Sciences
> Qualified as Solicitor in 1975; partner with Bower, Cotton and Bower, London. Founder member of New North London Synagogue. Married (Judith Tunkel, Homerton 1968-71), two children.

Shamash, Edward
Fitzwilliam, 1938-40
> 1941-46 R.A.F. ground staff with overseas service in Mediterranean countries, but hardly saw Palestine. Since war have worked in various offices in London. 1958-85 Guardian Royal Exchange Assurance Group, mainly on reinsurance contracts.

Sharman, Laurie (Dr.)
St. John's 1964-67
Natural Sciences

Qualified at The London Hospital; specialized in Kidney disease; appointed Consultant Physician and Senior Lecturer in Nephrology at St. Mary's Hospital, Portsmouth in 1983. Married, four children.

The Society had a notable effect on my religious observance and Jewish consciousness.

Sharpston, Eleanor Veronica Elizabeth
King's, 1973-76
Economics, Law, French

Did research at Oxford into economics and law; called to Bar 1980; since then have developed specialist practice in EEC law, working in London and Brussels. When not being a lawyer/economist, am generally to be found on the river (rowing) or playing music (classical guitar, violin).

Sheinfield, Meyer
Emmanuel 1936-39
Modern languages

After six years in the army joined Civil Service in 1946, retired in 1980 after thirty-four years service in Department of Employment. Served five years as Registrar of the Employment Appeal Tribunal.

Shribman, David M.
Jesus, 1976-77
History

Went up to Cambridge after A.B. in history at Dartmouth College, Hanover. Returned to America in 1977, and married in 1978. Worked as correspondent for Buffalo Evening News, Washington Star and New York Times before joining Wall Street Journal in 1984. Cover Congress and Presidential politics.

I cherish my time in Cambridge more with the passing of every year — valued friends, invaluable experiences, a way of looking at the world. Living abroad is the best way to learn about your own country.

Silk, Joseph I.
Clare 1960-63
Mathematics

Ph.D. in Astrophysics; worked on postdoctoral research in Cambridge at The Institute of Astronomy; returned to U.S.A. to Princeton; 1970 to present has worked at University of California, Berkeley. Publications include *The Big Bang* (Freeman, 1980) and *The Left hand of Creation* (Basic Books, 1983 and Heinemann, 1984). Married.

Avoided Jewish Society as much I could, and spent some effort developing the Zionist cause via the Israel Society. This culminated in a visit to Israel where the harsh realities of life on a kibbutz soon redirected my goals.

Silkin, Jeffrey (Yitzchok)
Christ's, 1966-69
Physics

Entered Commercial computing; M.Sc. (comp. sci.) Birkbeck 1973; spent 1982 in Melbourne; joined project SEED as London Director 1984. Lecture part-time in computing. Married, four children.

As a committed Jew the Society was a focal point of my Cambridge life in terms of food and prayer.

Silverman, Anthony H.
Gonville & Caius, 1974-77
Mathematics

> After four years with accounting and consulting actuary's firms, I joined my present firm of stockbrokers. Completed actuarial examinations in 1985. Married in June 1983.

Silverman, Warren
Churchill 1962-65
Natural Science

> Trained as a Patent Agent in London; joined Haseltine Lake and Company in 1968; has been a partner since 1979. Married, two children.
>
> *First Jewish Society member from Churchill. Appreciated role of Society as Jewish social centre. Memories of Mrs. Newman's cooking and certain undergraduates attempts at cholent making.*

Simon, Paul
Gonville & Caius,1976-79
Law

> Qualified as solicitor in 1982. Now in practice specializing in immigration and nationality law.
>
> *I was Secretary of J. Soc for a couple years....Most of the members in my day were also lawyers...*

Singer, Harold Samuel (Judge)
Fitzwilliam, 1953-56
Law

> After Bar finals in London in 1957 practiced at the Bar on the Northern Circuit till 1984 when I became a Circuit Judge, having been a Recorder of the Crown Court since 1981. Married, three children.
>
> *I was a President of the Society, but also Canteen Manager and save for Sundays ate all my meals there. Had many dear friends in the Society, which preserved an oasis of Judaism and friendship in Cambridge.*

Sklarz, Benjamin (Dr.)
Downing, 1953-59
Natural Sciences

> 1959-60 Post-doctoral studies at Brooklyn Polytechnic where I helped found the Yavneh group, on CUJS lines; 1961-68 Lectureships at Imperial College and Birmingham; 1969-83 Senior Lecturer at Bar Ilan University; since 1983 Research chemist with Abic Pharmaceutical and Chemical Co., Ramat Gan. Have published papers in organic chemistry and mass spectroscopy. Married, five children.
>
> *The JS was central to my life both on Shabbat and weekdays; the Friday night lectures and dinners, the more intimate group on Saturdays, the shiurim given and taken, the debates, the termly general meetings and committee work and the friendships formed.*
>
> *'Mr. Nichols' (Jack Handman) the jeweller of Bridge Street did much for many of us and for the Society. Raphael Loewe gave a scholarly shiur in Midrash at his house on Saturday afternoons. He inspired and guided the foundation of the Library — I was active in that and, I think, the first Librarian. Invigilation over exams on Saturdays and Holydays — Albert Cherns, Dr. Teicher, Dr. Rosenthal. I also recall the late Mrs. Margolis. May the JS remain as stimulating, dynamic and democratic as it was in my six year membership.*

Socolovsky, Mirit
Gonville and Caius 1981-84
Law

Law Society exams 1985; articles at Herbert Oppenheimer Nathan and Vandyk, London.

The Jewish Society was a good place at which one could meet both orthodox and unorthodox students; enjoy the special atmosphere on Shabbat and Festivals, and learn a lot about Judaism. I hope the society will continue to fulfil its aims and will go from strength to strength. I would also like to see a new shul building at Thompson's Lane.

Solomon, Allan I. (Dr.)
Peterhouse, 1959-60
Theoretical Physics (Postgrad)

1960-63 at Sorbonne, Paris; Principal Physicist, Republic Aviation, N.Y. 1963-66; Staff member, Brooklyn Polytechnic 1966-68; Tel Aviv University 1968-70; Institute for Advanced Studies, Dublin 1970-71 (currently Research Associate); Open University 1971-, where now Reader in Mathematical Physics. Visiting Professor: City College, N.Y.; Technion, Haifa; Institute for Scientific Interchange, Turin. Senior Warden, Watford Synagogue; Member, Board of Deputies. Married, two children.

As Synagogue Secretary, I was once approached by two young residents who offered to take the Service. I concurred, and later joined a most surprised congregation being treated to the first (and last?) all-Yemenite Shabbat at Thompson's Lane (1960).

Solomon, Nathaniel
Emmanuel 1944, 1947-49
Engineering, Economics

Unilever 1949-72; William Baird and Company, Director 1974-84; Associated Leisure P.L.C., Managing Director 1974-84; Pleasurama P.L.C., Chairman 1984-86.

I was a very infrequent attender of meetings of the Society. My main memories are of the excitement created by the establishment of the State of Israel.

Solomon, Norman (Rabbi Dr.)
St. John's, 1951-54
Moral Sciences, Music

Rabbi of various Orthodox communities, including Hampstead 1974-83; currently Director, Centre for the study of Judaism and Jewish-Christian Relations, Birmingham. Married, four children.

Spain, Philip Gabriel (Dr.)
Peterhouse 1962-66
Mathematics

Lecturer, University of Glasgow, since 1967. Married 1985.

Spencer, Paul S.
Downing, 1983-
Engineering, Electrical Science

Graduated 1986, returned to do Ph.D.

President-elect for Summer 1987

Spindel-Isserles, Norman (Isserles)
St. Catharine's, 1962-65
Engineering
>Settled in Geneva 1966; consultant in company organization and computing, working in French, German and English; developed proprietary methodology in my field, supported by software tools; established my own company for international diffusion. Married, three children.

Sprei, Michael Andrew
King's 1971-74
Engineering
>MSc in Management Science at Imperial College, London; spent 1975-1976 at Gateshead Talmudical College; joined British Airways in December 1976 as an O.P. analyst; joined Datamore in 1979 as systems analyst and became its technical director in 1981; joined Root Business Systems in 1986 as senior consultant. Married, four children.
>
>*The society was the focal point of Jewish life in Cambridge, it provided educational, social and cultural facilities to further knowledge and practice of Judaism. This included the provision of Services and kosher meals. Hopes for the future — the Society should attract as wide as possible a circle of Jewish students to participate in its activities.*

Squires, Gordon Leslie
St. John's, Trinity 1942-44, 1947-51
Physics
>Worked at Harwell in 1952 and subsequently in U.S.A.; returned to Cambridge in 1956 as a lecturer in Physics and Fellow of Trinity College. Author of two books and two Purim spiels. Married, two children.

Stamler, Anne Elizabeth (Mrs. Rosten)
Newnham 1976-79
Modern languages, History
>Course at Yakar Student centre. 1980 worked on social services project to improve aftercare in community of elderly patients discharged from Hospital. Worked at Yakar Study centre and teaching Jewish studies both at a Synagogue teenage centre and privately. Married, two children.
>
>*The Society was particularly helpful in providing security in the first bewildering months at Cambridge. It was an important source of friends throughout the three years. I hope it will continue to help Jewish students retain their identity and encourage interest and pride in their Judaism.*

Stamler, R.J. (Dr.)
Wolfson, 1984-86
Medicine
>Left England May 1986 to live in Israel. Currently working as House Officer at Sha'are Zedek Hospital, Jerusalem.

Stamler, Samuel
King's 1943-47
Modern languages, Law
>Called to the Bar 1949; took silk in 1971; Bencher of the Middle Temple; Recorder of the Crown Court. Currently a Trustee of the Cambridge Synagogue. Married, three children, three grandchildren.
>
>*CUJS was the alternative centre of life after, or even before, college for a substantial number of undergraduates. I wish it well: it will always be needed, I hope, as much as we needed it.*

Stanley, David
Gonville & Caius, 1954-57
Economics
> After various Sales, Marketing and Advertising appointments in UK and USA, have been running own importing company for last twelve years. Family is actively involved in N.W. Reform Synagogue and Manor House.

Stanton, J. (Mrs. Falk)
Girton, 1970-73
History
> Qualified as History teacher. Taught at Queen Elizabeth's Boys School, Barnet; Carmel College; Hasmonean Boys School. Married (A.Falk q.v.), three children.

Stecker, Simone
New Hall, 1982-85
Law
> Doing Articles in firm of Solicitors in Central London.
> *J.Soc was fun and interesting. Met people there who will remain lifelong friends.*

Steinberg, Shulamit (Mita) Rachel (Mrs. Charney)
QMC, 1942-43; LSE, 1943-45
Languages, Sociology
> Reunited with family Dec 1944 in New York. (Father, Dr.I.N.Steinberg, had spent WW2 in Australia, almost achieving the Government's agreement to a mass, cooperative, culturally autonomous Jewish settlement there.) Studied music — voice and early instruments in particular — in N.Y.C. Taught French and German at high school and college. In 50's and again 1974-87, founded, directed and sang in *a capella* quartet, Orpheus Chamber Singers. Have written articles, editing, and translating from Yiddish to English.
> *The Society enabled us to remain conscious, active Jews in the midst of our other, academic etc., concerns. The establishment of the kosher lunch cafeteria made possible kosher, nutritional and social lunches — one good meal a day, during the War, for the kosher-keeping Jews among us. I brought V.Gollancz and Dr.A.Steinberg et al to the Society, enriching my fellow students, and myself, with Jewish thought and discussion.*

Steiner, Sarah (Mrs. Meron)
Newnham, 1961-64
Classics
> Moved to Jerusalem 1965. Studied linguistics at Hebrew University. Part-time teaching at Hebrew University and at Tel Aviv University. Served on school committees. Currently completing Ph.D. thesis. Divorced, four children.
> *The only time I've ever stood in a synagogue in jeans, on three tables stacked one on top of the other was painting the Thompson's Lane synagogue ceiling in a team under the direction of Steve Lipson (then a physics research student who later taught at the Technion) one Long Vac.*

Stern, Marion (Mrs. Seidemann *formerly* Rettek)
Newnham, 1948-51
Mathematics
> Spent three years in family business (raw furs), then married and moved to New York. After the three children had grown out of nappies and were spending a good part of the day at school, I taught myself computer

programming, got divorced and joined a software business in the mathematical programming field. For the last two years I have been working for
A.T.& T. in a group that provides support for several internal groups that
put out computer based training. I have recently remarried. I have two
grandchildren.

*I was very active in CUJS during my three years at Newnham, and the
society and its members provided a large part of my social life. Also, for the
first time in my life I had the opportunity to eat kosher, be shomer shabbat
and mingle with other orthodox people of my own age, and I loved it.*

Stern, Ralph
Downing, 1958-61
Economics
> Came on Aliyah in 1962. Joined Bank Leumi, not fired yet! Married, four
> children.

Stone, Harold Victor Lever
Trinity, 1951-54
History and Law
> Qualified as a solicitor and joined father's firm. Continued in practice with
> same firm until established own practice in May 1981. In May 1980 married
> South African/Israeli Dr. Naomi Loon. Have three stepchildren and sailing
> yacht YAMMA.
> *As an orthodox/conservative member was horrified at intolerance shown
> by ultra orthodox to reform and liberal members, e.g. the objection to the
> repetition in English of the second paragraph of Olenu. Earnestly hope that
> this situation does not prevail today.*

Stonehill, Claire Aura (Mrs. Bar- Yaacov)
Girton, 1952-55
Modern and Medieval Languages
> Do freelance translating and editing. Married Nico Nissimoff *q.v.* Have three
> children.
> *Friday night at the Jewish Society was the highlight of the week.*

Sugarman, Peter Michael
St. Johns', 1979-82
History, Law
> President, Cambridge Union 1981; attended Yeshiva in Israel in 1982; joined
> Morgan Guarantee Trust Co. of New York; appointed Vice-President of the
> Bank in 1987. Unmarried, currently living in U.S.A.

Sunlight, Ben
Magdalene, 1955-58
Architecture
> Held first one-man exhibition at the Heffer Gallery, Cambridge while still
> an undergraduate in 1958. Received formal Art training at the Central
> School of Art & Design, London. Awarded Mural Diploma in 1962. Taught
> part-time, as an Artist, for a few years before practising entirely inde-
> pendently. Now feel that am at beginning of most mature phase of Artistic
> development. Married in 1979.

Szlezinger, Samuel
Robinson 1983-86
Law
> Law School 1986; accepted for articles in Macfarlane's for September 1987.

Tabor, David (Emeritus Professor)
Gonville & Caius, 1936-39, 46-

Left Cambridge early 1940 on War research in Australia. Active in Zionist movement. Started Habonim and first Jewish Student society (Melbourne). Returned to Cambridge 1946 as Assistant Director of Research, promoted to Reader (1956), appointed *ad hominem* Professor of Physics 1973, Emeritus 1981. Fellow of Gonville & Caius (1957), Fellow of Royal Society (1963). Served as Hon. Sec. and Chairman of Cambridge Jewish Residents Association. Married, two sons.

There was much excitement in 1937 at the consecration of the Synagogue by Chief Rabbi Hertz and the formation of the CUJS (I was first Hon. Sec.; Abba Eban — President). It was marvellous to have a permanent and attractive address for religious services and for cultural and social meetings. In the years approaching 1939 many Cambridge Jewish students were heavily committed to Zionism and to the saving of the Jews; my impression is that many of them now are more concerned with saving Judaism and maybe themselves.

Taub, Jonathan
Emmanuel 1978-81
Economics

Qualified as accountant in 1984; moved to Jerusalem to study at Mir Yeshivah; currently studying at Yeshivat Mercaz Hatorah, Jerusalem. Married, one child.

C.U.J.S. was the place for Jews to pray together, eat together, discuss and argue together. I hope that in the future it will be able to attract the majority of Jews in Cambridge who prefer to ignore their being Jewish, and will be able to play a role in the revitalization of the Anglo-Jewish Community. This can only be achieved by trying to raise the amount and level of Jewish education available in Cambridge.

Taylor, Lindsey
Sidney Sussex, 1977-80
Archaeology & Anthropology

1980-84 studied Prehistory at Hebrew University, then worked in Israel Dept. of Antiquities. Am now Editor of *Israel Exploration Journal* and translate and edit archaeological publications. Engaged to marry Norman Guthartz next year.

CUJS was very much the focus of my social life as a student, serving as a meeting place, opportunity to continue one's Jewish education and occasional pressure group for promoting Jewish causes, as well as providing the essential religious infrastructure; I hope it continues to play all these roles and extend its activities in the future.

Toeman, Edward Armand
St. Catharine's, 1946-49
History, Law

Practising Solicitor 1952-82. Appointed Registrar, Willesden County Court 1982. Married, two children.

Topper, Edwin Simeon
Corpus Christi 1975-78
Mathematics

Joined Refuge Assurance Co. as trainee actuary. Went to Cubie, Wood in 1982 where I qualified. Currently am Regional actuary in Manchester where I specialize in pension advice. Married.

I remember the Society with fondness, particularly the excellent Friday night speakers and the 'family Landy'. The food left a lot to be desired; my brother and I once prepared a vegetarian Friday night meal which made a handsome profit for the Society and was well received by the students! The close connection between the Society and the synagogue had its downside; it attracted, by and large, the more observant amongst the Jewish students. I would like to see a broader cross-section of the Jewish population taking an active part in the Society whilst not compromising on the religious front to achieve this end.

Topper, Jonathan Joseph
Corpus Christi, 1975-78
Engineering

Left Cambridge to resume work with my industrial sponsor, GEC High Voltage Switchgear Ltd. in Manchester. Gained experience in computer-aided design and programming. Left GEC in 1982 to work for SIA Computer Services in London. Married in Jerusalem where I have lived since January 1986. Am now training to be a Patent Attorney.

The Jewish Society pivoted about the Synagogue in Thompson's Lane. This was both a blessing and a curse. It encouraged student involvement in Synagogue affairs which was a good thing, but discouraged the vast majority of Jewish students from having anything to do with the Society, which was a gross failure. I hope that in the next 50 years the polarization will be reduced and that it will be possible for future generations of Jewish students in Cambridge to make a worthy contribution to the Jewish Society regardless of the level of their commitment to Jewish religious practice.

Tunkel, Judith (Mrs. Shaerf)
Homerton 1968-71
History and English

Deputy head History department at Pimlico School, 1971-74; qualified R.G.N. at University College Hospital 1987. Married, (Paul Shaerf *q.v.*), two children.

Member of CUJS 1968-71. Supper secretary 1970.

Ungar, Margaret Louise (Mrs. Drukker)
Girton, 1938-41
Mathematics

1941-45 Royal Ordnance Factories, Risley and Chorley; 1946-47 Scientific Officer, Fire Research Organization; 1955-56 London University, Institute of Education; since 1956 teaching Mathematics. Married, three children, eight grandchildren.

Valman, Hyman Bernard (Dr.)
St. Catharine's, 1952-55
Natural Sciences

Appointed Consultant Pediatrician at Northwick Park Hospital and Clinical Research Centre in 1972. Editor of *Archives of Disease in Childhood*. Published 5 books on aspects of Pediatrics. Married, two children.

As Canteen manager my greatest fiasco was when a special order of hamantaschen *arrived in a decomposed state two weeks after Purim, as the container had been unloaded from the train and left at the end of the platform in error. My greatest success was in persuading the late Henry Shaw, Director of Hillel House, to donate a fridge to the Society to replace the model that was continually breaking down.*

Vecht, Ann (Mrs. Rosen)
Homerton 1983-87
English and Education
> Appointed as teacher at the Michael Sobell Sinai School, 1987. Married (Stuart Rosen *q.v.*)
>> *Librarian, Social Secretary and Education officer C.U.J.S.*

Vecht, Jack
Gonville and Caius 1980-83
Natural Science, Electrical Sciences
> Aliyah 1984; since then has worked in electro-optical design and production

Wagner, Mark
Peterhouse, 1981-84
Mathematics
> Took M.Sc at Warwick University 1985. Working for Ph.D. at Hebrew University, Jerusalem.

Waimann, David R.
Downing, 1977-80
Economics
> Became a warehouse boy and after six months of back-breaking work joined the European Parliament on a scholarship. This was followed by three freewheeling months at one of the UN bodies in New York and then I packed my bags and scarpered off to Central Africa. After two years of volunteer work I surfaced again in the USA where I finished a degree in engineering. I am now trying to design (*illegible* HM) in the beautiful land of Israel.
>> *Best society there was. However, the food was better at the Landys and Reifs.*

Waley Cohen, Henrietta F.
Newnham, 1933-36
Natural Sciences, Pre-Medicine
> Went to Royal Free Hospital, but left after six months to marry, in 1937, O.R.M. Sebag-Montefiore. Have 3 children and 8 grandchildren. Son, Nathaniel was President of CUJS in 1961; grandson, Geoffrey Gestetner, is now up at Cambridge.
>> *We met behind a shop on Friday evenings and Saturday mornings, and undergraduates tok the services. After service on Friday evenings we went upstairs and had a fish meal together, and sang Jewish songs; sometimes we had visiting speakers at a meeting downstairs afterwards, including, once during my time, the Chief Rabbi Dr. Hertz. He came to tea in my bed-sitting room, on Saturday afternoon, walking there and back into Cambridge*
>> *One year I was responsible for organizing the Friday suppers. While I was up there were a number of wealthy Jewish undegraduates, including three Sebag-Montefiores, two Waley Cohens, Eddy de Rothschild two Burtons, and it was decided to buy the site of the Thompson's Lane Synagogue and build it.*
>> *It was always meant as an undergraduate synagogue, and the only town people who came were the boys at the Jewish house of the Perse school and their housemaster. I was usually the only female, but Ruth Besso came sometimes – she was one year junior to me at Newnham.*

Waley Cohen, Bernard (Sir)
Magdalene, 1933-36
History
> See *Who's Who.*

Walker, Anthony
Emmanuel 1978-84
Natural Science, Biochemistry PhD
> Worked for ICI agrochemicals for two years in Berkshire and Brazil; currently a management consultant with Arthur D. Little in London.

Wallman, Adrienne
Newnham, 1971-74
Japanese, History of Art
> Art Gallery and Museum Studies Diploma at Manchester University, followed by short spell in Travel industry. Since 1978 have been a production assistant and researcher at BBC Schools TV. Have travelled a lot and active in various campaigning groups.

Weil, David
Clare, 1985-
English

Wernick, Gary ('Gazza')
St. John's, 1984-
Natural Sciences, Management Studies

West, Geoffrey B.
Gonville & Caius, 1958-61
Maths, Physics
> Ph.D. Stanford University, California in Theoretical High Energy Physics 1966; post-doctoral work at Cornell and Harvard before joining the faculty at Stanford in 1970; since 1975 I live in Santa Fe, New Mexico where I head the High Energy Physics Theory Group at Los Alamos National Laboratory, part of the University of California system. I return to England roughly once a year for business and pleasure. Married, two children.

White, Andrew
Jesus 1979-82
Law
> National Coordinater Y.P.Z.; U.K. delegate thirtieth World Zionist Congress, 1982; Researcher, Nuclear Policy Studies Group, Bradford University, School of Peace Studies 1983-84; Research Consultant, Oxford Research Group on Nuclear Decision-making 1984-85; Course tutor in strategic Studies, Institute for Strategic Studies 1985-87; Doctoral student L.S.E.; L.L.M. in Law,1987; currently training to be a Solicitor. Publications include *The Terror of Balance* (Menard Press,1982) *Symbols of War; Pershing II and Cruise Missiles in Europe* (Merlin Press, 1983); *NATO in How Nuclear Weapon Decisions Are Made* (Macmillan: 1986). Founder member of JONAH, 1981; Co-founder; 'Sustaining our Visions' Jewish leadership project, 1984. Founder London Nuclear Research Group, 1985.
> *I loved the crowd of people at the Jewish Society on Friday nights. If there was a bad turn-out I would be dejected for the rest of Shabbat. Also, I learnt how many eminent Jewish speakers I had never heard of.*

Whyte, Caroline (Mrs. Lederman-Whyte)
King's, 1980-83
> Worked with Autistic children for a year in Israel; did Master's in Jewish Studies in Oxford in 1985; currently writing poetry; am about to resume Ph.D. at S.O.A.S. on Israeli war poetry. Married, one child.
>
> *My fondest memory of Cambridge is the J.Soc, a thriving exuberant Society. I hope that in future years Cambridge J.Soc will continue to represent the prosperous Jewish contingent at one of the world's greatest Universities.*

Wieselberg, H. Michael (Dr.)
Gonville & Caius, 1963-66
Medicine, Social Anthropology
> St. George's Hospital Medical School 1966-69; trained in pediatrics, before entering Maudsley Hospital to pursue psychiatry; clinical and research interest in childhood hyperactivity; currently Consultant in Child and Adult Psychiatry, University College and Middlesex Hospital Medical School. Married, two children.

Wilkes, Derek Lionel
Christ's, 1944-45, 47-49
English, Law
> Royal Navy 1945-47; called to Bar in 1949, and enrolled as Solicitor in 1956, and practiced since then. Formerly Chairman of Mapam in Great Britain, and was a semi-professional opera singer for some years.

Winegarten, Asher (Professor)
L.S.E. 1939-42
Economics, Statistics
> Served in the Admiralty; joined the Farmers Union as Chief Economist; became Deputy Director General and then Director General. C.B.E. (1968). Loved travel, Opera, Theatre. Died 1979. Married (Renee Aarons *q.v.*).

Wineman, Vivian
Gonville & Caius, 1968-71
Philosophy , History
> Career in Law and Business; founded own firm of Solicitors in 1981.

Winter, Felix
Trinity, 1936-39
Economics
> 1945 Economist Intelligence Unit; 1947 Dept. of Applied Economics, Cambridge; 1948 Ministry of Town and Country Planning; 1956 Remington Rand; 1959 London Transport.
>
> *I married in Thompson's Lane on 1st October 1948 and was told that this was the second marriage there, the first being that of Professor Hilda Himmelweit. The Society was very successful in stimulating interest in Judaism in persons who, like myself, had little Jewish knowledge. I hope it will continue successfully.*

Wiseman, Alex Simon
Churchill, 1976-79
Mathematics
> One year M.Sc. in Operational Research at Sussex University. 1980-84 Operational Research analyst at British Nuclear Fuels in Warrington. Since 1964 with Deloitte Haskins and Sells as a Management Consultant.
>
> *The Society fulfilled an important role in Cambridge as a meeting place for Jewish students and a focal point for Jewish life. The most interesting*

part of the evening was usually the invited speaker. The speakers were generally very good. I can recall a wide range, from Tom Sharpe to the Chief Rabbi.

Wiseman, Sara
Homerton, 1981-85
Education & Geography
> Teaching at a primary school in the London Borough of Newham.

Wittenberg, Jonathan
Kings, 1976-79
English
> Trained as English teacher and worked with young children in a multicultural environment. Began to train for the Rabbinate at Leo Baeck College in 1983.
> *I remember working in the garden at Thompson's Lane. At its most beautiful a large honeysuckle scented the path to the entrance. There were bulbs in season and patriotic blue and white alyssum and lobelia up the path. I have lovely memories of Florence Wright who, despite being in her seventies or eighties, helped us in the kitchen with good grace and kindness always.*

Wix, Phyllis (Mrs. Bloch)
L.S.E., 1942-44
> 1944 Conscripted and sent to Bletchley Park (code breakers); returned after War for final year at L.S.E.; 1949 married former RAF chaplain Sonny Bloch; on my husband's death in 1979 took over as MD of Soncino Press. Now more or less retired. Have four children and two grandchildren.

Wolfson, David (Sir)
Trinity, 1954-57
Economics, Law
> M.B.A. Stanford (U.S.A.) 1959; employed at Great Universal Stores 1964-78; Prime Minister's Office 1979-85; Chairman, Alexon 1982- 86. Married, three children.
> *Occasional visitor to Jewish Society. Like the Opera, attendance rare, but sorely missed if not there.*

Wolman, Lionel (Dr)
Peterhouse 1938-41
Natural Science
> M.B.ChB. 1944; M.R.C.P. 1946; D.P.M.1950; M.D.1952; Ph.D.1963; F.R.C.P. 1969; E.G. Fearnsides Research Scholar, Cambridge 1946; Canadian Mental Health Scholar, Toronto 1950-51; Squadron Leader R.A.F., Halton Bucks 1948-50; Consultant Neuro-Pathologist and Honorary Pathology Lecturer, University of Sheffield, 1952-69.
> Senior Warden Sheffield Great Synagogue; Chairman Jewish Education Committee, Sheffield; Vice Chairman Hillel House. Died 1969.

Yardley, Bernard N.
Trinity, 1983-86
Mathematics
> Started work as a trainee actuary — Cambridge was easy by comparison.
> *I remember being part of the clique that did the work but rarely held any major posts — voices behind the throne. May my type long continue! My hope for it are simply that it should continue to resist the left wing tendencies being much vaunted by UJS.*

Yoffey, Fiona (Mrs. Blumfield)
Newnham, 1971-75
Oriental Studies

Teacher training in London; lived in Jerusalem 1979-82; returned to London 1982 on marriage; taught at Classical Hebrew at Hasmonean High School 1982-85; teach at I.L.E.A. adult Ivrit classes since 1982. One daughter.

I still have nostalgic memories of Shabbatot at J. Soc., with the friendliness and homely atmosphere. It was lovely when quite a few faces from those days were at our wedding in Jerusalem, six and a half years after leaving.

Young,Esther (Dr. Marine)
L.S.E., 1942-45
Sociology

Came to U.S.A., married and obtained M.S.W. and Ph.D. at University of Pittsburgh, where am now Clinical Associate Professor; teaching and practising Child and Family Therapy. Three children, three grandchildren.

Great intensive Jewish experience at Thompson's Lane working with Rabbi Klein to found Kosher canteen. Cohesive group from Ehrentreu home involved in political activity to capture Board at Jewish Society.

Young, Marion (Mrs. Lupu)
Homerton, 1962-63
Education

Took part in the first IUJF Graduate scheme in Beersheba, before the present WUJS centre in Arad was established. In 1964 joined the staff of the Technion and in 1969 transferred to the University of Haifa. Profession: teaching English. In addition I edit material for academic journals and contribute occasional articles and book reviews to the Jerusalem Post.

Yudkin, John (Professor)
Christ's 1929-31
Biochemistry

Research in Biochemistry and Nutrition in Cambridge 1931-1943; RAMC 1943-1945; Professor of Physiology, London University 1945 — 54; Professor of Nutrition, London University 1954-71; now retired. Published many research papers in medical and scientific journals and several books. Active in Jewish-Israeli organizations. Married, three children, three grandchildren.

Yudkin, Mark (Dr.)
St. John's, 1980-83
Doctorate in Computer Science at the Computer Laboratory

Came to Cambridge in 1980 from Adelaide, S.Australia as an '1851' Scholar. Completed Ph.D., married a Swiss national and moved to Zurich in 1983. Worked for two and a half years in process control then moved into banking sector where I am currently active.

CUJS provided the central Jewish life in Cambridge, together with a series of speakers, and occasional social events. By providing religious services and kosher meals it looked after the religious needs of its members where required — even if there were always complaints about 'J.Soc. food'.

Yudkin, Michael D. (Dr.)
King's, 1956-62
Natural Sciences, Biochemistry

Harkness Fellow at Harvard Medical School 1962-64; Fellow and Tutor in Biochemistry, University College, Oxford 1965; University Lecturer in Biochemistry, Oxford 1966. Sabbatical leave at Stanford University, California

1971-72 and at Hebrew University, Jerusalem 1980-81. Co-Author of *A Guidebook to Biochemistry* and *Comprehensible Biochemistry*. Co-Chairman, Scientists for the Release of Soviet Refuseniks. Married, two children.

Zand, Michael (Professor)

Wolfson, 1979-80

Born 1927 in the U.S.S.R. Came on Aliyah to Israel in 1971. Since then Professor of Persian and Tajik at the Hebrew University, Jerusalem.

Zatz, Paul S. J.

Sidney Sussex 1958-61

Law

Qualified as a Solicitor and worked for a City firm 1964-81. Joined Clyde Petroleum plc, and is currently Legal and Corporate Director. Held office as Chairman of Wembley Liberal Synagogue. Married, two children.

I send good wishes for the future of the Society and hope that it will continue to provide a focal point for Jewish students from all ranges of the spectrum.

Ziderman, Adrian (Professor)

Downing, 1956-59

Economics

Went to Stanford University as a Fulbright scholar; returned to England 1961 to join academic staff of London University (LSE, QMC); specialist in the economics of manpower and of education; emigrated to Israel in 1975; head of Economics department, Bar Ilan University 1980; Visiting Professor, University of British Columbia, Vancouver 1985; joining World Bank, Washington D.C. in 1987 for two years as Senior Economist. In 1982 I moved from Petach Tikvah to Gimzu, a religious Moshav near Lod, with intention of combining an academic career with working our two acres of farmland. Married, four children.

For me CUJS provided an oasis of Jewish values and observance which fortified me during those critical, questioning years as an undergraduate. Looking back, I wonder how many Jewish undergraduates would have drifted away from Judaism had CUJS not flourished.

List of Deceased Jewish Graduates
COLLEGE INDEX

Non-Collegiate

Abendana, I.
[Bernard, H.H.]
[Bernays, A.V.]
[Bernays, L.J.]
Crool, J.
[Ferdinand, P.]
[Gompertz, J.F.W.]
Krebs, H.A.
Lyon, S.
Lyons, I. *sen.*
Lyons, I. *jun.*
[Michael]
Reuben, R.
[Scialetti, M.P.]
[Tremellius, J.E.]

Caius College

Abrahams, H.M.
Aron, F.A.
[Blumberg, F.W.]
Brodetsky, I.
[?Crespin, E.D.]
Davis, C.J.B.
Galkoff, L.
Gluckstein, I.H.
Hermann, J.
Hersch (Herschkowitz). I.H.
Hersch, L.H.J.
Jacob, J.
Kohan, R.M.
Kohn, W.H.
Myers, C.S.
Salomons, D.L.
Salomons, D.R.H.P.
Silverston, B.
Spiers, H.M.
Wiener, H.M.

Christ's College

Abrahams, I.
?Adler, P.S.
[Alexander, A.B.]
Arnold (Hoffmann), W.A.
[Bernal, R.]
Cohen, A.H.
Cohen, D.L.
Cohen, G.H.
[Cowen, C.H.G.]
Davis, I.

[Christ's College cont]
Edgar, L.I.
[Elton, A.]
?Eschwege, F.S.
?Feigl, H.E.J.
[?Fitz-Aucher (Rappoport), R.A.]
Fox, C.
Goldberg, A.D.
Gollancz, I.
?Gottschalk, G.J.
Isserlis, L.
Joseph, W.F.G.
?Kaufmann, B.
?Lange, F.W.T.
Lange, M.E.
Lehmann, H.
Levy, R.
Manasseh, S.D.E.
Mere, C.L.
?Moritz, C.
?Mosley, I.H.
?Nunes, F.
Oppenheimer, J.R.
Perlzweig, M.L.
?Pinto, M.S.
?Roth, G.K.
Sassoon, C.
Schechter, S.
Schiller-Szinessy, A.S.
Schiller-Szinessy, S.M.
Solomon, M.H.B.
Sosnow, N.M.
?Wayman, M.
Wolf, C.G.L.
Wolfe, J.A.
Woolf, W.R.M.
Yellin, A.

Clare College

?Adler, F.B.
[Alexander, G.H.G.]
Benjamin, J.A.
Benjamin, R.N.
[Bernal, C.]
[Gompertz, H.R.B.]
?Goodhart, E.J.
Gordon, H.H.
Hermann, L.
?Hirsch, J.G.
?Khayyatt, R.H.
Kisch, E.R.
Ladenburg, A.L.

[*Clare College cont*]
Lehmann, J.R.
Leon, E.J.
Leon, W.A.
?Levin, A.W.
Levy, L.A.
Lipschitz, J.
Lipschitz, J.M.
Lubbock (Abrahamson), I.
Nathan, J.
Nathan, L.
Oppenheimer, F.F.
Reif, A.E.
Rossdale, I.T.H.
?Rufford, M.J.
Samuel, C.H.
Sassoon, M.T.
?Stein, R.C.
Tanburn, W.L.
?Trier, N.E.
Werner, C.H.

Corpus Christi College

Barnett, R.D.
[Isaacs, A.A.]
Lipson, D.L.
Mindelsohn, K.
Rabson (Rabinowitch), M.

Downing College

Gainsbrough (Ginsburg), H.H.
Snowman, L.V.
Spero, L.

Emmanuel College

Abelson, E.G.
Abrahams, A.
Abrahams, S.S.
Arakie, E.A.
Bornstein, H.
Cohen, A.
Cohen, J.C.
Davis, H.N.
Eichholz, A.
Fridlander, E.D.
Golberg, L.
Greenhill (Greenberg), B.M.
Halsted, E.A.M.
Halsted, V.M.
Harris, H.
Harris, L.J.
Israel, D.D.G.
Jaffe, A.C.
Jaffe, W.E.B.
[Levien, E.G.]
Moses, V.S.
Salaman, A.G.

[*Emmanuel College cont*]
Spiers, C.H.
Waley-Cohen, R.

Fitzwilliam House

Chain, E.B.
Jung, L.
[Walters (Katz), W.P.M.]

Girton College

Ahrons, E.J.
Ayrton (*née* Marks), H.P.S.
Bennett (*née* Frankau), J.
Burnham (Burnheim, *née* Nachbar), H.
?Chotzner (*née* Lan Davis), E.K.
Churchill (*née* Myers), H.V.
Churchill (*née* Myers), S.
Cornforth (*née* Klugmann), K.C.
Davis, J.R.F.
Ellenbogen (*née* Alexander), E.H.
Fraser (*née* Harari), E.
Freund, I.
Gollancz, M.E.H.J.
Grabiner (*née* Stanley), E.
Guiterman (*née* Warburg), E. L.
Harris (*née* Jacob), N.I.
?Jaffe, E.
?Joachim, J.M.
Joseph, J.M.
Kirby (Klein), A.
Lange (*née* Bentwich), R.N.O.
Leavis (*née* Roth), Q.D.
Leon (*née* Soman), M.E.
Levy, F.
Libowitz, O.
Marcus (*née* Godinski), L.
Mayer (*née* Bentwich), H.R.
?Meynell (*née* Mendel), V.R.W.
?Michaelis, M.
Montefiore (*née* Ward), F.F.B.
Montefiore (*née* Schorstein), T.A.
Nathan (*née* Stettauer), E.J.C.
Salaman, E.E.
Shaw (Schwabacher), O.
Shorstone (Schorstein), B.V.
Spencer-Smith (*née* Greenhill), E.R.

Jesus College

Aron, E.M.
Bronowski, J.
Finley (Finkelstein), M.I.
Levine, A.
Levine, E.
Loewe, L.L.
Schiff, M.E.H.
Solomons, M.

King's College

Bein, A.B.
Bles, E.J.
Braudo, C.J.
?Braunholz, E.G.W.
?Braunholz, E.J.K.
Cohen, A.M.
Cohen, H.B.
Cohen, N.B.
Cohen, S.B.
?Ehrman, S.H.
Errera, A.J.J.H.
Fortes, M.
Inf(i)eld, H,
[Isaacs, S.]
[Isaacs, W.H.]
Jaffe, A.D.
Joel, D.J.B.
Ko(h)nstam(m), E.M.
Ladenburg, E.R.
Leon, H.C.
Lob, H.
Michaelson, S.M.P.
Mond, F.L.
Mond, R.L.
?Moritz, C.
Ortweiler, F.J.
Pass, A.P. de
Polack, B.J.
Pollak, L.E.
Rappoport, J.G.
Reitlinger, H.S.
?Rubens, H.V.
Sebag-Montefiore, J.M.
Solomon, E.H.
?Spielman, R.W.
Spielman(n), C.M.
Waley, (Schloss), A.D.
Waley, F.
Walston (Waldstein), C.
Weizmann, M.O.
Werner, C.A.
Wirszubski, C.
Zaiman, A.
[Zangwill, O.L.]

Magdalene College

[Benamor, J.H.]
Cohen, A.
Rossdale, F.A.
Stern, L.H.
Stern, S.J.
Wilk, J.
Wilk, L.

Newnham College

Altschuler (*née* Persitz), O.H.

[Newnham College cont]
?Ashauer, S.
Ashley (*née* Hayman), D.
Besso, R.
?Bolton (Sonnenschein), S.F.
Bridge (*née* Makower), U.
Chasanovitch, L.
Cohen, H.F.
?Cohen (*née* Hamill), K.
Cohen (*née* Cobb), L.M.
Cohen, M.
Donnison (*née* Singer), R.S.
Franklin, R.E.
?Friedeberg, E.L.
French (*née* Adler), H.
Gollancz, E.
Goodman (*née* Kay), C.P.
Greenwood (Grünbaum), I.F.
?Gregg (*née* Schreiner), F.L.
Grüner, A.
Haes, R.A.
Ha-Ezrahi-Brisker, P.
Hilton (Hildesheim), H.G.
Hirschfield, E.
Hubback (*née* Spielmann), E.M.
?Humphries (*née* Behrens), M.L.
Jacob (*née* Kisch), V.H.
?Joseph (*née* Myers), M.L.
?Josephy, J.
Kahn (?Cahn, *née* Bronner), L.
?Klein, M.C.H.
?Knight (*née* Oppenheim/Osborne), B.J.
Levi, A.K.
?Levin, E.M.
?Levin, H.M.
Levy, A.
?Lowenstein, M.L.
?Oppenheim, M.A.R.
Pearce (*née* Rosenhain), M.H.
Pereles (*née* Ullmann), M.W.
?Scott (*née* Schreiner), U.H.
?Sergel (*née* Streiff), H.
Taylor (*née* Cohen), H.O.
Vaughan-Morgan (*née* Joshua), C.M.
Weiss, H.
Werner, A.
Winter (*née* Geiler), L.E.
Wolff (*née* Jolowicz), M.S.
Ziman (*née* Gaster), N.F.

Pembroke College

[Cohen, J.]
Diringer, D.
[Edersheim, A.]
[?Goldman, P.]
Harari, R.A.
Levinstein, G.E.
Mosseri, F.N.

[Pembroke College cont]
Mosseri, L.N.
Nahum, E.A.
Sebag-Montefiore, J.
Spielmann, H.L.I.
Wassey (Wassilevsky), S.
Zaiman, B.A.

Peterhouse College

Abrams, L.G.
Benjamin, L.E.
?Blumberg, S.H.G. d'A.
Cohen, A.E.
Cohen, O.H.L.
Friedman, M.
[Gompertz, S.]
Mendel, H.L.
Mond, A.W.
Mond, F.L.
Nathan, R.
Postan, M.M.
Salamon, M.W.H.
?Silberrad, C.A.
[Solomon, R.]
[Solomon, W.H.]
Wolman, L.
?Woolf, J.L.

Queens' College

Birnberg, J.
Blackburn (Schwarzman), R.I.
Cohen, E.
Cohen, J.I.
Cohen, S.G.
Gordon, S.
[Herschell, J.F.I.]
Inf(i)eld, L.
Israel, J.D.
Jackson, J.
Loewe, H.M.J.

St. Catharine's College

Besso, D.
Craig (Cohen), S.I.R. (S.H.)
[Ginsburg, B.W.]
Hertz, S.M.
Hyamson, D.J.
[Kahn, C.J.]
[Kahn, F.J.]
[Kahn, J.]
Levy, I.
(Loewe, H.M.J. *see* Queens')
?Posener, E.A.

St. John's College

Adler, H.M.

[St. John's College cont]
Alexander, A.
Alexander, M.
Bender, A.P.
Bloch, A.
Chotzner, A.J.
Davis, F.A.
Green, S.M.
Jacobs, J.
Kahn, A.
Leon, J.
Levy, S.I.
Lewis, H.S.
Lipkind, G.
Maccoby, E.M.
Marmorstein, E.
Miller, E.
Mond, A.M.
Mordell, L.J.
Nissim, J.
Norman (Neumann), S.T.
?Paiva, H. de
[Pass, H.L.]
Polack, A.I.
Polack, E.E.
Rosenhead, L.
Rosenheim, M.L.
Smouha, E.H.
Sylvester, J.J.
Trachtenberg, M.I.
Valentine, D.H.
Wilmers(doerffer), J.G.
Yates, G.A.

Selwyn College

[Adler, A.L.W.]

Sidney Sussex

Price, H.L.
(Spero, L.) *see* Downing

Trinity College

Barnett, L.D.
Beer, A.H.
Bentwich, J.S.
Bentwich, N. de M.
Berlyne, D.E.
[Bernal(-Osborne), R.]
[Bernays, A.E.]
Besicovitch, A.S.
Billig, L.
Blackman, M.
Brodetsky, S.
Cherns, A.B.
[?Crespin, A.J.]
Diamond, A.S.
Edelman, M.

Roll of Members
COLLEGE INDEX

Cambr. Coll. of Art & Technol.

Roth C.
Rudie H.

Christ's College

Atkin R.
Balfour-Lynn P.
Berry E.
Bronstein M.S.
Chayen J.
Edgar L.I.
Gamse I.
Goldberg J.
Goldinstein E.
Kaye A.
Lovitch L.
Magrill H.R.
Marcuson R.
Pearlman A.
Rickayzen G.
Roth G.J.
Samet P.A.
Sattin G.
Senior B.
Silkin J.
Wilkes D.L.
Yudkin J.

Churchill College

Amias J.A.
Florentin C.
Gilroy K.S.
Jacobs L.
Landy J.
Merzer A.M.
Pearlman R.H.
Silverman W.
Wiseman A.S.

Clare College

Baum D.
Doran A.
Ellison M.
Goorney N.J.
Kaye A.
Kessler D.
Landy R.
Maroudas C.E.
Podhoretz N.
Rashba J.D.

[Clare College cont]
Rose R.A.
Rosen J.A.
Rosenthal C.
Savitz A.M.
Silk J.I.
Weil D.

Corpus Christi College

Crystal J.D.
Rubinstein E.
Samuel A.P.
Topper E.S.
Topper J.J.

Darwin College

Katz J.I.

Downing

Lass J.D.
Aaronson I.
Alexander N.P.
Cohen M.H
Falk A.
Goodhardt G.J.
Green A.L.
Greenwood J.
Kohorn E.I.
Lewis J.M.
Lyons A.B.
Morris G.K.
Nemeth C.
Sklarz B.
Spencer P.
Stern R.
Waimann D.R.
Ziderman A.

Emmanuel College

Baker P.
Bernstein I.A.
Bornstein I.
Caller A.
Caller M.
Fromson B.
Goldstone A.F.
Goodwin S.P.
Jaffe V.
Korn P.
Lang C.A.

[Emmanuel College cont]
Lawson D.N.
Nathan L.D.
Newman A.
Poyser C.A.
Rabinowicz E.
Rayner J.
Richardson M.
Schonfield A.E.D.
Sheinfeld M.
Solomon N.
Walker A.

Fitzwilliam College

Acker M.
Brownstein M.
Drake S.K.
Filer D.S.
Kuper C.G.
Lassman J.
Nagel W.
Nissimoff N.
Rothschild W.L.
Shamash E.
Singer H.S.
Taub J.

Girton College

Aarons R.
Alexander E.
Ben-Israel H.
Briscoe S.
Fineberg N.
Friedman J.E.
Furst L.
Gottlieb A.
Hubert S.
Montagu J.M.
Rossiter M.A.
Rubinstein A.
Samuels P.J.
Sanders V.
Stanton J.
Stonehill C.
Ungar M.

Gonville and Caius College

Ayrton S.
Ballheimer A.M.
Braun L.
Citron D.B.
Coleman C.I.
Darcy K.
Davis R.
Doll-Steinberg A.
Eilon D.
Fox S.M.

[Gonville and Caius College cont]
Frankenberg R.J.
Glass A.J.
Goodman P.
Hill O.W.
Jay B.
Joseph N.
Levy D.M.
Lopian J.B.
Lyons L.
Raphael D.
Rosenberg D.
Sacks B.
Sacks E.
Saltman A.
Sasieni P.
Shaerf P.
Silverman A.H.
Simon P.
Socolovsky M.
Stanley D.
Tabor D.
Vecht J.
West G.B.
Wieselberg H.M.
Wineman V.

Homerton College

Berkman L.
Ebner J.
Marks F.K.
Michaels J.
Tunkel J.
Vecht A.
Wiseman S.
Young M.

Jesus College

Benady S.
Bernstein P.
Charkham J.D.
Cohen B.J.R.
Cohen D.
Cohen E.G.
Ehrenstein J.
Fireman B.A.
Fox K.F.
Halpern V.
Kleinman P.
Landy A.
Landy B.
Landy F.
Loewe L.L.
Marsden J.
Michaels L.
Nagler N.A.
Podro M.

Priestley M.B.
Rydz S.L.
Selby P.
Shribman D.M.
White A.

King's College

Abulafia D.S.H.
Blain M.A.
Brooks S.
Chinn T.
Ellenbogen G.
Goldhill S.D.
Goldstein G.
Heymann M.
Huttner B.
Jedwab M.R.
Kahn R.
Kochan A.
Lewis M.H.
Lieberman Leigh S.
Mond D.R.
Polack B.H.
Rose D.
Sebag-Montefiore N.
Sharpston E.V.
Sprei M.A.
Stamler S.A.
Whyte C.
Wittenberg J.
Yudkin M.D.

London Hospital

Mushin B.

London School of Economics

Allen S.
Bennun N.
Fairmont M.
Frankel W.
Margulies W.
Nyman R.
Rappaport R.
Ross P.E.
Winegarten A.
Wix P.
Young E.

Magdalene College

Cowan J.M.
Games S.
Goldstein R.B.
Hoffman I.M.
Jackson P.L.
Moschi G.

Myers B.J.
Rosenne S.
Sandelson B.H.
Sunlight B.
Waley-Cohen B.

New Hall

Baum N.
Halpern A.
Levin S.
Stecker S.

Newnham College

Abrams H.
Altmann E.D.
Baker M.
Berlyne A.R.
Bier H.
Blaukopf R.
Cole L.
Domb A.
Fliegelman M.
Gaba P.
Glass J.
Isaacs G.D.
Landes S.
Lee A.
Levy I.C.
Lightstone L.
Linger A.M.
Lipton J.A.
Margulies A.
Mollett B.
Nabarro R.
Rosenfeld S.S.
Sampson E.
Sands J.
Stamler A.E.
Steiner S.
Stern M.R.
Waley-Cohen H.F.
Wallman A.
Yoffey F.

Pembroke College

Benjamin J.C.
Cohen C.
Davidson J.
Diamond J.
Domb C.
Eban R.
Freedman C.
Gergel S.
Goldenfeld N.D.
Goldrein N.C.
Guttman E.

[St. John's College cont]
Blackburn D.M.
Bradlow E.P.
Colb S.
Finlay R.A.
Gottlieb P.
Hayman Z.
Jayson R.V.
Keidan J.M.
Kelly V.
Loewe R.J.
Miller D.
Miller R.J.
Pearlman C.
Pearlman J.
Philipp E.
Rappaport C.D.
Rosenhek S.F.
Rosenstock M.
Schwartz J.S.
Sharman L.
Solomon N.
Squires G.L.
Sugarman P.
Wernick G.
Yudkin M.

Trinity College

Alberman K.B.
Albert S.C.
Bar-On R.R.V.
Ben-Nathan C.
Ben-Nathan M.J.
Berkowitz I.
Bower M.H.
Brecher D.
Brittan L.
Brown B.D.
Brown M.J.
Burton R.M.
Casper B.M.
Cherns A.B.
Citron N.
Cohen S.B.
Cohn P.M.
Collins S.P.
de Rothschild E.L.
Edelman J.M.
Elata C.
Epstein E.N.
Filer P.A.
Fox H.
Freeman A.
Freeman H.
Garcia P.
Gillis J.

[Trinity College cont]
Glynn S.R.
Goldstein M.
Green S.
Greenberg D.
Greenberg M.
Haberman P.
Haberman S.
Joseph A.
King-Cline A.
Klug A.
Kopelowitz L.
Kornberg J.A.
Mendoza E.
Mestel L.
Miller B.
Moleman J.M.
Naftalin A.P.
Oppenheimer A.
Rosenfelder W.J.
Ross J.J.
Rudolf A.
Sachs L.
Saffman P.G.
Schwab H.
Schwab W.
Sciama D.W.S.
Seaton A.T.
Stone V.H.L.
Winter F.
Wolfson D.
Yardley B.

Trinity Hall

Berkoff B.
Berkoff N.A.
Cantor R.
Conway A.M.
Ellis D.L.
Fluss Z.S.
Freedman L.S.
Gruder J.N.
Halford M.
Heller C.
Janner D.J.
Janner G.
Sassoon R.M.E.

University College (London)

Herzog V. (Chaim)

Wolfson College

Casson K.
Stamler R.
Zand M.